M. W. Wiseman

The dynamics of Religion

An Essay in English Culture History

M. W. Wiseman

The dynamics of Religion
An Essay in English Culture History

ISBN/EAN: 9783337131036

Printed in Europe, USA, Canada, Australia, Japan

Cover: Foto ©ninafisch / pixelio.de

More available books at **www.hansebooks.com**

THE
DYNAMICS OF RELIGION

AN ESSAY

IN ENGLISH CULTURE HISTORY

BY

M. W. WISEMAN

LONDON

THE UNIVERSITY PRESS, LIMITED

16, JOHN STREET, BEDFORD ROW, W.C.

1897

CONTENTS.

PROLOGUE vii

PART I. THE REFORMATION.

Chapter I. GENERAL ESTIMATES 1
    II. LUTHER AND THE PAPACY 10
    III. PRIMARY PROTESTANTISM 14
    IV. THE PERSONALITY OF HENRY VIII . . . 29
    V. THE MORAL AND INTELLECTUAL SEQUEL . 47

PART II. THE RISE AND FALL OF THE DEISTIC MOVEMENT.

Chapter I. THE BEGINNINGS 71
    II. THE ATHEISTIC PHASE 80
    III. THE ANTI-ATHEISTIC PROPAGANDA . . . 94
    IV. THE PIONEER DEISTS 107
    V. THE HERESY OF LOCKE AND NEWTON . . 118
    VI. THE PROFESSIONAL DEFENCE 130
    VII. BENTLEY AND ANTHONY COLLINS . . 144
    VIII. BUTLER AND AFTER BUTLER 165
    IX. THE MORAL AND INTELLECTUAL OUTCOME . 182

PART III. MODERN THOUGHT.

Chapter I. THE TRANSITION 193
    II. THE BEGINNINGS OF THE BROAD CHURCH . 215
    III. THE TRACTARIAN REACTION 234
    IV. UNBELIEF WITHIN THE CHURCH . . . 250
    V. LAY RATIONALISM 277
    VI. THE BALANCE OF FORCES. Conclusion . 308

INDEX 335

PROLOGUE.

THAT *Man is not a veridical animal* is a truth oddly lost sight of in nearly all serious modern discussion on the course of social things. His Reverence Dean Swift, whose own intellectual life so signally helps to prove it, laid angry stress on the fact in his bitter allegory, failing however to realise from his own habit how profoundly true was his own saying, and going on to abate its point by representing his Houyhnhnms, in contrast to man, as spontaneously truthful. Now, as we know the horse to be an animal prone to fallacy, we have really no good ground to regard him as devoid of deceit; and in any case, to conceive falsehood as a mere invention of man, like printing and gunpowder, is seemingly to favour an undue hopefulness about its withdrawal from the plot of human affairs, whether by force of that "simplification of life" which some reformers preach, or of that moralisation of it which is wrought for by others. The scientific attitude towards the instinct of intellectual fraud is that of study and precaution, as of the physician towards disease. It is indeed a partial resort to this attitude that has led to our losing scientific sight of the nature of the force considered. Last century, the Christian priesthood habitually set down to "priestcraft" the progress and permanence of all religions save their own; and it has been well noted as deeply instructive that the current academic view, according to which priests as such have no craft, has arisen only since the academic priesthood itself has been tried by the code it had framed for others. Students who know perfectly well that their brothers and comrades, or it may be themselves, play the parish priest as Cicero played the augur, are naturally moved to take a new view of all augurship, as a procedure suspected to be directly inefficacious, yet gone about in a kind of ceremonial good faith and in a public spirit.

The trouble is that such students are not psychologically consistent, and will never bring themselves to see in one light the Mexican hieratical butcher of bound victims, the Romish priest receiving the nun's vow of renunciation, and the English bishop consecrating alternately a church and a battle-flag. They will never consent to feel towards the bishop as towards the Toltec slayer with the obsidian knife, or the priest of Dionysos in Andros who turned water into wine on the feast-day of the God, and gave out that void wine-jars were filled overnight by miracle. They may declare on pressure that every tearer-out of hearts on the Mexic hill regarded his business of butchery in some high and holy light, and devoutly trusted in its supernatural necessity and efficacy; for which humane conception they find help in Flaubert's vision of the brawny blackbearded priests of Moloch, flesh-fed by many sacrifices, tossing the babes into the mouth of lurid brass, and jeering at the pale votary of the Moon-Goddess, whose very aspect put aside hope of fortune in battle. They may even contrive to conceive that the Dionysiak miracle-monger, age after age, forever felt himself to be doing a sacred work, like some early Christian scribe piously interpolating a manuscript of the First Gospel. The truth is that by thus violently and unscientifically assuming a perfect single-mindedness in all ancient instruments of religious delusion, they hope to save all question of the single-mindedness of the Christian priest of to-day. Yet all the while they set a difference not merely in degree but in kind between the bishop on the one hand and the medicine-man and the sacrificial priest on the other.

Now, it is surely time that, instead of bringing an assumed pristine veracity in ancient priests to the factitious vindication of the priesthoods of to-day, we bring our actual knowledge of the double-mindedness of the average man and the average priest in our own day to the explication of the religion-makers and mongers of the past. To ascribe an ideal sincerity to these in the lump is to imitate Swift's ascription of it to the Houyhnhnms of his allegory, an irony which forgot to be ironical. We know as a matter of intimate fact that men habitually proclaim as vital truth what is primarily the doctrine of their self-interest, the utterance of which brings them or preserves for them their incomes and their status. Why then should we believe that in ages when the moral sense in other respects showed itself to be much more crude than it commonly is to-day, the work of delusion was gone about entirely or in the main unconsciously? It is really a monstrous assumption. Perfect sincerity, true single-mindedness, is a quite abnormal thing in mankind, as abnormal as perfect sweetness of temper and utter unselfishness. It may be that such abnormal types have now and then been concerned in starting a religion; but even that seems unlikely; and in any case the work of propagation and of maintenance must always be largely in the hands of men who have at least one eye to their purse, or their power, or their reputation.

Of course there is a confusion of consciousness in the matter. Men fighting for their own interests under the guise of abstract truth and righteousness do not as a rule regard themselves as deceiving anybody. And it is a superficial view of the quasi-sincerity of their state of mind that has led our amateur psychologists, the sentimental historians and essayists, to set up their facile kingdoms of sheep and goats, sincere people and insincere, species without hybrids. They imagine an ideal liar or Jesuit, Talleyrand or Bishop Blougram, or, if they be Nonconformists, Lord Beaconsfield; and against that type of dark insincerity they relieve the candour of the other. Yet it is a commonplace for all schools alike that all men are faulty in general; and it might surely be assumed on that footing that an imperfect truthfulness, in matters more complex than plain buying and selling, is an average defect. Howbeit, we are faced on all hands by that current optimism of estimate which substitutes " sincere error" for craft and dissimulation in all historical indictments; and as it happens, plausibility is lent to that view by the intellectual character of many who take the old line of charging with sheer dishonesty all who notably differ from them. Your Protestant who holds all Catholics for liars, and your Catholic who holds all Protestants for wilful wrong-doers, seem alike too stupid to permit of any verdict being passed on them but that of insusceptibility to light; and so they come to figure as types of religious and withal unamiable sincerity. It is just here, however, that the edge of a true analysis may begin to correct preconception, beginning with the discovery of the simple fact that the very bigot in general is so partly in virtue of the element of unveracity in him.

To show this to some extent historically is the task of the following treatise. The thesis is, not that religion is in all ages sustained by unmixed insincerity, but that in a period of advancing knowledge it is seen to pass from a state in which ill-enlightened men adapt or adopt their creed under varying political pressures and pecuniary temptations, conscious of compromising and dissembling on special points of doctrine, to a state in which the more intelligent are more or less clearly conscious of distrusting the main body of their doctrine, yet still maintain it, privately or inwardly professing to think they thus do more harm than good. The real sustaining forces at work all along are certain bases of primary superstition, religious and political; certain vested interests in the direction of these; and certain varying political forces disturbing or controlling these interests. Against or among these, the forces of growing knowledge and criticism play with varying effect, according as the sustaining forces support or injure each other, and as the critical spirit waxes or wanes with new knowledge, perplexity, difficulty, or encouragement, whether intellectual or social. Such rise and fall of the spirit of criticism we see in the pre-Reformation Protestantism of the Lollards, politically suppressed; in the " Italianate " unbelief of the age of Elizabeth, disappearing for lack of intellectual air; in the Deism and Atheism of the seventeenth and eighteenth centuries, flagging under perplexity philosophical and social, till the French

Revolution brought eclipse in one social zone and new activity in another.

At length, in our own day, we find ourselves in presence of an unmeasured development of rational criticism, partly open and aggressive, partly furtive or unavowed, permeating in the latter form all the churches, which nevertheless maintain as much as may be of their doctrine and machinery, glosing where absolutely necessary and evading challenge wherever possible, trusting to the simplicity of many and the nonchalance of more for a sufficiency of support, moral and material. In this state of virtual discredit of the essentials of religious belief, and of unquestionable dissimulation on essentials by thousands of clergymen, we get a clue to the state of mind of their predecessors in times when not the essentials but the forms of supernatural doctrine were mainly in question. And of course, seeing that in our own day many are fanatical for the essentials, it is the more clear that in the past many were fanatical for the forms, though the fanatics depended then as they do now for their power of coercion and ostracism on the complicity of the timid insincere. All this best comes out in the tracing of the actual history, which is hereinafter set forth in its main outlines with, it is hoped, less bias from a rationalistic leaning than is normally involved in leanings of another kind. The general view above indicated emerged from the study, and did not induce it. Indeed some readers may fail to find in the historical study the proof of the conclusions here drawn.

It is then the more advisable to press from the outset the doctrine that the customary notion of veracity and unveracity partakes of the mystical, and rests upon no proper objective study of men and affairs. Our psychology, in fact, is on the side of ethics still quite unscientific, mainly because our ethical science, so-called, remains traditional and transcendental. Our experts seem to fear being charged with immorality, as Beccaria was accused of sympathy with crime, if they do not affect a certain moral warmth and a camaraderie with the average sentimental citizen; as might happen with good Conservatives called upon to denounce the Armenian atrocities. They apparently recall with misgivings the ill names cast upon Mandeville and Helvétius, and they seemingly resolve to make themselves safe by repudiating all ethical theories which journalists, those romantic and unsophisticated men, would call "cynical". The present writer can only hope that more sophisticated people, having seen so much of the sentimental method, may be the more ready to tolerate an attempt to present history in a spirit which, despite a possible air of cynicism, is really, so far as it goes, rather one of science.

PART I.
THE REFORMATION.

CHAPTER I.

GENERAL ESTIMATES.

THE people of England possess, in the records of their "Reformation", a body of instruction as to the springs of action, religious and political, by which they have never profited as they might. To know that episode aright would be to know how the ways of nations may be made to part, the culture and thought of a whole era to take a new colour, and the peace and well-being of a continent to be broken and shaken to their foundations, by the unforeseen concurrence of small and great causes, and the personal equations of a few powerful men. But a great many things conjoin to prevent the people of England from understanding "what happened at the Reformation". Ever since, it has been to the interest of the most powerful professional class among them to make them believe that what happened was a passing away from certain "errors" and an embracing of certain "truths", the errors including immoral monasteries and the mass, and the truths including the Scriptures, done into English. It is a quaint enough process of mythology. Physicists avow to us that, in the mutations of matter, nothing really happens as they teach us to conceive it, our scientific ideas being only a kind of shorthand, or series of symbols loosely corresponding with what probably goes on. The proposition is perhaps not so philosophic as the physicists suppose, since it is not clear how they can really tell that our ultimate ideas are imperfectly symbolic, when in the terms of the case they do not know how otherwise to imagine the facts. But, however that may be, it is understood all round that science tries to get as near the image of the actual natural process as our senses can carry us. In our history, on the other hand, the normal effort is to keep more or less anxiously away from it. The condensed histories do not even indicate the concrete facts, but fuse them into masses in which their shape and substance are lost: the detailed histories seek carefully to swathe them in a picturesque haze of posthumous moral sentiment, which adapts them to the moral-æsthetic sense, even as the fog transforms factories to palaces, and slums to cathedrals. In the end, a body of well-established, interesting, and intelligible facts are made collectively as unplausible as a bad novel, and about as interesting. Perhaps the mere boredom of the old process may by this time reconcile at least a few people to tolerating the unpopular course of seeking to get at the bare truth. Last century science draped some of the angular facts of physics in the mystic abstractions of Caloric and Phlogiston; and in our own day, after having brushed aside the too satisfying conception of "Nervous Debility", the doctors are conceding to the public's psychological needs, and their own, with the more subtly coloured formula of "Neurasthenia". The historians are certainly no further forward, though the psychological compulsion is surely less. In any case, it can hardly be less interesting to look at things as they are, once in a while, than to look at them as the fog makes them all the time.

As it happens, one Englishman, whom many people would call "typical", William Cobbett, once took it upon him to blow the fog away from the Reformation. It is instructive as to the accuracy of "typical" conceptions, however, to find that Cobbett's *History of the Reformation* is even less read by his countrymen to-day than any of his other works, which is saying a good deal. Posterity does not seem to be "careful of the type", in this instance. Father Gasquet has not secured much Protestant attention for his recent editions of the *History;* and, though the Catholics of Ireland reprint the book at sixpence, from battered stereo-plates, it is much to be doubted whether they in general so far depart from their ordinary practice concerning books as to read it. In fact, a little of it is probably enough to countervail a great deal of average Protestant propaganda, so perfectly fitted is its sledge-hammer hitting to establish the unread Catholic in the faith that his side has the best of it. In England, for the same reason, we do not read it; and, indeed, with its eternal italics, it is not readable. Cobbett generally wrote in a passion, and in this case he was older than he once was, and angrier than ever; so that the steam blown off by him in blowing away the fog soon becomes as tedious as the fog itself, besides being less cooling to the eye. In fact, the old reformer was inspired in his passion against one fog by his devotion to another, inasmuch as he undertook[1] to prove that "that beggary, "that nakedness, that hunger, that everlasting wrangling "and spite, which now stare us in the face, and stun our "ears at every turn," were put upon us by the Reformation, "in exchange for the ease, and happiness, and "harmony, and Christian charity, enjoyed so abundantly, "and for so many ages, by our Catholic forefathers". Fog for fog, that was on the whole as good as this. One feels that, as Heine said[2] of him, Cobbett was a watchdog who turned with the same fury on everything that disturbed him, and that the very perpetuity of his barking prevented his being heeded when he bayed at a real thief. In this case the "dog of England" merely made his next-door neighbours put their fingers in their ears. We cannot even say of the book, what Coleridge said of an earlier writing of its author's, that it is "in the best bad style of this political rhinoceros, with his coat of armour of dry and wet mud, and his one horn of brutal strength on the nose of scorn and hate; not to forget the flaying rasp of his tongue;" though the characterization is partly pat, and has a further interest as an assiduous attempt at out-cobbetting Cobbett.

[1] *History*, Letter I.   [2] *Englische Fragmente*, ix, end.

To know what the Reformation was, we must get out of earshot and eyeshot of Cobbett, with his "red scolding face". Other voices hint guidance. A German historian, Dr. Hassencamp, tells us,[1] for instance, that "while in "Germany the work of the Reformation was evoked, by "an internal religious need, in the British Isles the "separation from Rome was accomplished at the beck of "a violent and sensual monarch, who, by the aid of "servile counsellors, himself assumed ecclesiastical supre- "macy, and like an Oriental despot, under menace of the "most cruel penalties, utilized the power thus obtained "to enslave the consciences of his subjects". This is perhaps a little better. Still, it is a little too Cobbettic. For Henry, when all is said, is really not known to have been a particularly sensual man; and, again, it is not so clear that matters progressed in such an absolutely spiritual way in Germany. Luther, in the matter of verbal violence, seems to have held his own even against Henry—"bellowing in bad Latin" is Hallam's account of it;[2]—and in view of the later proceedings of the Lutheran Anabaptists, and of Luther's own denunciations of his Protestant contemporaries, it can hardly be said that Reformation Germany was marked by that idyllic chastity ascribed by Tacitus to the Germans of his day. Mr. Hallam[3] and Sir William Hamilton[4] have put together some of the evidence which goes to show that, not merely among the so-called Anabaptists, but among the Protestant communities generally, there was what Hamilton calls a "fearful dissolution of morals". Luther, shortly before his death, calls Wittemberg, the very scene of his especial exploits, "a Sodom"; Professor Musæus, of Jena, also a Protestant, soon after pronounced it, in Latin, a "stinking Devil's-sewer"; and, a little later still, the Protestant Walther declared that in the university

---

[1] *History of Ireland*, trans. p. 9.
[2] *Literary History of Europe*, ed. 1872, vol. i, p. 377.
[3] *Id.*, p. 306.
[4] *Discussions on Philosophy and Literature*, 2nd ed., p. 497.

town of Marburg "the rule of morals is such as Bacchus
"would prescribe to his Mœnads, and Venus to her
"Cupids". Finally, we have Luther's own express admission[1] of the truth of the Catholic charges against his
followers: "No sooner did our Gospel arise and get a
"hearing than there followed a frightful confusion. . . . .
"every man at his free pleasure would be and do what he
"listed in the way of pleasure and licence, so that all law,
"rule, and order were utterly overthrown; this is, alas,
"all too true. For licentiousness in all ranks, with all
"sorts of vice, sin, and infamy, is now much greater than
"formerly, when the people, and above all the rabble,
"was generally held in fear and restraint, whereas now it
"lives like an unbridled horse, and does whatever it
"would without apprehension". As we know that it
was the popular and aristocratic support given to Luther
that carried him through his struggle, it does not thus
appear that the predilections which effected the Reformation in Germany were altogether loftier than those of
Henry VIII.

Nor is that all. The first count against Henry is that
he broke with Rome in order to break with his first wife.
But if he had been of the school of Luther, he need have
been at no such trouble. Luther and Melanchthon, we
are told, privately counselled him, when he applied to the
Universities for advice, "not to divorce his first queen,
"but to marry a second over and above". The same
piquant advice, as it happened, had been given to Henry
by the Pope; but the reformers could not have known
that. And when Philip, Landgrave of Hesse, champion
of the Reformation, similarly applied to them a few years
later for licence to take a second wife, on the score that
he was tired of the first, they first lengthily discoursed on
the nature of the divine law, and solemnly deplored those
scandalous habits to which his Highness had unreservedly

---

[1] See the letter cited in the original German by Mr. Baring Gould in his *Lost and Hostile Gospels*, pp. 28-29, from Walch's ed. of Luther's Works, v, 114.

confessed in his *Instructio;* then gingerly deprecated the marriage, as tending to scandal among the "enemies of " the Gospel"; but decided:—" In fine, if your Highness " be fully and finally resolved to marry yet another wife, " we judge that this ought to be done secretly .... so " that it be known only to your Highness, to the Lady, " and to a few faithful persons obliged to silence, under " the seal of confession; hence no attacks or scandal of " any moment would ensue. For there is nothing un- " usual in princes keeping concubines; and, although the " lower orders may not perceive the excuses of the thing, " the more intelligent know how to make allowance." This delightful document[1] was signed by Luther, Melanchthon, Bucer, Corvinus, Kraft, Lening, Wintferte and Melanther; and the discreet nuptials of the Landgrave, which duly followed, were witnessed and presided over by Melanchthon, Bucer, Melanther and others. Nor was there any forced contravention of principle on their part in the matter, the reverend doctors having long been one and all of opinion that polygamy in certain cases was lawful, while some of them gave and took[2] a quite patriarchal latitude in the matter. In earlier days they had not even blenched at publicity; on that head they had, however, grown more prudent with age, advising a secresy in Philip's case which they had not suggested in Henry's.

It really does not appear, then, that the German Reformation was so signally spiritual in comparison with the English. To the English eye, when it views the facts, the German procedure is at least as scandalous as is the English procedure to the German eye. Cranmer is recorded to have remonstrated with his brother-in-law,

---

[1] See it partly given in translation by Hamilton, as cited, p. 497, *sq.;* and in full, in the original, with a translation, at the end of Liv. VI of Bossuet's *Histoire des Variations des Eglises Protestantes.*

[2] Melanther and Lening, it seems, had the task of persuading the second wife to accept the situation; and Hamilton records for us that Melanther was himself the husband of three wives at once.

Osiander, on the laxity of the German Reformers' views of the institution of marriage; and from the whole dispute there emerges the pleasing probability that the country in which the Reformation most nearly approached the austerity which good Protestants would fain ascribe to it was licentious Gaul—unless, indeed, the known preference of Henri Quatre for domestic arrangements *without* the formality of the nuptial tie be held to discredit Huguenot principles.

CHAPTER II.

LUTHER AND THE PAPACY.

WHILE we are upon this part of the question, it may be as well to examine further into the "religious need" said to have underlain the German movement. What, exactly, was it? The beginning of the strife, so far as Luther was concerned, was Tetzel's sale of indulgences. Tetzel was not the direct agent of the Pope, as we are often told; the Pope had in reality sold or given the right of vending indulgences according to use and wont to the Archbishop of Mainz, who owed him 45,000 thalers for the pallium, and could not pay. Albert was to meet his debt by the sale of the indulgences, which property he in turn sold to the capitalist Fugger of Augsburg, choosing, however, the monk Tetzel to do the advertising, as it were. The business had thus become one of those sacred and prescriptive rights of property on which Burke in a later age declined to lay sacrilegious hands. No doubt the fact remains that His Holiness got through it some of the money he wanted for St. Peter's; but it is to be noted that he resorted to proceedings of the kind because he could not otherwise get the funds he wanted from Germany. That is to say, in Germany as in England the people had begun to be very restive under the constant money exactions of the Church. Multitudes of them, however, bought the indulgences; so that the "religious need" in the case would seem to have been that of those who did not buy. Luther's position on this one theme, indeed, though suddenly and spasmodically taken up, was soundly ethical, and probably no less soundly scriptural, although it has never been quite clear what was really meant by the power instantaneously to remit sins, claimed by the Founder, and understood to have been transmitted by him through Peter to the Church. The weak part in Leo's case, from the point of view of the normal moralist, was that he gave absolution for cash, irrespective of repentance. But then Luther in turn, when dealing with the main issues of practical morals, laid it down in the most emphatic way, on the one hand, that he who had found grace could not sin, and on the other hand that good action was not in any man's power, the human will being as a mere hackney which was alternately mounted by God or Devil, according as God chose. The matter has been so often debated that it is needless to go into the details again; and it may suffice to note that Dr. Julius Köstlin, the universally accepted Protestant biographer of the Protestant hero, has admitted[1] that Luther went dangerously far, and had at length to draw back. But that was later in life; and we are bound to suppose that while he denounced Tetzel he held a doctrine which implied that the things which Tetzel did could have no effect, good or bad, upon conduct. We are not to suppose for a moment, of course, that Luther and his fellow reformers were, as Cobbett has it, "a nest of atrocious miscreants," such as "the world has never seen in any age"; they certainly had no design to corrupt morals, as the phrase goes. But then had Leo and Tetzel any such design either? Does any Protestant to-day believe they had? And if it be admitted that they had not, wherein had Luther any moral or religious superiority over them, save inasmuch as they were bent on making money and he was not? And since he bitterly complains, in the advice to the Landgrave, that the bulk of the nobility who supported the Protestant movement were mainly bent on despoiling the Church, even the charge of self-seeking recoils upon his cause. To this complexion the matter must come. Whatever may have been the moral motives stirring the always confused and turbulent brain of Luther; whether

[1] *Life of Luther*, trans. p. 382.

or not he began the fight in a mood of vexation at the drawing away of his congregation by the rival attraction of Tetzel; certain it is that the popular force of his movement lay in nothing that can without unseemly sarcasm be called a "religious need", but in simple common-sense resentment of the new Papal device for collecting funds, and in the zeal of the most astute to secure funds in another manner. For if by his own showing his followers immediately took far more advantage of the abstract and gratis indulgence given them by his doctrine than the buyers of indulgences had taken of those they had paid for, the moral difference between the two parties was at least not on the side of the "reformers". Nor can it be pretended that the general tone of Catholics was less ethically scrupulous than that of their opponents. Tetzel's expedition was sufficiently scandalous; but when the general sense of the Church was later collected in the Council of Trent, it declared for the doctrine of moral freedom, which the Protestant Churches since Luther's time have mostly seen fit to embrace, either officially or otherwise.

It will probably be suspected by an ingenuous Protestant reader at this point that the present line of criticism is framed in the interests of Catholicism. But a little patience will avail to remove the misgiving. We simply take up the position of Mr. Hallam,[1] that "The "doctrines of Luther, taken altogether, are not more "rational, that is, more conformable to what men "*à priori* would expect to find in religion, than those of "the Church of Rome; nor did he ever pretend they did "so". And if Mr. Hallam be viewed askance, as suspected of Deism, we may take rather the verdict of Dr. Beard, that Protestantism, a rebellion against Catholic scholasticism, built up a new scholasticism of its own, upon assumptions hardly less arbitrary;[2] or the verdict of the Rev. Mr. Green,[3] that Luther "despised reason

---

[1] *Literary History*, vol. i, p. 307.
[2] Hibbert Lectures on *The Reformation*, 1883, p. 37.
[3] *Short History of England*, p. 315.

"as heartily as any Papal dogmatist could despise it. . . .
" He had been driven by a moral and intellectual com-
" pulsion to declare the Roman system a false one, but it
" was only to replace it by another system just as
" elaborate, and claiming precisely the same infallibility.
" . . . Luther declared man to be utterly enslaved by
" original sin, and incapable through any efforts of his
" own of discovering truth, or of arriving at goodness.
" Such a doctrine not only annihilated the piety and
" wisdom of the classic past. . . .; it trampled in the
" dust reason itself." But, while it may be argued that
this frame of mind is expressive of a "religious need",
we must finally decline to say as much of the Protestant
community in general, since that, as we have seen, relied
on the common moral sense, which is a phase of reason,
in its first hostility to the Papacy, and afterwards a good
deal on its carnal instincts, which are always understood
to be condemned by Scripture.

CHAPTER III.

PRIMARY PROTESTANTISM.

WE may now approach the English Reformation with tolerably open minds. It is broadly true that the event came about at the "beck" of Henry, who was a violent man, but whose "sensuality" does not appear so aggressive in comparison with the reigning models of Lutheran Germany. What it behoves us to ascertain is why Henry becked. And a perusal even of Mr. Froude's History, with the rapidity of which its substance permits, but with the critical diligence which is befitting over everything its author has written, will satisfy any candid person that Henry's motives were at once strictly personal and reasonably conscientious, as king's motives go. There can indeed be no pretence that his majesty suffered from a "religious need", save in the sense that he was in a quasi-religious difficulty for which he wanted a religious solution. Mr. Froude, who had a gift for the publication of unwelcome facts that was only partially counteracted by his faculty of misstating their significance, has made it fairly clear that if Henry had had a healthy family by his first queen, England would never in his time have broken with the Papacy, and Anne Boleyn and Catherine Howard would have died with their heads on their shoulders. This is really the central fact in the history of the English Reformation. Whatever of popular anti-Romish feeling had previously existed in England, as in Germany, turned wholly on two grievances, one being the extortionate ways of the priesthood, and the other, the fact that they spent their gains so largely on their personal pleasures. It is not in human nature to see priests levying all manner of clerically authorised assessments, " signs of private interest enough "to mortify the most lively faith," as Hobbes put it later, and turning the proceeds to the account of comforts, and offspring, which on clerical theory were not entitled to exist. When the professedly self-denying saints of non-Christian cults have been found to indulge themselves like other people, they have been known to be put to death out of hand by the other people, shocked at such depravity. Christian charity forbids such extremities of resentment, always reminding us not to nail the sinner's ears to the pump; but it does not exclude financial rectifications. This is all that the "Protestants" of Henry's day and realm seem to have in general protested against. The Church's theology and ritual suited them well enough. The previous movements of Wycliffe and the "Lollards" had come to nothing, intellectually speaking, most men being quite undisturbed by disputes about transubstantiation, or even by the phenomenon of priests' concubines, so long as the Church courts did not fleece them too outrageously, or the priest did not transgress all ethical etiquette in his amours.

It is instructive to keep in view this doctrinal peace in pre-Reformation England. Whatever vigorous discontent we can trace in Church matters, from the Conquest onwards, is of a strictly practical kind, befitting the nation that was one day to be reputed the most utilitarian in Europe. William Rufus anticipated and exceeded Henry himself in his aversion to Papal control; but any defect of orthodoxy on his part was a matter of constitutional bias to profanity, not of doctrinal unsoundness. The occasionally anti-clerical attitude of Henry the Second, again, is sufficiently accounted for by the fact that he found the archdeacons' courts levying by their fines every year more money than the whole revenue of the crown; and all manner of appeals being made to Rome on issues outside the Church's declared province.[1] About 1230, a number

---

[1] See Mrs. Green's *Henry the Second*, pp. 84-85.

of the priests themselves combined with certain of the nobles in a kind of anti-Rome league; but it was with a strict eye to business, the object being to boycott and terrorise Papal nominees holding English benefices.[1] Even when nationalist feeling was added to financial, doctrine remained unaffected, and the "errors of the "Church of Rome" were the creed of Englishmen, as of Italians. As it has been put in dignified Johnsonese by the late Professor Le Bas,[2] writing of the period before Wycliffe, "the exactions and usurpations of the Ponti- "fical court could be readily estimated by those who "were profoundly indifferent to her aberrations from the "primitive purity of faith. And hence it was that "England, though a citadel of orthodoxy in matters of "mere belief"—such is the latitudinarian expression of the reverend gentleman—"was in those times by no "means the seat of contented allegiance to the Apostolic "See". This Protestant authority even thinks that "she might perhaps have been satisfied to slumber for "centuries longer under the sedative influence of the "Romish superstition, if the burden of Romish dominion "had been less galling and oppressive." It is a sound surmise; and some of us venture to go further still, and suspect that she would have been Roman Catholic at this day but for the personal equation of Henry VIII; and this in virtue not of anything specially sedative in Romish superstition, which is really not more dormitive than the Protestant variety, but of the smallness of the sway possible to men of ideas in English life, then as now.

In the reign of Edward I, long before Wycliffe, we find asserted by certain enthusiasts of the province of Canterbury the principle that men were not bound by the authority of the Pope, or even of the ancient Fathers, but solely by that of the Bible and "necessary reason".[3] But that idea could not find safe harbourage in England

---

[1] Matthew of Paris, ed. Madden, vol. ii, p. 337.   [2] *Life of Wiclif*, p. 88.
[3] Wilkins, *Concilia*, ii, 124.

till after three hundred years, when the Church had been politically broken down, and a body of citizens freed from Papal authority had begun Bible-reading for themselves. So with the teaching of Wycliffe on transubstantiation. His attacks on begging friars with full purses and large estates would naturally appeal to most laymen; but when it came to taking one view rather than another of a dogma on which no common-sense view was compatible with Christianity, his exposure of "error" was, politically speaking, a beating of the air. Certainly, there grew up a party of Lollards, just as there was a party of heretics in Italy itself; but their mainly doctrinal criticism of the Church could no more serve to overthrow it in England than the efforts of the later reformers could maintain the Reformation in Italy and Spain. The (supposed) chronicler Knyghton, who was canon of Leicester, in Wycliffe's time, and so in the sphere of Wycliffe's influence, complained that you could not meet two persons in the street but one of them was a Lollard;[1] and in 1395, while Richard II was posing as king in Ireland, the party sent to Parliament a petition in twelve heads in which they challenged the authority of the Papacy; condemned monasteries, clerical celibacy, nuns' vows, the "feigned miracle of the sacrament", exorcisms and benedictions, special prayers for individual souls, pilgrimages, prayers and offerings to images, confession and absolution, war and capital punishment, and "unnecessary" "trades". The rationalist of to-day will see here vigorous and interesting beginnings of the free play of judgment on religious things; while Churchmen, with the late Mr. Massingberd, will see, along with "the seeds of great and "saving truths", "many things which no well-informed "mind can approve". But what here concerns us is the residual historical fact that the persecution of Lollardism by Henry IV and his son sufficed to destroy it.

The facts are, indeed, a little obscure, and are rendered

---

[1] Massingberd, *The English Reformation*, 4th ed., p. 157.

more so in the vivacious narrative of Mr. Green, who always seems to have written up each period before he had studied the next, and after he had partly forgotten the one before. Indeed, his memory at times fails him badly in the course of a page. To follow his narrative is to find more vicissitudes in human affairs than even they admit of. As thus: " With the formal denial of Transubstantion which Wyclif issued in the spring of 1381 began that great movement of revolt which ended, more than a century after, in the establishment of religious freedom, by severing the mass of the Teutonic peoples from the general body of the Catholic Church."[1] " Within Oxford
" itself [directly afterwards] the suppression of Lollardism
" was complete, but with the death of religious freedom
" all trace of intellectual life suddenly disappears."[2]
" From that moment [of Wyclif's death—1384] Lol-
" lardism *ceased to be in any sense an organised movement,*
" and crumbled into a general spirit of revolt. . . . .
" But it was this want of organization, this looseness and
" fluidity of the new movement, that *made it penetrate*
" *through every class of society.* . . . . The movement had
" *its own schools;* its own books; its pamphlets were
" passed everywhere from hand to hand."[3] " Powerless
" as the efforts of the Church were for purposes of
" repression, they were effective in rousing the temper
" of the Lollards into a bitter and fanatical hatred of
" their persecutors. The Lollard teachers directed their
" fiercest invectives against the wealth and secularity of
" the great Churchmen. In *a formal petition to Parliament*
" [1395] they mingled denunciations of the riches of the
" clergy with an open profession of disbelief in transub-
" stantiation," etc.[4] " The projects of the Lollards
" shaped themselves into more daring and revolutionary
" forms. . . . ."[5] " Sir John Oldcastle . . . . threw
" open his castle of Cowling to the Lollards as *their*

[1] *Short History of the English People,* p. 234.
[2] P. 236.   [3] Pp. 251-252.   [4] P. 253.   [5] P. 253.

" *headquarters*. . . . . With the death of Sir John
" Oldcastle [1418] *the political activity of Lollardism came
" suddenly to an end;* while the steady persecution of the
" bishops, if it failed to extinguish it as a religious move-
" ment, succeeded in destroying the vigour and energy
" which it had shown at the outset of its career."[1] " In
" the presence of Lollardism, the Church had at this time
" [1422] ceased to be a great political power and sunk
" into a mere section of the landed aristocracy. . . . .
" *Lollardism still lived,* in spite of the steady persecution,
" *as a spirit of revolt;* and [in 1431] we find the Duke of
" Gloucester traversing England with men-at-arms for
" the purpose of *repressing its risings* and hindering the
" circulation of its invectives against the clergy."[2]
" Lollardism, as a great social and popular movement,
" had ceased with the suppression of Cobham's revolt, and
" little remained of the directly religious impulse given by
" Wyclif beyond a vague restlessness and discontent with
" the system of the Church. But, weak and fitful as was
" the life of Lollardism, the *prosecutions whose records lie so
" profusely scattered* over the bishop's registers failed
" wholly to kill it."[3] " All spiritual life seemed to have
" been trodden out in the ruin of the Lollards."[4] " So
" utterly had Lollardism been extinguished that not one of
" the demands [of the complaint of the Commons of Kent
" —1450] touches on religious reform. The old social
" discontent seems to have subsided."[5] " *The persecution
" of the Lollards,* the disfranchisement of the voter . . . .
" the shame of the long misgovernment, told fatally [in
" 1460] against the weak and imbecile King [Henry VI],
" whose reign had been a long battle of contending
" factions."[6] " From the time of the Lollard outbreak,
" the attitude of the Church is timid as that of a hunted
" thing. . . . The Church still [1471] trembled at the
" progress of heresy."[7] Then, finally: " The awakening

[1] P. 260.   [2] P. 267,   [3] P. 342.   [4] P. 268.
[5] P. 275.   [6] Pp. 277-278.   [7] P. 285.

"of a rational Christianity, whether in England or in the Teutonic world at large, begins with the Florentine studies [1493] of Sir John Colet."[1]

Now, Mr. Green was unquestionably a gifted historian, with a great power of making his subject fascinating; but we must all agree that this is not how history ought to be written. It is clear that he did not really know things to have been as he said, but made generalisations from hand to mouth as he went along. If he could thus miss real knowledge, there is evidently no small risk that the rest of us may be misled if we do not go warily. But this at least comes clearly enough out of his long zig-zag of erring narrative: the action of Wycliffe was *not* the beginning of a movement that culminated in the Reformation. The power of the Church, which Mr. Green at times wrongly represents as paralysed throughout the century, and at others as in active play, had really sufficed, with the support of the fourth and fifth Henries, to crush aggressive Lollardism. The same power had been a main factor in putting down Richard II (who was lenient to the Lollards, and whose wife, Anne of Bohemia, either directly or indirectly brought Wycliffe's writings in the way of Huss) and establishing Henry IV; and when Henry VIII came to the throne there was no coherent heretical movement in England. Perhaps the whole truth would include the view that Lollardism had finally gone to the wall, as art and letters did, through the uncivilising effect of the Wars of the Roses. About 1450 we find Lollardism still so pushing that Bishop Peacock could bring upon himself a prosecution for heresy, ending in his imprisonment for life, by simply attempting to oppose the heretics with temperate argument instead of abuse, making a few moderate concessions by way of carrying the Church's point against them. That episode, which Mr. Green omits to notice, would seem to show that the Lollard movement was not so dead after Oldcastle's time as

[1] P. 298.

he asserts. A bishop would hardly publish in those days a series of tracts and books to combat a moribund cause; and it can hardly have been that his books secured their end when he himself was disgraced for writing them. But, however that may have been, the England of Henry VII was soundly Catholic in creed. The heresy of ideas, of elementary critical reason, had come and gone, leaving transubstantiation and clerical celibacy, and images and pilgrimages, and all the rest of it, in full credit. And when we find Henry VIII beginning to quarrel with the Pope on the question of the divorce, the nation was substantially as orthodox as he, though, perhaps, more on edge than he against the priests, as having more cause for complaint, and, perhaps, more expectation of profit from any interference with Church property. Of Protestantism in the modern sense there was only so much as existed in the Society of Christian Brethren, organised in 1526, "with a central committee "sitting in London; with subscribed funds, regularly "audited, for the purchase of Testaments and tracts; "and with paid agents, who travelled up and down the "country to distribute them;"[1] and according to Mr. Green, following Fox, these innovators "fled in crowds "over sea" in 1527, when Wolsey imprisoned some of their party at Oxford, and burned a heap of their Testaments in St. Paul's Churchyard. Much more formidable as enemies to the temporalities of the Church was the party among the middle and upper classes who in 1529 were "so confident of the temper of the approaching Parlia-"ment, and of the irresistible pressure of the times, that the "general burden of conversation at the dinner-tables in "the great houses in London was an exulting expectation "of a dissolution of the Church establishment and a con-"fiscation of ecclesiastical property".[2] But even these persons, like their congeners in Germany described by

---

[1] Froude, *History of England*, ed. 1872, vol i, p. 170.
[2] *Id.*, p. 167.

Luther and his colleagues in their memorable counsel to the Landgrave of Hesse, were speculative in a financial sense only; and we may accept Mr. Froude's account of the state of parties in so far as it asserts this. The forces of the moment were, he says, "the English party who "had succeeded to power, and who were bent upon a "secular revolt," and "the Papal party, composed of "theoretic theologians like Fisher, Bishop of Rochester, "and represented on the council by Sir Thomas More. "And both of these were united in their aversion to the "third party, that of the doctrinal Protestants, who were "still called heretics."[1]

Now, it is easy to see that it lay with the king, fear of whom hypnotised the majority, to decide whether the party of confiscation should or should not prevail. The plan of confiscation was of old standing. In the reign of Henry IV, the House of Commons had been avowedly in favour of some measure of secularization of endowments.[2] That, indeed, may be taken to have been the normal frame of mind of the baronage of the Middle Ages; for it cannot be too plainly or too paradoxically said that devotion to the Catholic Church really did not exist among lay Catholics until Protestantism arose to develop the feeling as a counteraction. This is a paradox in the proper sense only, that of a statement of truth which has the semblance of being untrue by reason of an air of contumacy to common sense. When the matter is looked into, the proposition is seen to be almost a truism. Before there was a real schism in doctrine and ritual and communion, churchmen might and would be zealous for their own corporation; and some laymen might be Pope's men rather than king's or emperor's men; but a devotion to the Church as Church could not exist outside of its own walls, inasmuch as all men held the same theology, or else, if any were unbelieving, they were as likely to be churchmen or Pope's men as laymen or emperor's men.

[1] *Id.*, p. 173.   [2] *Id.*, pp. 77, 93.

As Burke has it, the Guelphs and Ghibellines "were "political factions originally in favour of the emperor and "the Pope, with no mixture of religious dogmas: or, if "anything religiously doctrinal they had in them origin- "ally, it very soon disappeared; as their first political "objects disappeared also, though the spirit remained".[1] That the ordinary Christian knight and diplomatist had as such no normal or inveterate respect for things ecclesiastical is made clear by a hundred episodes, from the sacking of Constantinople by the Crusaders to the capture of Rome and the Pope by Charles V. Mr. Mallock has put in the mouth of one of his characters the attractive thesis that the modern sense of humour is, as it were, a precipitate of the Christian religion, which had put mystery and sacro-sanctity where paganism saw only natural facts. The theory is not fully reconcilable with the Christian dearth of humour between Lucian and Rabelais; but it is so far psychologically sound that it posits the principle of the mutual generation of contraries. Of that principle there is a clearer historic illustration in the case under notice. Before the Reformation, in Italy itself, there were violent movements of schism within the Church, Dominicans and Franciscans in mass quarrelling over dogmas, and "Spiritual" Franciscans in turn battling with the worldly ones. But, though such strifes paved the way for the Reformation, they would never have sufficed anywhere to destroy the Church; and the Protestant movement substantially throve by reason of lay defection. The class pride and *esprit de corps* of priests, in countries where they were not so numerous as to overpower society, first generated an anti-priestly spirit among orthodox laymen; and an anti-Catholic theology among such laymen first generated a positive Catholic devotion among lay Catholics. So that the rise of schism and clash of belief in modern times has been the main means of regenerating on a large scale a really fervid

[1] *Thoughts on French Affairs*, Works, Bohn edition, vol. iii, p. 352.

Catholic devotion, of the type of that of Augustine, who kept his incandescent by his unfailing source of exercise in combating Old Pagans and Neo-Christians.

The strongest argument, of course, for the inevitableness of the Reformation, is that set up by this fact of the undoubted readiness of whole classes of believing Catholics to fall upon the Church's property. It would seem as if, in those countries more remote from Italy, where the clerical population was less dense almost in the ratio of the distance and the difficulty of communication, its fat revenues must in the long run have been confiscated by the combined action of the greater and leaner nobility. It was morally impossible that the clergy should ever put down envy by collectively reforming their lives in accordance with any ideal whatever. No endowed corporation whatever, started with whatever purity of zeal, can long do more than partially escape the normal effects of the possession of idle wealth. As regards that ground of anti-clericalism the Church was chronically made more or less concerned, of itself or in spite of itself. It was, in fact, always being reformed, as Protestant historians show, with an imperfect sense of the significance of the fact. As soon as the last new broom was worn morally bare, some of the rulers of the Church would try another, being admonished thereto as much, often, by their own or their subordinates' critical sense as by the grumblings of the laity or the secular power. The Articles of Reformation drawn up by the University of Oxford in 1414, by order of Henry V, provided with equal vigour for the checking of ecclesiastical abuses and the suppression of Lollardism, showing that the call for reform came not from heretics but from the powers that were, whether ecclesiastical or civil. We may say, indeed, that the vices of the Church during the Ages of Faith, barring those which grew out of the institution of celibacy, were relatively not a whit worse than—let us not say those which sprang up so rankly and so instantaneously in Lutheran Germany, but—those which flourished later under the respectable roof of Anglicanism itself; "relatively," we say, meaning that the whole moral code of the feudal ages was grosser, and the ideal of justice lower, than that of later times. The burden of celibacy, indeed, makes a monstrous practical difference between the moral aspects of old Catholicism and modern Protestantism. It was quite impossible that in the small populations of the Middle Ages, when for the most part only the more robustly animal organisms could pass the perils of disease from birth onwards, there should be men and women enough with a real vocation for celibacy to fill the monasteries and nunneries of the period with suitable inmates, and enough additional men of the requisite type to supply the priesthood in general. The variations in the repute of the priesthood in different ages and countries may be explained from this point of view. In our own day, in Ireland, the Catholic clergy are understood to be above scandal to a degree unknown in either France or Italy; and the explanation probably is that, on the one hand, the hostile neighbourhood of Protestantism compels the heads of the Church to peculiar vigilance, and that, on the other hand, the abundant field for selection among the children of the dutiful peasantry makes it easy to secure types of the sort required. In France, where the priesthood is relatively so much less popular, there is no such facility of choice; and in Italy there is less sense of the need to make it. As regards modern monasteries and nunneries, they necessarily tend more and more to be tenanted only by men and women with a vocation for celibacy. But in medieval and Renaissance Europe there could be no effective choice of material whatever, inasmuch as the monasteries were a refuge for all manner of men seeking a shelter and a maintenance, and all manner of women similarly pressed, or forced to take the veil for the convenience of their families. There would naturally occur in a certain proportion of cases the breaches of vow of which Protestant historians make so much. But precisely as the growth of population and industry and the spread of law and order made regulation easier, and lessened the miscellaneous pressure on the convents, there seems to have been a general tightening of their discipline, and the Church was on this score probably less lax at the time of the Reformation than ever before, though still inevitably open to attack.

On the financial side, certainly, the case was sufficiently hopeless. The Church was a tax-levying poperty-holder, with the strongest tendencies to accumulation; and nothing could hinder that either the exactions of the priests and the ecclesiastical courts should irritate the people, or the benefices of the Church should be sought for and disposed of as simple sources of income; while all along the preponderating mass of the laity with similar financial views would find in the Church's wealth unfailing matter for envy. The history of the Church on the financial side, usually written by Protestants with the purpose of connecting all forms of "corruption" with the imagined "spirit of Catholicism", is in truth a simple lesson in economic sociology. Apparently, all the orders of friars in succession were established with the hope that each would give the world an example of self-denying devotion where all previous forms of sacerdotalism had failed. There was in Francis of Assisi, as Mr. Massingberd has put it, with the incomparable aplomb of the Anglicanism of the last generation, "a sincere and self-"devoted, however ill-directed piety";[1] and Francis in particular enjoined on the friars of his order a *celsitudo altissimae paupertatis*, a peculiar absoluteness of poverty, forbidding them under any circumstances to possess money, denying them even the power to hold lands collectively, as did the earlier orders, and making even their begging conditional on their inability to get work. But ere a generation was over, not only had work disappeared from the programme, but the order had

---

[1] *The English Reformation*, p. 98.

everywhere begun to possess fixed wealth in the form of monasteries and churches, and a large revenue of the surest kind in fees as well as in alms. The vested interest was already too strong to be overruled by the wishes of the founder; so Pope after Pope lent himself to the views of those of the order who sought to modify its rules, finally forcing most of the others into silence or secession; the latter course constituting a powerful preparation for the later Protestant movement everywhere.[1] Thus, though the insurgent Jack Straw proposed to spare the "begging friars" in England when making a clean sweep of all the rest of the clerical species—a favour which may suggest either their having a hand in the insurrection or the survival of real or seeming pauper virtues among some of them—they kept Wycliffe in a state of chronic exasperation, and by keeping up the sharp opposition of their interests to those of the regular clergy, divided the forces of the Church against each other, while giving all the more scope to lay criticism.

Here then was indeed an obvious opening for an attack on the Church's temporalities, but not an easier one than had existed for hundreds of years and been all the while guarded by the kings, whose own obvious interest in turn was to take care that the Church and the baronage were kept in balance, as powers to be usefully played against each other. As a general result, " England had for above " three hundred years been the tamest part of Christendom " to the papal authority ".[2] A king with a clear title had gone down before the Church's hostility. A king with a doubtful title therefore would not be likely on mere abstract principles to seek to upset an institution which counted for so much in his favour in the case of a revolt among the baronage, and from whose plunder at best he could only hope to secure a fraction, unless he were to drive the baronage into the arms of the Church by refusing them the main share. And all the while the Church

[1] So Mosheim, *Eccles. Hist.*, cent. xiii, Part ii, ch. 2, § 38.
[2] Burnet, *History of the Reformation*, Part I, Book i.

represented a great numerical force. It is one of Mr. Froude's extravagances to say that the "Papal" party consisted only of "theoretic theologians" like Fisher and More. To say nothing of the homicidal practicality of More's arguments against heretics, the later history of the country shows, by the admission of Protestant historians, that there was a dogged Catholic majority of ordinary untheoretic citizens, not only then but long afterwards; and that only the two circumstances of fear of the king, and slowness to see how religious matters were going to turn, prevented this majority from revealing itself more fully. Indeed, at the very moment of which Mr. Froude writes, it was More who had "succeeded to power" on the fall of Wolsey; and the party bent on "secular revolt", if more complacent, was really not any stronger than before.

CHAPTER IV.

THE PERSONALITY OF HENRY VIII.

We must turn, then, to the personality and the personal equation of Henry VIII for the real causes of the political beginning of the Reformation, on which only after a generation did the sacerdotal and theological changes follow which made the practical historic severance between Catholicism and Anglicanism. It may be worth while to go once more over the familiar but yet often misapprehended details. The trouble, it is clear, began with the question, at once domestic and diplomatic, of the lack of a male heir to the throne, and the circumstances under which the lack came about. Her Majesty, Queen Katharine, had been brought to bed half-a-dozen times, with the only surviving result of one sickly princess; and in the case of a marriage so peculiar, the wedding of a deceased brother's widow, religion gave an abundant backing to the qualms which the mere political situation could very well raise. In the Europe of the sixteenth century, kings and subjects alike could in all good faith feel what the modern Englishman does not without reflection realise, that a throne whose heir was a girl was in a very serious plight; and when that girl, herself sickly, was the sole survivor of six infants, four of them males, born of a mother who had successively married two brothers, king and subjects could further feel, perhaps more intelligibly for a pious posterity, that there was an aspect of divine displeasure over the situation. What the bulk of the people really did feel is another question, not easily settled. Mr. Froude of course decides, on his general principles, that public opinion was mainly on the King's side. Mr. Hallam points to the letter of Bishop Bellay, the French ambassador, late in 1528, declaring that the divorce was so unpopular as to make a revolt conceivable.[1] The general likelihood is that the problem, lit only by the equally dark lanterns of the spirit and the letter, divided opinion all round.

It was, indeed, an exquisitely dramatic illustration of the power that lay in the Christian creed to misguide nations where mere heathen common-sense would have saved them. Pagan Emperors of Rome, placed as was the English Defender of the Faith, would have been in no difficulty as to their course. They would have adopted a son at choice, and, a monarch being in either case an absolute necessity for a nation unable to rule itself as a republic, the adopted son would have had as good a title as one born in the purple. But the "purer faith", as our clerical historians still term it, brought with it such a paralysis of political invention that no such expedient could suggest itself to any Christian person. Even the course of legitimising his own illegitimate son was felt by Henry to be a desperate expedient, to be attempted only as a last resort, if the Pope would permit of it at all. Whatever were the general practice and influence of Churchmen, the teaching and practice of the Church on matters of paternity had come to be so influential for Europe that a prince born out of wedlock ran a great risk of having his title disputed, whether or not the Pope had legitimised him; so that a process which would have inflicted no practical wrong on anybody was several degrees more inexpedient than one which would inflict on one woman at least a sense of wrong unspeakable.

She, again, on her part, illustrated the crudity of the Christian ethic on another side. For her, there was only one question to be considered—that of her technical

---

[1] Burnet, *History of the Reformation*, Part III, Book ii. Nares' edition, vol. iii, p. 66.

rights under the normal marriage law. The fate of the kingdom was as nothing in the balance. As a princess she knew, poor lady, that her great function was to provide an heir for the throne; and that in lacking a son she lacked the one thing needful; but she must needs stand on her rights as an ordinary woman under the marriage bond while holding a place of power and privilege that set aside ordinary human rights. She would be a queen with none of the moral penalties of queenship; nay, after having been married in clear contravention of the normal marriage law by the express dispensing power of the Pope, reluctantly exercised, she held it to be an outrage that the same dispensing power should be called upon to annul the tie. And the typical good Christian, professing to know only one moral code for monarchs and subjects, after cancelling the principle of moral equality by the very acceptance of hereditary monarchy, saw then and still sees the case with Queen Katherine's eyes. At the time of her marriage such observers had actually revolted from the act; but that revolt was now forgotten. She and her sympathisers alike, in short, did what we find all parties doing in this as in so many other historic dramas—made their interest and their sympathy the first and last test of action, finding that course to be absolutely right, religiously and ethically, which simply expressed their wishes, and refusing to look from other people's point of view at all.

It is necessary to insist on this normality of egoism all round if we are to know the Reformation episode as nearly as possible for what it was, without idealising one side more than the other. Queen Katherine in her youth seems to have been a completely consenting party to the diplomacy which wedded her first to the Prince Arthur, and shortly afterwards, on his death, to the Prince Henry; and when we note the sufficiently hard facts that Henry VII, after some religious and superstitious hesitations, agreed to the transfer by way of keeping in his treasury the dowry the Princess had brought with her, and that the younger Henry had at least to some extent the same end in view, we are not to lose sight of the equally hard fact that the Princess consented to marry her young husband's boy-brother a few months after her young husband's death. Her insistent plea that her first marriage had never been consummated, though partly valid as an appeal to Henry, does not affect the other bearings of the case. Arthur had been only fifteen, an age hardly to be reconciled with a serious choice on the part of a bride of seventeen or eighteen; but at Arthur's death Henry was only twelve, an age which puts serious feeling on her side out of the question. At best, we must say of the unhappy lady that in youth she had to let herself be made a shuttlecock of monarchic politics; and that when in mature age she sought to insist on her personal rights she ignored the fact of her former surrender of them for a price. It was a marriage within the prohibited degrees, and as such so repellent to thoughtful Catholics that even the Pope's dispensation left many misgivings. On the other hand, probably nobody in that age had any misgivings about the purely human side of the matter, the facile transfer of affection, the dispensing with the sanctions of the heart. Such thoughts were not current in the ages of Faith and of the Reformation. In our own day, however, it would seem only consistent to let modern ethics he heard on the more spiritual point as well as on that of the legal rights of Katherine against her husband.

When we thus approach that question, it is seen that Henry really had at the outset an arguable case, as a king and as a man. Even the New Woman of our day must in consistency admit that his first marriage was one of those which had better be dissolved, having substantially failed in all their objects. We must not let our sense of a man's odiousness in later life affect our judgment of his beginnings; nor must we let our sense of Mr. Froude's ethical untrustworthiness (as shown, for instance, in his suppression of the plea of Catherine's virginity[1] at her second wedding) put us upon rejecting every plea he advances. By the moral lights of his day, Henry was in a grievous perplexity. The Levitical law[2] said in so many words "If a man shall take his brother's "wife it is an unclean thing. . . . They shall be childless". True, the same inspired code elsewhere expressly provided (what Mr. Froude ignores) that a brother *must* endeavour to have offspring by his childless brother's widow;[3] and it so happened that this other precept had been used to urge on, as it was afterwards used to justify, the second marriage.[4] Henry took anxious counsel on the subject; and Bishop Burnet has preserved for our entertainment[5] the conflicting views of Bucer, Œcolampadius, Paulus Phrygion, Zwingli, Grineus and Calvin, who respectively held, the first, that the Levitical text was binding on all mankind; the second, that it was not; the third, that it was; the fourth, the same, but with a saving clause on behalf of Katherine; the fifth, that the Levitical law was valid, but that the marriage ought not to be dissolved; and the sixth, that the law being decisive, the marriage should be annulled. The one thing agreed upon by all the Protestant theologians was that the Pope had no power in the matter; and the trying text in Deuteronomy, founded on by the Papists, was by the other side in the main judiciously shelved as a divine mystery, it being left to later times to reach the prosaic explanation that the Law of Moses is a medley of many codes, framed at many times, by many hands, in more lands than one. For Henry, the main religious fact was that his bed was cursed. He could remember, or those about him could

---

[1] Mr. Froude chooses to follow Burnet. The edifying pros and cons may be studied in Herbert, *Life and Reign of Henry VIII*, Murray's Reprint, pp. 378-382, and p. 115; Polydore Vergil, lib. 27 *ad init.*; Burnet, Part I, Book ii, *ad init.*; and Hallam, Ch. ii, note *h*.
[2] *Leviticus*, xx, 21.
[3] *Deuteronomy*, xxv, 5.
[4] Polydore Vergil, *Hist. Angl.* L. xxvii.
[5] *History of the Reformation*, Part I, Book ii (Nares' ed., vol. I, pp. 150-151).

recall, how when his mother died just after his bethrothal to his brother's widow, and his father was struck with illness, the double trouble was held for a sign of divine displeasure, and the contract was sought to be renounced. He might well think that there had fallen upon him a more comprehensive punishment because his father and he had refused to profit by their former lesson. The idea of ascertaining *how* it was that Queen Katherine came to have one miscarriage or still-birth after another, and how the males she did bear living died immediately, probably did not enter into even the medical speculation of the time; but if it did, it would not affect the religious problem.

The ethic of to-day, however, especially as wielded by the new moral authority above mentioned, can hardly let pass the medical clue. For, when the matter is looked into, there is seen reason to doubt the explanation of Henry that the Queen's inability to bear viable male children was due to "certain diseases" from which she suffered. The trouble really seems to have come from the other side. The relevant facts are: (1) that of all Katherine's pregnancies only one girl-child survived, and she sickly; (2) that Henry's illegitimate son, created by him Duke of Richmond, died in adolescence, apparently from the same kind of constitutional malady as later destroyed Edward VI; (3) that Anne Boleyn, like Katherine, bore to Henry a stillborn female and a stillborn male child; (4) that Anne's daughter Elizabeth, though not sickly, was in her turn, according to contemporary scandal, incapable of child-bearing;[1] (5) that Edward VI, born of Jane Seymour, began to pine in early boyhood, and died at puberty, of some deep-seated congenital disease; and (6) that by Catherine Howard and Catherine Parr Henry had no other issue. 'Twere to consider too curiously to seek to know at this time of day the medical explanation, though to a medical eye the

---

[1] Ben Jonson's conversations with Drummond of Hawthornden.

problem has fascination. Suffice it that there is no need to surmise acquired disease on Henry's part.[1] His father, Henry VII, was the only child of a mother who had three husbands; and of the eight children of Henry VII, two sons and two daughters died in childhood, and Arthur in late boyhood; while of the two surviving daughters Margaret gave birth to a son, James the Fifth of Scotland, whose children mostly died immediately after birth. It is all rather interesting as showing how population was kept down in the Middle Ages, king's children dying at such a rate; but it also suggests that there was in Henry's stock one of those obscure heredities whose significance has begun to be recognised in modern fiction, if not yet in ethics.

And the matter is so far practically relevant to this inquiry, that we find Henry to have been a singular extension or decadence, so to speak, of his father's tendencies. 'Of Henry the Seventh, Bacon tells us that "it is a strange thing that, though he were a dark "prince and infinitely suspicious, and his times full of "secret conspiracies and troubles; yet in twenty-four "years' reign he never put down or discomposed coun- "sellor or near servant, save only Stanley, the lord "chamberlain. . . . . He was indeed full of appre- "hensions and suspicions. But as he did easily take "them, so he did easily check them, and master "them; whereby they were not dangerous, but troubled "himself more than others.'"[2] In the son, we have the suspiciousness carried to an extreme, without the power of sitting in judgment upon it. For the rest, while Henry VII was one of the most minutely laborious of kings, the Father of the English Reformation was

---

[1] Mr. Froude has cast a dramatic light on the subject by his bold but not injudicious hypothesis that the reckless infidelities of Anne Boleyn, which cost her her life, were inspired by the desperate desire to have a male child, which the King, in her opinion, was unable to give her. *The Divorce of Catherine of Aragon*, 1891, pp. 426-427.

[2] *The Reign of Henry VII*, Murray's ed., pp. 400-401.

distinctly a pedant. The elder Henry, as Bacon puts it in his magistral way, "had nothing in him of "vainglory, but yet kept state and majesty to the height; "being sensible that majesty maketh the people bow, but "vainglory boweth to them".[1] The son, on his part, was a zealous contriver of the interludes and other laborious entertainments which his father viewed with sad civility; and when he went to war, it was with a preposterous parade which anticipated that of Napoleon the Third, and would have made his soldierlike father stare. When he went over seas in 1513 "his house of timber went about "with him in fourteen waggons; he had a tent of cloth of "gold besides several scores of minor tents and pavilions "for his retinue. The non-combatant part of this follow- "ing was absurdly large—scores of cooks, confectioners, "lavenders, butlers, scullions, and henchmen. His ward- "robe alone was calculated to occupy 'a hall of forty-five "feet long by fifteen broad'. He took with him his "Master of the Jewel-house, with many strong boxes "full of jewellery. But perhaps the most astonishing part "of his train was the complete choir of his chapel-royal, "to the number of no less than 115 chaplains and singers. "With such a horde of useless follows, requiring hun- "dreds of waggons and thousands of horses, Henry "seems almost to vie with Xerxes in his absurd and "unpractical ostentation."[2] Naturally, the campaign came to nothing: indeed, it would have been still more natural had it ended in Henry's utter destruction. And this, be it remembered, was the king in whom Mr. Froude, under the tuition of Mr. Carlyle, learned to see the ideal Strong Man for the Strong Man's task of "reforming" the Church in England.

If any general explanation be needed for the details of Henry's course, this of his innate pedantry will suffice. His policy in fighting for his divorce is of a piece with his

[1] *Id.*, p. 399.
[2] C. Oman, in Mr. Traill's *Social England*, iii, 73.

diatribe against Luther, in Latin, which (though probably not wholly His Majesty's) Mr. Hallam did not assert to be any better than Luther's own; and with his queer Mystery Play of 1527, in which the schoolboys of St. Paul's played, among other things, " Religio, Ecclesia, " Veritas, like three widows, in garments of silk, and suits " of lawn and cyprus; Heresy and False Interpretation, " like sisters of Bohemia, apparelled in silk of divers " colours; the heretic Luther, like a party friar, in russet " damask and black taffety"; and " Luther's wife, like a " frow of Spiers in Almayn, in red silk ".[1] That Luther should have a wife was for the English Father of the Reformation even such a scandal as his own later matrimonial measures have become for posterity; and for the Defender of the Faith the general teaching of Luther was damnable heresy, pure and simple, for which he would have burned the heretic out of hand, even as he besought the Bavarian king to do. It moves Mr. Froude to sage reflection that this play, representing the Pope as wickedly put in captivity and the Church as trodden under foot by the Emperor, was played at Greenwich only three years before—with Wolsey dying in disgrace— "'the Pope's Holiness' was fast becoming in English " eyes the plain Bishop of Rome, held guilty towards " this realm of unnumbered enormities, and all England " was sweeping with immeasurable velocity towards the " heretic Luther". That is Mr. Froude's lively way of keeping up the interest of his narrative. To a plain reader, the velocity of development alleged to be going on in 1530 is no more perceptible than the unnumbered enormities of Pope Clement, who, unhappy gentleman, would readily enough have given Henry his divorce were it not for fear of the irresistible Emperor (who happened to be Katherine's nephew), and would as readily have declared straightforwardly against it were it not for fear of alienating Henry, lately laurelled as Defender of the

---

[1] Froude, vol. i, p 75.

Faith. For if Henry had his perplexities, the Pope no less had his; and when we read of him avowing that he had never been able to find the key to that totality of divine and human law which was declared to have been locked in his official breast by the Holy Spirit, we are apt to-day to find him the least unsympathetic of the whole group of intriguing egoists concerned. Henry, professing to be the champion of the Church as against Charles, cared not in the least whether the Pope were ruined by granting the divorce; and Charles, champion of the faith in his own way, did not care whether England was driven into schism by the withholding of it. His Holiness seems to have been unfeignedly anxious to oblige either of the bullying potentates who made his life a burden by their exigencies, provided only that his concession should not upset him; and he finally decided simply to choose the less of two evils. England had to be politically lost to the Church, lest otherwise the Church should become the bondmaid of the Empire. He even went so far as privately to advise Henry at more than one time to marry Anne Boleyn without more ado, leaving it to His Holiness either to undo the first marriage at his leisure or legalise both[1]—a scheme which after all need not finally deprive him of our sympathy, and which Henry rejected rather from suspicion than from scruple.

As for the king's second marriage, that was in the end illegally accomplished in just such a fashion; the king after all his years of litigation finally doing what he would not do when Pope Clement had privately advised it before. The royal pedant furtively married Anne Boleyn (and that none too soon)[2] before any form of divorce

---

[1] Herbert, as cited, pp. 349, 445.

[2] Mr. Hallam sternly observes: "I think a prurient curiosity about such "obsolete scandal very unworthy of history" (ch. ii, note g); but he so far relents as to supply us with details. A letter of Cranmer proves that the king's marriage, which the historians before Burnet dated Nov. 14, 1532, did not take place till about Jan. 25, 1533 (Ellis's *Letters Illustrative of English History*, vol. ii, p. 39). Cranmer did not even know of it till a fortnight after that. The birth of Elizabeth, again, is definitely proved to

between him and Catherine had been gone through, thus committing bigamous adultery on no higher sanction than the favorable opinions of six foreign universities, obtained, as Mr. Hallam decides, "not always without a little "bribery, even as those of Oxford and Cambridge were " not given without a little intimidation ". What Cranmer did was not to marry Henry to Anne but to pronounce Catherine divorced afterwards, an act of gratuitous decorum on his part which cost him dear in the end. It would seem as if after all the Pope might have stood to his own advice had he not been made to understand that acquiescence at this stage would not check Henry's policy of separation; and then came the Pope's excommunication, followed by the English Parliament's renunciation of his authority,[1] of which the first effects were the withholding of His Holiness's former perquisites on the appointment of bishops, and the deprivation of two bishoprics held by Italian Cardinals. All this was progress on the line of least resistance, as was the appeal of Convocation to the king for a new translation of the Bible.

Yet even then, when the suppression of the monasteries and nunneries was at length proceeded with, there arose insurrection on such a scale that even after its repression the king saw fit to secure his position by bestowing the confiscated lands freely among the nobility and other landlords, a step which at once put on his side the great conservative power in matters political, a sufficient vested interest. Without that, he could not feel secure. Henry,

have occurred on September 7, 1533 (Hallam, as cited); "so", in the words of the sagacious Bishop Burnet, "there not being full eight months " between the marriage and that birth, which would have opened a scene of " raillery to the court of Rome, it seems the day of the marriage was then " said to be in November," *History of the Reformation*, Part III, B. ii (Nares' ed., vol. iii, p. 107). For further scandal concerning Queen Elizabeth's mother, the uninformed reader may consult Dr. Lingard (*History of England*, ed. 1849, vol. v, p. 1, *note*); and the efforts of earlier Catholics are duly commemorated by Bishop Burnet (Part I, B. ii, vol. i, p. 66).

[1] On this compare Anthony Harmer on the *Errors and Defects of Burnet*, 1693, p. 19.

indeed, at all times showed a surprising susceptibility to popular opinion, considering his attitude towards his ministers, having once made a public explanation and sent Anne Boleyn away from court in deference to the murmurs of his subjects;[1] but we cannot suppose him to have yielded in either case without good cause, whether subjective or objective; and in the case of the rebellion there was solid pressure enough. As against the mixed state of things in the south, where the innovators did most of the talking, there was in the north a mass of determined adherents to the ecclesiastical cause. So that, whatever prejudice there may have been against the monasteries, it could not conceivably have availed to overthrow them had the king been on their side. The monasteries after all had more friends than enemies; and they could buy defence.

We are finally led, then, to the conviction that the English Reformation was made possible through the fact that the English King needed a divorce which the Pope did not dare give him. But for this, there could have been no "English Reformation" in the sixteenth century; and in that case the whole course of English history in the seventeenth would have been profoundly different. As Bishop Burnet saw two hundred years ago, the preliminary work "could hardly have been done but by a "man of his humour". If such a proposition seems to clash with the modern conception that great historic episodes are always the results of great general causes, that conception must just be modified to suit the facts; for the facts here are clear. Certainly, wider causes came in later to widen the breach set up by Henry's action; but their operation was clearly contingent on that action. The Father of the Reformation was emphatically anti-Protestant, anti-Lutheran, to the day of his death. He set his face rigidly against marriage for the clergy; he stood fast for transubstantiation; he caused the heretic

[1] Herbert, p. 362.

Lambert to be burned by way of showing that the King of England had not "embraced the new doctrines lately "circulated in Germany"; he rigorously forbade the translation of the New Testament by Tyndale and Coverdale, and all other translations save that which he had authorised; he forbade the circulation of the treatises of Wycliffe, Tyndale, and Frith; and he seems to have come near executing Catherine Parr, his last wife, who, like Anne Boleyn, read the prohibited works, and further had the hardihood to argue about them with her aging lord while "the anguish of a sore leg" was added to his normal infirmities.[1] The one point in which he had wrought "reformation" was in the suppression of the monasteries, a proceeding which, even before the searching investigation of Father Gasquet, was seen by non-Catholic students to have been conducted in the spirit of the Wolf versus the Lamb, whatever may have been the Lamb's carnal transgressions. Dr. Beard emphatically decides that the spoliation "was so entirely a "financial expedient as to be altogether unworthy of notice "in any religious connection; whatever may have been the "sins and laxities of the monasteries, no one who looks at "the character of the King, the agents whom he employed, "and the uses to which the proceeds were put, can believe "that they were dissolved for that reason".[2] Mr. Massingberd's Anglican account of last generation led to substantially the same conclusions as are reached by the Catholic historian[3] in this—namely, that most of the larger monasteries were conducted in strict conformity to their ideals; and that their suppression was an act of political rapine, largely inspired and directed by Thomas Cromwell, and authorised by Henry partly by reason of his then pressing need for money, which could thus be obtained without troubling Parliament, and partly with

[1] Herbert, p. 735.
[2] Hibbert Lectures, as cited, pp. 306-307.
[3] Gasquet, *Henry VIII and the English Monasteries*, 2nd ed., vol. i, pp. 329-340.

the desire of winning new moral support among his subjects, or some of them. It would be some comfort to him under his sense of having broken with the historic Church to feel that a number of his people hailed him as the conscientious reformer of a corrupt monasticism.

As for the actual effects of the suppression, they were of course neither so beneficial as is made out by the Protestants nor so deplorable as is made out by the Catholics. Monasteries are at best a kind of intellectual poorhouses, of workhouses for the poor in spirit; and as managed in the Middle Ages they bred the spiritual poverty they undertook to relieve, whatever they may have done as regards the poverty of the body. Father Gasquet, in addition to being a scholar and a gentleman, is a monk; and as such he of course cannot share our lay indifference to the mere stoppage of so much ritual machinery in an age which needed quite another sort of activity to purify and renew it. If Henry had set up scholarships and fellowships, even in moderate number, in place of the monkeries he upset, there would have been a clear gain to culture. The remarks of Mr. Hallam on this head are interesting memorials of the Whig creed of *laissez-faire*, which when he wrote was in its idealistic and irresponsible youth, nourished on the gospel of Adam Smith, and strong in the moral ineptitude of the Tory adversary. Against those non-economic writers who had denounced the bestowal of the Church estates by Henry on a crew of courtiers and land-grabbers, and who had dwelt on the gain that would have arisen from their devotion to the endowment of schools and colleges, he felt bound to make Smithian demurrers, which are yet all undermined by his avowal that the partition actually made subserved only private greed.

Behind Mr. Hallam's wavering argument there is nothing but the primary dogma of the wrongfulness of any public endowment of culture; and it ends in the Whig confession of faith: "nor are we to forget that the "class to whom all the abbey lands have fallen have been "distinguished at all times, and never more than in the "first century after that transference of property, for their "charity and munificence".[1] To which, without unduly crying over spilt milk, we may briefly answer that the "Protestant" spoliation of the monastery lands—a process which in our own day the descendants and representatives of the impropriators would describe as "robbing God"— contrasts very badly with the course previously taken by Wolsey, who, robbing God in God's name and the Pope's, used the wealth of suppressed convents to found Christ Church College; and further that the "charity "and munificence" of the receivers of the filched lands is a myth, which, in face of the agrarian depopulations of Henry's and Elizabeth's reigns, is at least as unacceptable as the Catholic mythology of Cobbett and Dr. Lingard. The real lesson of the suppression of the monasteries is neither that a large landed aristocracy, endowed no matter how, is the best machinery for promoting culture, nor that Protestantism brought in individualism and poverty where Catholicism had established socialism and comfort; but just this: that a feudal king could best upset a religion by endowing a large number of powerful and covetous persons with the plunder; or, in other words, that religious dynamics and statics are alike to be understood in terms of pecuniary interest.

The modern Socialist eulogy of the monastic system is of course to be set aside as one of the caprices of the partisanism of schools. The economic problem had begun to force itself on men's eyes in the previous reign; and a system of secular provision for the poor had to be begun while the monasteries were still in force, the Catholic system having failed in that as in other respects. As for the dispossessed monks and nuns, they seem to have been pretty regularly pensioned, and may be supposed on the average to have lost little happiness by their return to normal life. It is thus not clear that there was not some gain to civilisation in the way of a

[1] *Constitutional History of England*, ed. 1863, vol. i, p. 81.

replacement of a certain proportion of mental albeit delicate life in a population chiefly notable for appetite and muscle, the restored element counting for something in the rapid flowering of mental life in the England of Elizabeth.

But, however that may be, the suppression of the monasteries was clearly no expression of a new moral growth among the English people. In the case of Thomas Cromwell, though his is too obscure a character to permit of our conceiving him with any confidence, there was perhaps a certain idealistic hostility to the power, as apart from the creed, of Rome; but in the case of the lay impropriators in general there was no more of spiritual impulse than had moved the baronage of previous ages when in its impenitent moods it coveted the Church's wealth, cursing the ancestral piety which had bestowed it. Whatever the Reformation may have later done for the higher civilisation, it mainly proceeded at the outset on the lowest—or shall we say the first?—orders of motive. Only in so far as the spirit of criticism then abroad gave Henry's benificiaries additional courage to commit their sacrilege, was there any intellectual element in the case. It was in England very much as in Germany, where, as Dr. Beard admits, so soon as the suppression of the Peasants' War the Reformation passed "very much into the hands of the "Princes", who "saw that its effect must be the "secularization to a large extent, of the Church pro- "perty, a process of which they wished to secure the "control".[1] And in Scotland the process was still more nakedly one of expropriation of a rich clergy by a greedy baronage. The nearest analogue to the episode, thus far, was the chronic spoliation of the Jews by kings and mobs in earlier ages, when the sense of a religious and therefore of a moral grievance had gilded somewhat the primeval instinct of plunder.

[1] Hibbert Lectures, p. 176.

As for the secular clergy, so called, they made no clean breach with their past. Under menace of a prosecution by the king over some technical treason committed by them under Wolsey, they paid the subsidy he wanted, and at the same time agreed to make no further "canons" without his assent. That was all. That the king was the fountain of all non-ecclesiastical law was a principle already accepted; and the Church at this stage acknowledged no more. And so far was its organisation from having lost its old power over opinion, that in 1532 we find it burning Thomas Bilney for his preaching against vows, pilgrimages, and prayers to saints, though Bilney was so far from Lollardism, or the later Puritanism, as to insist on the necessity of ordination by bishops, or confession, and on the priestly power of absolution. Others were burnt in the same year for such heresy as denying purgatory and condemning expiatory masses; and Cranmer in the following year could not save Frith, who had denied transubstantiation. And so little of congruous Protestantism was there in the new dispensation, that Henry's policy of murderous self-assertion is still best typified in the scene of the simultaneous execution by his orders of six men, three of them for maintaining the Pope's religious supremacy, and the other three for calling in question the Pope's religion; an episode which brings out with a special salience the fact that cruelty in the name of religion, so often set down to "sincere fanaticism", is in large part the expression of an animal rage which can hardly be said to have anything to do with intellectual conviction.

Church and Parliament alike again slavishly ratified every one of Henry's caprices and cruelties, and at the same time enforced the creed of the Church of Rome with all the cruelty that Rome could possibly have put into the work. Here, we may say, the insincere persecuted the sincere. Sir Thomas More died for his too thorough devotion to Church and Pontiff: Queen Catherine the Third could not save her gentlewoman, Anne

Askew, from torture and death for some refinement of interpretation which varied from the Roman dogma; and the Six Articles, voted by a Parliament which would as readily have voted sixty, affirmed at the stake's point and the rope's end all the cardinal doctrines of the Dark Ages, from which Lollardism had tended to swerve. It was a carnival of callous savagery such as no other country north of the Alps had yet seen within the era of nominal civilisation; and the one moral fact which now stands out from the whole broil of affirmation and denial is the power of the Christian superstition of kingship to override all others,[1] and to degrade the nation most boastful of its spiritual and political freedom into the most enslaved herd of loyalists that northern Europe could show. It was in the most absolute obliteration of freedom of thought, speech, and life, that the English Reformation took root.

---

[1] "The strange thing is," writes Dr. Beard, "how little the nation "counts for, how much the Prince" (*Hibbert Lectures*, p. 304. Cf. p. 403).

CHAPTER V.

THE MORAL AND INTELLECTUAL SEQUEL.

WHEN we carry into the succeeding reigns our inquiry as to "what happened at the Reformation", we do but find fuller reason to describe the process as a struggle in which the personal bias of the Crown, or of its ministers, set one ecclesiastical doctrine up and another down by turns, till at last political expediency kept one in place. In this process "spiritual need" was the least of all the factors. Vested interests were so much stronger that they in a measure controlled even the action of the Crown; whereas religious ideas, critical or constructive, can be seen to have triumphed politically only in so far as they lent themselves either to the vested interests or to State policy.

The proof of the essentially political and financial nature of the change comes out most vividly in the contrast between the reigns of the young Edward VI and his sister Mary. Throughout the first, religious persecution went on in the name of the "reformed" faith as it had gone on under Henry. Joan Bouchier was burned for denying that Christ was man, and Van Barre for denying that he was God. These novelties of heresy point to the instant result of a general circulation of the Bible in the vernacular. Of course, there had been English translations in use before Henry VIII, just as there had been German translations before Luther, and French and Spanish versions likewise. From the independent study of these versions came much of what early heresy there was; and when, in a time of peace and discussion, the translations were spread more widely, there was a proportionate increase of heretical doctrine, no other result being possible where people were taught to find absolute and supernatural truth in a chaos of primitive myth, history, law and theosophy. The old trouble about transubstantiation in particular went from bad to worse. That otherwise credulous Christians ever began to doubt the abracadabra of the "Real Presence" (plainly enough asserted in the "*Hoc est corpus meum*", from which modern inquiry deduces the "hocus-pocus" of to-day) can only be explained by the fact that the strict Scriptural doctrine was a main means to the aggrandisement of the clergy. It was probably not that the innovators loved reason the more, but that they loved the priest the less; and that became for them the true doctrine which most minimised the sacerdotal function.

Mr. Hallam has observed in his draconic way that it would have been well if the reformers had learned "by "exposing the absurdities of transubstantiation, not to "contend for equal nonsense of their own".[1] But what else could they do? The fountain of trouble lay in the sacred books. Here was a crude survival of primitive barbarism, only in our own times understood as such, made sacrosanct and awful for half-civilised and intellectually childish Christendom by the whole authority and tradition of the faith. Men might get the length of protesting that bread and wine remained bread and wine whatever a mumbling priest might do; but if they held by the sacred books at all they could only vary the dogma. Thus we find the Wycliffite William Swinderley, protected by John of Gaunt, propounding "that the sacrament of "the altar is bread *and* Christ's body";[2] from which fantasy, the "consubstantiation" of later Lutheranism,[3] others proceeded to the vaguer notion of a "spiritual" presence, depending on the act of communion, and not on the office of the priest; and yet others, as Zwingli and Œcolampadius, to the quasi-rational tenet (current in

---

[1] *Constitutional History*, 10th ed., vol. i, p. 89.
[2] Massingberd's *English Reformation*, 4th ed., p. 167.
[3] Mr. Hallam is clearly in error in saying that Luther "invented" this.

the pseudo-science of our own day) that the ceremony was one of simple commemoration, the bread and wine being merely symbols. At this last stage, clearly, the theological and the ecclesiastical elements alike are rarefied to the vanishing point; and the strife to which the proposition gave rise, as Mr. Hallam notes, nearly wrecked the Reformation on the Continent. Churchmen, if they would remain such, must perforce put the doctrine in a form which yielded some importance to their office, and due deference to the sacred text. The safe course, as Mr. Massingberd has urged, is that of those who "do not profess to explain the matter, but to "adopt the language of Scripture without explanation"; and this was the course of the notoriously judicious Hooker; whose doctrine is more evangelically expressed in "the well-known language of Bishop Ken":—" Oh, " God Incarnate! *how* thou canst give us thy flesh to "eat, and thy blood to drink; *how* thy flesh is meat "indeed; *how* thou who art in heaven art present on our "altar, I can by no means explain; but I firmly believe "it all, because thou hast said it." Applied to doctrine, the principle squared with that of the legendary scholar who said: "When I do not understand a passage, I "translate it literally;" and for the ordinary believer, the principle came to be of the nature of that expressed in the more modern formula: "We believe in baptism "because we have seen it done."

Whatever was done in the way of doctrinal change, accordingly, was determined by the two opposite pressures of resistance to the old political danger from the party of Rome and resistance to the religious radicalism which would have impoverished the Church. Thus it was that Cranmer, as Mr. Green says, "drifted" into doctrinal Protestantism, playing into the hands of the anti-Papal nobility by adopting one by one doctrines which marked the English Church off from Catholicism; and guarding the Church from disintegration by burning, in the true Roman manner, those who sought to carry matters further still, as he had previously burnt those who first pushed the doctrines which he himself was later to subscribe. The ruling nobles, whether of Somerset's party or Warwick's, were alike committed to opposing any return towards Rome, which would mean to them risk of loss of the appropriated Church lands. But they were as far from being "reformers", in any genuine sense, as from being Papists; and the fact that Somerset framed for himself on his assumption of the Protectorship a "beautiful prayer", taken in connection with his later practice in pulling down Churches to build himself a palace, only serves to remind us what a twy-natured thing was the religiosity of those ages, as of our own. Such leadership as his and Warwick's could only undermine whatever moral authority the "Protestant" cause had as yet acquired among average men; and the wrangles of the bishops on points of creed (Gardiner refuting Cranmer, and Cranmer sending Gardiner and others to the Tower), joined with the riotous indecorum of the innovators who went beyond Cranmer as he did beyond Gardiner, soon overtasked the limited progressive power of the bulk of the nation. The "Reformation" had spent its credit as rapidly as did the "reign of the saints" a century later.

When, accordingly, after six years of rapacious and persecuting Protestantism, the Princess Mary, daughter of Katherine, came to the throne, a full two-thirds of the nation was as ready to re-embrace the old Catholicism as was its posterity later to restore royalism after the Commonwealth. This is not now disputed by any historical school. And, though in the ordinary view of the "sincerity" of religious movements such a somersault is a mere freak of nature, it becomes transparently intelligible when we state it in terms of all the ideas that have weight with masses of people in the Christian stage of culture. King Henry had begun his course on a question of Scriptural law, surmising that he lay under God's curse for obeying one of the two contrary texts to which Christendom looked for guidance in such a case as his marriage. To people who believed in a ruling Providence, it might well seem clear as noonday that he had read the divine law backwards, and that the curse really fell when he put his first wife away. Anne Boleyn had died on the scaffold, after bearing first a daughter and a still-born son. Jane Seymour had died in childbed, and her son had perished in his still tender youth, as his illegitimate brother had done. Next, the king, having married Anne of Cleves, divorced her on pretexts which to the normal conscience were utterly lawless, and proved him to have got far past the stage of primary religious scrupulosity; so that the very Church and Parliament which yielded him the divorce had immediately passed a law to prevent similar divorces on the part of his subjects. Next, his marriage with Catherine Howard had but revealed a new fatality of dishonour, and brought another victim to the block. Finally, the marriage with Catherine Parr had had no issue; and after so many efforts to bar her succession, the despised daughter of the one lawful wife had come to her inheritance. Never did a prince come to the throne with such a semblance of divinely established destiny; and nothing but the inveterate passion for persecution, inseparable from all irrational faith, and the more insane in her case because of the intensity of her Catholicism, could have caused the Catholic Church yet again to lose ground in her short reign.

The completeness of the recantation made by Church and State at her enthronement is an instructive commentary on the familiar doctrine of the stedfastness and "sincerity" of the English character. The Parliament which at Henry's order had renounced the Papal supremacy, and divorced his wives as occasion called, now solemnly welcomed the Papal Legate, promptly voted a return to Papal obedience, received absolution on its knees, and repealed the whole ecclesiastical legislation of the two previous reigns. But one thing it would not do. It would not surrender one yard of the Church lands that had passed into private keeping; and the only renunciations made were those effected by the Queen herself, at a cost to the crown of a large part of its annual revenue. To have seized the stolen lands would doubtless have cost Mary her throne; as the attempt to recover the Scotch tithes in the next century was the beginning of the end for Charles I. Tithes and income were the realities of religion for the average man then as now. We cannot have a statistic of the number of men who cared enough for their creed to do more on its behalf than persecute its opponents; but we may surmise that those who would restore property to the Church on either side were rather less numerous than the builders of churches.

Once the landholders felt safe, only an extreme virulence of persecution, coupled with the imposition of the Spanish influence, could undo the Queen's popularity; and even that conjunction would not have served to restore Protestantism, had not her successor been in a manner committed to Protestantism by the hostility of the Catholic powers. But, that being so, Church and State turned one more somersault and re-embraced Protestantism, albeit gradually, the Queen herself being far from Protestant orthodoxy. What really built up the Protestantism of Elizabethan England from the Queen's accession on, was on the one hand, the Crown's need to rely on the people as against Spain or France, and on the other hand the tendency of the people to add to their new hatred of Spain a hatred of Spain's religion. This is an element in creed-building which now comes first into prominence. A national devotion to any creed as such takes a good deal of cultivation; but racial animosities have the spontaneity of animal passions and the durability of a vice. The mere idea of the advent of a foreign king had enraged the common people alike in the early part of the reign of Henry VIII, when there was a prospect of his being succeeded by the King of Scotland, and at the advent of Mary, when, having put down the faction of Lady Jane Grey, she insisted on marrying Philip of Spain.

Scotland was the ancient enemy, and Spain the modern; but the new hatred mounted in the ratio of the power and importance of the adversary. For Spain, regarded formerly with friendly eyes as the enemy of the power of France, was become the enemy of Elizabethan England in the sense in which Holland was that of Reformation England, and France that of Georgian England—the commercial and maritime rival, the would-be supplanter, or the prior claimant to coveted lands. The Drakes and Frobishers hated the Spaniards as spontaneously as one gamecock does another; and, religion being one of the great channels for malignant passion in the ages of faith, it was impossible that such a ground of creed-difference as already existed should not be improved on both sides. No view as to the rival theories of the sacred bread and wine; no sense of the unfitness of private masses and confession and priestly celibacy; not even the enthralling strife over the wearing of surplices, could spread a Protestant ferment as fast as the simple consciousness that the great national enemy was the great champion of Popery. And, as even Mr. Froude has been moved to remark, the complacent English conscience gave itself a new ground, in the recital of Spanish cruelties, for hating Rome as the Church of blood, at the very time that English and Protestant cruelty was seeking to stamp out Irish Catholicism by massacres such as capped the bloodiest deeds of the worst adventurers of Spain.

In the year 1580, the Jesuit Campian "was able " to preach with hardly a show of concealment to a vast "audience in Smithfield"; and the Catholic gentry received the Catholic missionaries with open arms; but after 1588, when the Catholic nobles led their retainers to Tilbury, and Lord Howard of Effingham led the English fleet against the Armada, the day of Catholic reaction was over, and the country was definitely Protestant. Made non-Papal by the personal equation of Henry and the class interest of the Protectorate; made Papal again by the loyalism under Mary, the English nation was at length made definitely anti-Papal by the concurrence of its ecclesiastical policy and its Queen's interest with its new national enmity to Spain in the days of Elizabeth. Even the growing doctrinal asperity of the new school of divines trained at Geneva (where the system of Rome had to be fought with a system as definite, if Protestantism were to be saved) could never have hardened and nerved the Protestantism of England as did the play of the primitive passions of racial separateness and hate.

When Mr. Green declares[1] that "it was with the "unerring instinct of a popular movement that, among a "crowd of far more herioc sufferers, the Protestants fixed, "in spite of his recantations, on the martyrdom of Cranmer "as the death-blow to Catholicism in England," he does but put, as too often happens in his pages, rhetoric for reasoning. "The Protestants" could not possibly have had any such "instinct" at the time of the event ; but if they had, it would have been no more unerring than the much more popular instinct which had welcomed back Catholicism under Mary. "It is from that moment", says Mr. Green, "that we may trace the bitter remem-"brance of the blood shed in the cause of Rome which ". . . . still lies graven deep in the temper of the "English people." Mr. Green is always setting up epoch-making "moments" of this sort. In this case, at least, it must be perfectly clear to every student that the statement is fantastic. Cranmer's case can never have seemed peculiarly outrageous to any one who knew his record, with its six recantations and its own tale of burnings of truer men who did not recant ; and the fact that he had been the instrument to divorce Mary's mother, and to illegitimatise herself, must have been felt in her day to give his execution the quality of a not altogether unjust vengeance. If his name has in later times been singled out as that of a leading Protestant martyr, it has been in virtue not of any "unerring

---

[1] *Short History*, p. 360.

"instinct of a popular movement", but of the simple partisanship of the Anglican Church, which looks to Cranmer as its clerical founder.

In the matter of tyranny and cruelty, the Protestant regimen of Elizabeth fell little behind that of Mary. The Marian bishops showed all the stedfastness which Protestants have been taught by Fox to associate with their own infallible cause; while at the outset of Elizabeth's reign "the Protestant minority among the clergy were already disgusting the people by their violence and greed".[1] In those years the Queen's ministers shed little blood; but when they began to execute the Jesuit missionaries they went on until the list mounted to something near two hundred, apart from the scores who died in jail.[2] Short of bloodshed, the tyranny was continuous. "No Archbishop of Canterbury since the days "of Augustine had wielded an authority so vast, so "utterly despotic, as that of Parker and Whitgift and "Bancroft and Abbot and Laud. The most terrible "feature of their spiritual tyranny was its wholly personal "character." "Whitgift strove to force on the Church the "Calvinistic supralapsarianism of his Lambeth Articles. "Bancroft, who followed him, was as earnest in enforcing "his anti-Calvinistic dogma of the Divine right of the "episcopate. Abbot had no mercy for Erastians, Laud "had none for anti-Erastians. . . . . All preaching or "reading in private houses was forbidden."[3] It was simply a change of tyrannies; and if more lives were taken under Mary than under Elizabeth, it was due not to any humanity of temper in Protestants, but to the fact that Elizabeth herself was absolutely irreligious, and had no faith for which to be fanatical. What she disliked most was the air of presumption in the lower orders; and on that score she vetoed the "prophesyings" which some

---

[1] *Short History*, p. 371.
[2] *Id.*, p. 402. Soame (*Elizabethan Religious History*, p. 597) admits 180.
[3] *Id.* p. 438.

of her bishops encouraged. The ease with which they were suppressed[1] is one more proof of the facility with which even fanaticism can be put down when the proper means are used, at the proper time. For the rest, the serenity with which the Queen contemplated the "religious destitution" of her people serves as well to demonstrate her own freedom from piety as did her remark to the complaining Archbishop Grindal that three or four preachers in a county were plenty.[2]

And when we look into the details, it cannot be said that she was without grounds. Neither the conforming nor the nonconformist clergy seemed to count much for civilisation, the first being in large part dishonest and the others in large part disorderly. The celebrated Browne, founder of the Brownists, who became the Independents, "assaulted the constable of his parish in demanding a "rate from him, and was committed to Northampton "gaol, where he quickly died. He used to boast that he "had been detained in thirty-two prisons, some so dark "that he could not see his hand at noonday. Death in "the thirty-third, under a charge of assault, throws a "shade of suspicion over all his former committals, "though he so far abandoned his principles as to hold the "rectory of Achwich, in Northamptonshire, yet he never "preached. . . . He quarrelled with his wife, and lived "apart from her during many years."[3] On the other hand, the scandal about a certain Archbishop of York, compromised with an inn-keeper's wife,[4] suggests that conformity was no security for propriety. But, apart from all special scandals, it is clear that the priesthood in these, the heroic days of Protestantism, was in the main either consciously insincere in its conformity or ignorant and unqualified. "Of the Popish [Anglican] clergy . . . . the vast majority were destitute of all useful knowledge,

---

[1] "Their obnoxious name was heard no more." Soame, *Elizabethan Religious History*, 1839, p. 226.
[2] *Id.* p. 225.   [3] *Id.* p. 229.   [4] Froude, *History*, vol. xii, p. 5.

and could read little Latin." "It would be easy to multiply testimonies . . . . to the papist inclinations of a great part of the clergy in the first part of this reign. They are said to have been sunk in superstition and looseness of living."[1] "A disorderly state of the Church, arising partly from want of any fixed rules of discipline, partly from the negligence of some bishops and simony of others, but above all from the rude state of manners and general ignorance of the clergy, is the common theme of complaint in this period, and aggravated the increasing disaffection towards the prelacy."[2] But if we turn to hear the disaffected, as represented in the Martin Marprelate tracts, we are led with some rapidity to conclude that the doctors, if they had had their way, would have been rather worse than the disease.

The question finally arises, then, in what sense the whole Reformation episode can be made out to have been a gain to civilisation? The naïve dogma of the Protestant Churches, that it put "truth" in place of "error", is now outside serious discussion, save in so far as we may admit that image-worship is less favourable to any play of intelligence than the doctrine which in the name of religion condemns it. For rational students of history the question must resolve itself into these: Were the mental and the moral life of the nation in any way advanced by the ecclesiastical change; and was its political development advantageously quickened? It ought now to be possible to discuss such questions judicially; and to some extent they have been so discussed, even in popular Protestant works. Thus, we find Mr. Green very candidly putting it that "The real " value of the religious revolution of the sixteenth century " to mankind lay not in its substitution of one creed for " another, but in the new spirit of inquiry, the new

---

[1] Hallam, *Constitutional History*, vol. i, p. 183, citing Strype's *Annals of the Reformation*, vol. i, p. 166.
[2] Hallam, vol. i, p. 191.

"freedom of thought and of discussion, which was "awakened during the process of change. But," he adds, "however familiar such a truth may be to us, it "was absolutely hidden from the England of the time."[1] Not only is the last clause true: it would be true if it were so expanded as to annul the one before. The truth in question has not become "familiar" even in our day. It is acceptable only to educated people, and remains a vain saying alike to the Nonconformist conscience and to the Conformist; for the High Church cannot any more than the Low see the value of the spirit of inquiry, and the Broad Church misapprehends it.

Nor was the kind of "inquiry" set up among the religious population such as availed much for light. In the first days of Protestantism, under the Protectorate, the phenomena were mostly those of mere unintellectual license, as in Lutheran Germany. "Ecclesiastical order "was almost at an end. Priests flung aside the surplice "as superstitious. Patrons of livings presented their "huntsmen or gamekeepers to the benefices in their gift, "and pocketed the stipend. All teaching of divinity "ceased at the Universities; the students indeed had "fallen off in numbers, the libraries were in part scattered "or burned; the intellectual impulse of the New Learning "had died away. One noble measure, indeed, the "foundation of eighteen grammar schools, was destined "to throw a lustre over the name of Edward, but it had "no time to bear fruit in his reign. All that men saw "was religious and political chaos, in which ecclesiastical "order had perished, and in which politics were dying "down into squabbles of a knot of nobles over the "spoils of the Church and the Crown."[2] In the next reign, what of free inquiry went on in the name of the Reformation was free only in the sense that it was independent of the Thirty-nine Articles. In place of the authority of the living Church it set up that of the dead

---

[1] *Short History*, p. 352.   [2] *Id., ib.*

Bible, interpreted with the same insane confidence as went to the work of the Inquisition. Bibliolatry is on the whole probably more unfavourable to free thought than Mariolatry and the worship of saints. Up to a certain point the Calvinists, no doubt, thought and read harder than the Catholics; but that point once reached, the new presbyter was really a more efficient strangler of speculation than the old priest, besides being quite as malevolent. To say nothing of the Presbyterian tyranny in Geneva and Scotland, the same school in England exhibited itself as the negation of all variety of opinion. " Never had the doctrine of persecution been urged with " such a blind and reckless ferocity " as by the new school of Presbyterians. " I deny," wrote Cartwright, ".that upon repentance there ought to follow any pardon "'of death. .... Heretics ought to be put to death " now. If this be bloody and extreme, I am content to " be so counted with the Holy Ghost."[1]

A little scientific reflection will show, indeed, that no Reformation of the Church, even were it disinterestedly gone about, could have the effect of either widening men's minds or raising their morals. The documentary basis for both Churches was the same; and the evangelical moral theory of the innovators was, as we have seen, positively more immoral than that of the quasi-corrupt conservatives, who compounded for indulgences by a certain amount of penitential discipline. To interrogate the Bible afresh was merely to turn to ancient ignorance for guidance to modern, the one-eyed consulting the blind. The impression which still prevails to some extent even among agnostics, that there was a lifting moral element in Puritanism, is a misconception set up by the mere phenomena of austerity and asceticism, phenomena which had existed in all civilised ages, Pagan and Christian. Puritanism was but a partial transference to lay life of the ascetic ideal of monasticism; and the lay effort broke

[1] Green, p. 456.

down like the clerical, for similar reasons. At its highest point, that is, long after the Reformation, it certainly did not produce a stricter sexual practice than subsists to-day among the Catholic peasantry and priesthood of Ireland; and in the directions in which real moral progress was most needed it seems to have counted for nothing, the Protestant being as much given as any one else to compounding for the sins he was inclined to by insistence on a few factitious virtues. His policy in Ireland, under one Protestant monarch after another, is the decisive proof that in civic wisdom and sympathy he went back rather than forward. Not that the Catholics of the time show a whit more ethical insight or elevation than the Protestants. More's deterioration from the luminous rationalism of his youth to the darkened fanaticism of his later life shows what the Catholic atmosphere could do. And in the intrigues of the palace which put Henry's reign in more respects than one on a level with that of a Mohammedan despot, the Catholics played as base a part as did their supplanters. Even as the anti-Papalists plotted against Catherine of Aragon and Catherine Howard, so did the anti-Lutherans plot against Anne Boleyn and Catherine Parr. The anti-Papal but Catholic Chancellor Wriothesley, father of Shakspere's patron, tortured the gentle Anne Askew with his own hands; and Mary's bishops were as cruel in a general way as any men of their age.

On the side of ordinary commercial morals, it is clear, there was no change for the better. Mr. Froude, who at the outset of his history paints a sufficiently fanciful picture of the rigid rectitude of the English people under Henry, on the strength of the many laws to put down the frauds which abounded among them, unconsciously reduces his general argument to absurdity by assuring us that this pristine righteousness gradually dwindled till the old trade companies perished for lack of honest men. " There were no longer tradesmen to be found in suffi-
" cient numbers who were possessed of the necessary

"probity; and we may perhaps in part connect the "phenomena with the deep melancholy which in those "[closing] years settled down on Elizabeth herself."[1] This is of course not to be taken seriously; but when, on the other hand, Professor Gardiner represents English statesmen of that age as being conscious that England had grown in moral stature by reason of the breach with Rome, it is difficult, if not to take him seriously, at least to conceive what he has in his mind. If he had said that England had gained in intellectual breadth and depth, that her literature had passed almost at a bound from the medieval bareness of the period after Chaucer to a modern complexity and subtlety, he would be intelligible. Even then, he might be challenged to say whether any work of the Elizabethan period showed a greater originality and modernity of mind than the *Utopia* of More, produced before Luther was heard of. But the very mention of that work recalls us at once to the true sources of the mental expansion of England in the latter part of the sixteenth century. To that expansion religious Protestantism contributed practically nothing; and if there had been no other new culture force at work there would simply have been no noticeable expansion at all. Mr. Froude, after delivering himself as above quoted on the trade morals of Elizabeth's latter days, forgetfully declares: "I believe the Reformation to have been the greatest incident in English history; the root and source of the expansive force which has spread the Anglo-Saxon race over the globe, and imprinted the English genius and character on the constitution of mankind".[2] If this were true, the Protestant Dutch and the Lutheran Germans ought to have done in an equal degree the things done by the English. Evidently Mr. Froude's rhetoric supplies no explanation whatever. But in view of the sociological facts the English expansion is in-

[1] *History of England*, edit. 1875, vol. i, p. 61.
[2] *The Divorce of Catherine of Aragon*, 1891, p. 18.

telligible enough. It clearly came of the new secular culture and the commercial stimulus set up by the new contacts of English with continental life, in the state of peace which Elizabeth generally contrived, by dint of much lying, to maintain as between England and the continental powers. The peace promoted foreign intercourse, both through trade and through individual travel, and the Elizabethan culture is obviously stimulated on all sides by the results of such intercourse. The new country-houses and gardens were built on Italian models; the new poetry was as much influenced by Italian models as by the classic culture spread by the new grammar-schools; and Italian fiction was the great storehouse of artistic motives for the new drama. Scolding old schoolmaster Ascham storms against the multitude of books newly translated out of the Italian, and pronounces them all lewd alike; but when he comes to details he lets slip the diverse facts that the readers of these translations " have in more reverence the Triumphes of Petrarche " than the Genesis of Moses. They make more account " of *Tullies* Offices than *S. Paule's* Epistles; of a tale in " *Bocace* than a storie of the Bible. Than they counte as " Fables, the holie misteries of Christian Religion. They " make Christ and his Gospell only serve Civill pollicie: " Than neyther Religion cummeth amisse to them. . . ."[1] That is to say, the Italian books set men thinking of ethics and rational politics as well as of things amorous; and they included Petrarch as well as Boccaccio.

The angry old moralist[2] goes on to throw a light on the beginnings of rationalism in England that is here worth looking to :—

" For where they dare, in cumpanie where they like, " they boldlie laugh to scorn both protestant and Papist. " They care for no scripture: They make no counte of

[1] *The Scholemaster* (written about 1563), Arber's reprint, p. 82.
[2] " It would be satisfactory," writes Mr. Arber, " if he could be cleared from the suspicion of a too great love for cock-fighting " (*Chronicle* prefixed to reprint of *Toxophilus*, p. 6).

THE MORAL AND INTELLECTUAL SEQUEL. 63

"generall councels: they contemne the consent of the
"Church: They passe for no Doctores: They mocke the
"Pope: They rail on *Luther*: They allow neyther side:
"They like none, but onelie themselves: The marke they
"shote at, the ende they looke for, the heaven they desire,
"is onelie their owne present pleasure and private proffit:
"whereby they plainlie declare of whose schole, of what
"Religion they be: that is, Epicures in living, and ἄθεοι in
"doctrine: this last worde is no more unknowne now to
"plaine Englishe men than the Person was unknown
"somtyme in England, untill some Englishe man took
"peines to fetch that develish opinion out of Italie."

This very explicit testimony gives no precise idea of the extent to which the new freethinking had permeated Elizabethan society; but the dying words of the elder Essex (Walter, father of Robert), though doubtless exaggerating through strong emotion, prove that it had gone far. Speaking of the intellectual life of his countrymen, the dying Earl averred that "The Gospel had been "preached to them, but they were neither Papists nor "Protestants; of no religion, but full of pride and "iniquity. There was nothing but infidelity, infidelity, "infidelity; atheism, atheism; no religion, no religion."[1] So that in the period of intellectual expansion which we associate in particular with the names of Bacon and Shakspere, the "psychological climate" was rather that of educated Italy than that of the Puritan England of tradition. Even among the common people there were stirrings of rationalism, for we find a Norfolk ploughwright, Matthew Hammond, burned at Norwich in 1579 for persistently declaring the New Testament "a fable, "Christ a mere sinful man, erected into an abominable "idol, the Holy Ghost a nonentity, and the sacraments useless".[2] Doubtless, the breach with Rome made way for the new freedoms of thought; but the thought itself

---

[1] Froude, *History*, vol. xi, p. 199, citing *MSS. Ireland*.
[2] Soame, as cited, p. 234.

went mainly on lines aloof from theology of any sort. Nor can the effect have been to make men politically worse than Essex himself, who was as cruel an exterminator of Irish as any English leader of his cruel age. If there was ever a period in which England was restless without being intellectual, literary without being progressive, productive without genius, and controversial without profit, it was in the period between the irreligious Elizabeth and the Civil War. "With the close of the "Elizabethan age," confesses Mr. Green, "the intel-"lectual freedom which had marked it faded insensibly "away: the bold philosophical speculations which "Sydney had caught from Bruno, and which had brought "on Marlowe and Raleigh the charge of atheism, died, "like her own religious indifference, with the Queen. "'Theology rules there,' said Grotius of England, "only ten years after the Queen's death; and when "Casaubon, the last of the great scholars of the six-"teenth century, was invited to England by King James, "he found both King and people indifferent to letters."[1] This was the time of which Mr. Green in the same breath asserts that "a new moral and religious impulse "spread through every class". It would have puzzled him to show any valuable moral result, abstract or concrete.

On the commercial side, finally, it is clear that the English advance owed nothing to the change of creed, save in so far as England profited by the peace which was maintained by the diplomacy of the Queen or her ministers. Here again Mr. Froude, in his inimitable way, lets us see the truth while asserting the fallacy:—

"Protestantism on the Continent had brought with it "war and misery. In England, the affinity between the "more genuine creed and material prosperity *had* "*opportunity to show itself*. The manufacturers of Ghent "and Bruges, leaving the grass to grow in the streets of

[1] *Short History*, chap. viii, sect. i, p. 449.

"their own splendid cities, had transferred their capital
"and their arts to London and to Bristol. For every
"languid English gentleman who had fled to France to
"enjoy the consolations of the Catholic religion, a
"hundred Flemish artizans sought the Island where they
"could toil in safety with their families, worship after
"their own fashion, and eat the fruit of their labours.
"The thousand ships which in the old times had sought
"annually the waters of the Scheldt, now discharged
"their cargoes on the wharves between London and
"Blackwall; and the great English commercial corpora-
"tions were absorbing the trade of the world, while the
"Castiles were drained of their manhood to feed the
"Flanders armies, or defend the Empire of the two
"Indies."[1]

From all which it appears that the Thirty-Nine Articles had nothing causal to do with the case. The trade of Antwerp came over because Antwerp had been besieged and taken by Philip's general; and England's commercial expansion could as well have come about under a Catholic sovereign who should have had the skill or luck to keep out of war as Elizabeth did. The beginnings had been made long before. "As far back as the reign of Henry "VII a commercial treaty had been concluded with "Florence, and the trade with the Mediterranean which "had begun under Richard III constantly took a wider "development."[2] If "Protestantism on the Continent "brought with it war and misery", Protestantism obviously had no special affinity with or power of inducing commercial prosperity, especially if it involved such a decline in commercial probity as Mr. Froude himself alleges.

As between Catholic and Protestant claims, then, our conclusion is clear enough. The Catholic, pointing to the Anabaptist movement in Germany and the scandalous chronicle of the domestic life of Henry VIII, affirms that Protestantism was but an expression of a corrupt yearning

---

[1] *History*, vol. xii, p. 1-2 [2] Green, p. 387.

for moral license, even as the Anglican and Dissenter in turn assert it of the Freethinker. The Protestant champion, on the other hand, points to the licentiousness of medieval Catholicism, and falls back on the paralogism of Mr. Froude: "The era of Elizabeth was the out-"pouring of the movement which Henry VIII com-"menced; and it was the grandest period in English "history. Is it credible that so invigorating a stream "flowed from a polluted fountain?"[1] According to Mr. Froude's own narrative, it must have done so, or else the moral transformation he alleges is a chimera. On the one hand he maintains that the old Catholicism was corrupt; on the other hand he insists that Henry and Thomas Cromwell, who lived and died Catholics in creed, were not "polluted", and that Cranmer, who made six recantations, was not worse but better than other people. Then, whatever moral and mental improvement took place was a result not of change in dogmas, but of new knowledge and culture apart from dogmas. The plays of Shakspere and the treatises of Bacon owed no more to Protestantism than did the theorem of Copernicus and the experiments of Galileo, Catholics both.

And, what is more, religious Protestantism drew as little from the new movements of thought as they from it. It is common to suggest, in modification of the false formula which credits the new culture to Protestantism, that Protestantism was a phase of the new culture. But the above survey of the facts leads us to no such conclusion, as regards either England or Germany. Henry was doubtless a well-educated king for his time; but it was not his education that moved him to break with the Pope. Mr. Green sets up a grotesque misconception when he writes that during the Civil Wars and the reign of Henry VII the world around was passing through momentous changes, among which he specifies these: "Its physical bounds were suddenly enlarged. The

---

[1] *The Divorce of Catherine of Aragon*, p. 12.

" discoveries of Copernicus revealed to man the secret of
" the universe. . . ."[1] In this way there is suggested a
new intellectual source for the Reformation. As a matter
of fact, the treatise of Copernicus, though meditated for
thirty-six years, was not published till 1543, when it was
brought out at the earnest request, as everyone knows, of
Cardinal Schomberg, and dedicated to the Pope. And, as
Mr. Green observes later,[2] without correcting his previous
blunder, "it was only in the later years of the sixteenth
" century that the discoveries of Copernicus were brought
" home to the general intelligence of the world by Kepler
" and Galileo".

So we come back to the personal equation of Henry, as
above traced, and to the other practical solutions forced
on us by the later steps of the Protestant development.
And that these give us in the main a true conception is
finally made the more credible by the undisputed fact
that in the next century even the religious movement,
after producing a political convulsion, spent itself, in
England as elsewhere. To summarise the summary of
Mr. Green: "The progress of Protestantism gradually
" ceased. It wasted its strength in theological contro-
" versies and persecutions, above all in the bitter and
" venomous discussions between the Churches which
" followed Luther, and the Churches which followed
" Calvin. It was degraded and weakened by the
" prostitution of the Reformation to political ends, by the
" greed and worthlessness of the German princes who
" espoused its cause, by the factious lawlessness of the
" nobles in Poland, and of the Huguenots in France.
" Meanwhile the Papacy succeeded in rallying the
" Catholic world round the Council of Trent. . . . . The
" enthusiasm of the Protestants roused a counter-en-
" thusiasm among their opponents. . . . . Even learning
" passed gradually over to the side of the older faith. . . .

---

[1] *Short History*, ch. vi, sect. iv, p. 297.
[2] Chap. vii, sect. vii, p. 412.

" Southern Germany . . . was the first country to be re-
" Catholicised. . . . In the Low Countries, the Re-
" formation was driven from the Walloon provinces, from
" Brabant, and from Flanders. In France, the conver-
" sion of the King [Henri IV] was followed by a quiet
" dissolution of the Huguenot party."[1] And what
happened in England, where the " Reformation" held its
ground in the shape of an unprogressive Protestantism
divided into warring sects, was that intellectual evolution
went on very much as it did in France, thanks neither to
Protestantism nor to Catholicism, but to the very fact
that under both systems alike the strife of sections
repelled a certain number of thinkers to other ground,
stimulated their distrust of the theology which bred such
constant dispeace, and to some extent left them free to
think on their own behalf. It would be a violent effort of
the imagination that should figure religious sects as
mellificantes, honey-making; but if they ever were so in
any sense it was to the end of the bees, " not for
" themselves ".

[1] Chap. viii, Sect. ii., *beginning*.

PART II.
THE RISE AND FALL OF THE DEISTIC MOVEMENT.

CHAPTER I.

THE BEGINNINGS OF DEISM.

What may be termed the second "psychological "moment" in modern English religious history is that of the rise of non-Biblical or Naturalistic Deism, a peculiarly interesting intellectual phase, which lies broadly between the Restoration and the French Revolution, Deism being only inferribly and inactively existent before the English Rebellion, and being seen to dwindle and disappear on the literary side before the outbreak of the profounder convulsion in France, which was the new birth of so many innovating principles. Interesting as the Deistic movement is, and close as it lies to the modern intelligence in point of ideas as well as in point of time, its history has been much less discussed in the present century than that of the Reformation. Indeed, the disparity in the amount of attention given in recent times to the two themes is so great as to become extremely significant. Of English works on the Reformation period there is a whole popular library, and every history of the period deals with it at great length. Of the Deistic movement there is no satisfactory account; indeed, there is barely a mention of it in any English history, commonly so-called, though there are several works of culture-history which deal with it more or less fully. The first systematic study of it in recent times was the German Lechler's *Geschichte des Englischen Deismus* (1841); the most luminous English sketch is Mark Pattison's essay on the *Tendencies of Religious Thought in England (1688-1750)* in the *Essays and Reviews.* After Lechler, perhaps the best synopsis of the literary course of the movement is that given in Dr. John Hunt's *Religious Thought in England from the Refor-*

mation,¹ all along a remarkably fair account, as coming from a clergyman. The shorter survey in J. J. Tayler's *Retrospect of the Religious Life of England*² has similar merit. On the other hand the treatment of the subject in the Bampton Lectures of the late Mr. Adam Storey Farrar (1861), courageously entitled *A Critical History of Free Thought*, is duly Bamptonian, though possessing a certain freshness in virtue of its claim to have fully attained the scientific spirit by making the assumption that all Freethought is to be studied as a form of disease. Lighter and brighter is the work of M. Edouard Sayous, *Les Déistes anglais et le Christianisme* (1882), also written from the orthodox standpoint. The work of the late Principal Cairns, again, on *Unbelief in the Eighteenth Century* (1881), as might be surmised from the title, is a respectable expression of the Christian uncharity which thinketh little or no good of any non-Christian; and may be said to leave the discussion further from the plane of argumentative amenity and good sense than we find it in some of the orthodox replies to the Deists in their own day, such as Butler's *Analogy* or even Leland's *View of the Principal Deistical Writers*. Mr. Leslie Stephen's elaborate *History of English Thought in the Eighteenth Century*, which comprehends the Deistic movement, is of course a very different performance, wanting only greater thoroughness of study, unity of scheme and of judgment, and perhaps a breath of philosophic genius, to make it a classic. As it is, it is neither a definitive work of reference nor a convincing body of doctrine and criticism; and it has a vacillating way of throwing sirloins to Cerberus, of hedging a verdict with a contradiction, and of betraying alarm lest the author should be thought civil to people whom it has been customary to treat with insolence, that somewhat chills an open-minded reader, while bringing home to him the difficulty of being impartial on purpose. Mr. Stephen's critical rectitude is

---

¹ 3 vols., 1870-1873.   ² Second edition, 1876

somewhat as that of the Indian's tree, which was "so straight that it leant the other way". So that one is fain to salute his work respectfully and go prospecting unpretentiously on one's own account.

The manner of the beginning of the Deistic movement is indeed one of the most interesting and instructive of studies. We have seen how the Reformation in England was primarily the work of a despotic king, who instead of desiring a change of doctrine was ready to put innovators to death, but who by his action on political grounds opened the way for changes of doctrine; how at nearly every stage of the process men's pecuniary interest had far more share than any process of religious reasoning in shaping their creed, or at least their Church; and how the Church of England thenceforth was demonstrably an organism that could be made to take almost any form or colour of creed under due pressure from the civil power. After matters had apparently shaken down to a settled footing, the newly developed bibliolatrous fanaticism, being joined with the decisive motive of anger against fresh taxation, brought about precisely such a civil convulsion as Wycliffe had confidently declared would never arise through the putting of the sacred books in all men's hands. And this convulsion it was which practically began the unsettlement of all religious belief in our modern England, though the process has been one of ebb and flow, and the financial forces which originally told against the Catholic Church have for two centuries been made to tell in favour not only of the Anglican but of the Dissenting. Of which more anon.

Mr. Pattison, broadly sketching the Deistic movement and that of reasoning orthodoxy which followed on it, places their rise and fall between 1688 and 1830, regarding the Tractarian movement of his own day as marking the end of the second. This may be in some ways a convenient and helpful account of the matter, but it leaves out of sight several things worth keeping in view. One of them is the fact that the Deistic movement as a social phenomenon really began on the heels of the Civil War, and spread noticeably soon after the Restoration. Exactly how it began, of course, we cannot tell, though we can specify the first Deistic writer. Theistic and pantheistic speculation there must have been in England at least as early as the reign of Elizabeth, when we find Marlowe labelled an atheist, and Shakspere obviously enough no Christian; indeed, much nearer Atheism in his philosophy of life than Marlowe ever seems to come. Wherever such doctrines as those of Giordano Bruno found any harbourage, concrete Christianity must have begun so far to suffer shrinkage, only to be repaired through the decay of the conditions of speculative life. We have seen Acham's outbreak against the Englishmen of his day who were made freethinkers by Italian travel and Italian books; and we have heard the testimony of the elder Essex as to the virtual Atheism of many of his educated contemporaries—testimonies borne out by actual declarations of reasoned unbelief from the working-class, where reticence has never been greatly cultivated. And we know from Montaigne's eloquently equivocal defence of the *Theologia Naturalis* of Raimond de Sebonde that there were already in his day some French freethinkers, doubtless formed by Italian influence, who made no account of the pleasing paralogisms either of the essayist or of the theologian. But in that age the position of Deism or Theism—" Godism," as the iconoclasts of our own day unmusically term the general position—was the furthest stretch of freethinking that could well be taken by any minds not of the rarest intellectual temper; to say nothing of its being the only form of anti-Christian heresy that a man dared be known to harbour even in the age of Hobbes. Leland, sketching the history of the Deistic controversy in 1754, traces the name Deist back to 1563, when the French Protestant Viret, in the epistle dedicatory to the second volume of his *Instruction Chrétienne* " speaks of some persons in that time who

"called themselves by a new name, that of Deists.
"These, he tells us, professed to believe a God, but
"showed no regard to Jesus Christ, and considered the
"doctrine of the apostles and evangelists as fables and
"dreams. He adds, that they laughed at all religion,
"notwithstanding they conformed themselves, with
"regard to the outward appearance, to the religion of
"those with whom they were obliged to live. . . . . He
"adds that many among them set up for learning and
"philosophy, and were looked upon to be persons of an
"acute and subtil genius; and that not content to perish
"alone in their error, they took pains to spread the
"poison, and to infect and corrupt others by their
"impious discourses and bad examples."[1] As Viret thus
early makes much more account of the Deists than of the
Atheists, whom he also mentions, the Deistic movement
of the next century in England cannot be regarded as
a sequel from either atheistic or pantheistic beginnings;
but must be taken as a spontaneous revolt from all
current forms of clericalism and of dogma. And it is
very instructive to find that it successively arose in very
similar circumstances in France and in England—that
is, in each case as a sequel to a period of furious religious
war and manifold fanaticism, such as had previously
elapsed in Italy, where in the same way there arose by
way of reaction a distrust of religion in general. We
gather from Pascal's *Pensées*, very much as we gather
later from Berkeley's *Dialogues*, or Butler's *Analogy*, that

[1] *View of the Principal Deistical Writers*, ed. 1752, pp. 2-3. See the passage more fully and faithfully cited by Bayle in Note D to his article *Viret*. Though Bayle does not trace the connection, it may be surmised that the French Deists to some extent derived from the influence of Laelio Sozzini (uncle of Faustus), who in 1546-1552 travelled in France, England, Holland, Germany, and Poland. In 1552, Calvin warned him that his *pruritus quaerendi*, if not corrected, would bring on him *gravia tormenta* (Bayle, s.v. *Marianus Socin*, the first, *Note B*). The Italian connections of Deism are among the themes unexpectedly omitted from the late Mr. John Owen's treatise on *The Skeptics of the Italian Renaissance* (1893). But one or two clues are given by Burckhardt, *Civilisation of the Renaissance in Italy*, end.

the writer finds himself in a society in which religious conviction has lost credit; and that he is bitterly bent on making sure that though the doubters are smart people he can reason better than they on their own ground. It is on record, too, that Pascal's own father had little regard for religion; and it has been surmised that the elder Pascal was one of those "good fellows who had for "breviary the Essays of Montaigne".[1] Of such general distaste for Christian dogma in the France of 1650, and in the England of 1660-1730, there seems to be only one explanation, namely, that the very extremity of religious feeling, the long frenzy of mutual malevolence, the stupendous failure of a professedly love-inculcating religion to make men so much as consent to let each other alone, much less to love each other, had set many men on questioning whether the game was worth the candle; whether this creed which caused blood to flow like water was any more divine in its special dogmas than that of Mahomet, or those of pagan antiquity. Educated men simply grew sick of the religious temper, of religious phraseology, of religious books, of religious principles; and even those who remained orthodox tended to take on a new tone of secular ratiocination, seen alike in the scientific and the apologetic writings of Bishop Wilkins. Of the English Royal Society, founded in 1648, partly through Wilkins' instrumentality, Dr. Wallis wrote that its business from the first "precluded matters of theology "and State affairs". Its members would discuss the circulation of the blood, but not the indwelling of the Spirit. "God and the Soul," Dr. Sprat records, were for them tabooed subjects. A similar temper was evidently abroad earlier in France; and it must have been on the Continental side—very likely in his intercourse with the Dutch, among whom also there must have been a recoil from fanaticism and dogma—that Charles II underwent the influences which made him what he certainly was when in

---

[1] Faugère, édit. of *Pensées*, 1844, Introd., p. lxxviii.

health, and what he probably remained in heart at the end, while receiving Catholic absolution—a simple Deist. He may, indeed, have got his lead from Hobbes when Hobbes taught him mathematics in his exile at Paris; but his acquiescence in the expulsion of the philosopher from his court, on the publication of the *Leviathan*, suggests that he had not then formed his views. There is, however, no room for doubt that in later life he was a Deist.[1] And in this sufficiently known heterodoxy of Charles, which rather promoted than narrowed his popularity among the middle and upper classes, we have a sufficient reason for dating the English Deistic movement rather from 1660 than from 1688, and for seeing its main source rather in the great brain of Hobbes than in the orderly and prudent intelligence of Locke, who may be taken as the founder of rationalistic orthodoxy, but hardly of rationalistic criticism, in England.

If there were no other reason, the mere discredit into which the Church had clearly fallen at the Restoration would suffice to establish by inference the vogue of some form of heterodoxy. That discredit, long ago dwelt upon by Lord Macaulay and Mr. Buckle, and indignantly denied by Mr. Gladstone on the strength of vicarious research, seems to have been once more sufficiently made out in a recent work of a somewhat ponderous character,[2] which multiplies controversy over many fields. It seems impossible that the clerical profession should ever be treated with such general disrespect as fell to its lot in England after the Restoration, unless educated men had come in general to make light of what the clerical profession taught. Its mere impoverishment, of course, would go some way to keep it in low esteem, in a commercial community; but the very fact that it remained impoverished so long, under a government on which

[1] See the annotations to Burnet's *History of His Own Time*, beginning of Book II.
[2] *Buckle and his Critics*, by J. M. Robertson, chap. viii, § 2. Compare Pattison in *Essays and Reviews*, p. 315 (9th ed.)

churchmen had special claims, shows that there were other influences at work. The story of the gradual turning of the tables, the ultimate establishment of the clergy on a fair financial footing, with the result of finally making orthodoxy as fashionable as heterodoxy for a time had been, will be traced later. From the first, however, it will be found that the power of a religion, once squarely challenged by intelligence, to keep its hold over men, practically resolves itself into the power of setting up pecuniary interests, which are sure to be defended by those concerned.

No doubt a shrewd observer, any time between the Restoration and the publication of Butler's *Analogy*, could have predicted how the strife of ideas, or what passed for such, would end or tend. On the one hand was the lean but indestructible army of churchmen, with its "black "dragoon in every parish", bound to subsist, however poorly, sure to fight for its corporate interest day by day and year by year, and so committed to maintaining by hook or crook the creed it was paid to preach. On the other hand were the straggling troops of brilliant amateurs, the wits and clever men and lovers of reason, who saw through and ridiculed the clerical claims, and for their own part looked to Hobbes as their philosopher, but never dreamt of aught save a desultory and skirmishing attack upon the enemy. At its lowest, the faith had its well-salaried and high-placed leaders, with their cathedral-castles, their palaces, and their walled towns; while the head of the freethinkers was in the dangerously apostolic position of having nowhere to lay his head save on the sufferance of a patron. If Hobbes on private grounds could get a pension from the king, that was the most that rationalism could look for. Such a struggle could only end in one way, in an age in which there was no machinery capable of multiplying knowledge, as against the machinery for counteracting it, to wit, the Church itself. It was now impossible that there should be any such general secular jealousy of the Protestant

Church as had weakened the Catholic Church before the Reformation. The Protestant Church itself figured as the champion of religious liberty against the designing "Popery" that always gesticulated menacingly in the background of the national imagination. The clergy were further the sworn supporters of the monarchy, and thus stood equally safe as between king and people. And as there was no chance of the common people, the main sources of population, ceasing to be superstitious; as the upper-class freethinkers themselves did not wish that they should, it was only a question of waiting till the undrilled intelligence of the educated class should gradually lose the distaste for religion it had acquired in the Civil War, and should accept the State clergy as an inevitable neighbour with whom it was well to be on friendly terms.

CHAPTER II.

THE ATHEISTIC PHASE.

For us to-day, the main interest of the retrospect lies in following the steps of the readjustment, and noting how, as in the previous age, the fortunes of religion are determined by ignorance, by avarice, by self-interest, by fashion, by carnal organisation, by anything rather than reason, argument, conviction, or good faith. All along, perhaps, the cause of the rationalists was in some measure hampered and hindered by the tendency of their method to lead the reason beyond Deism into Atheism; a step which only a few could confidently take even in their own hearts, which none dared plainly avow, and which even those who took it seem to have regarded as safe only for the highest intelligences, to wit, their own. Rationalism, like every other process of mental differentiation, begins with a certain arbitrariness; so that we find a writer professing an all-round attitude of philosophic scepticism, such as Glanvill, exhibiting an obstinate *a priori* belief in spirits and witches while going about to challenge apriorism and traditional ideas in general.[1] With such opposition from even normally liberal thinkers, the few deeper doubters might well practise a prudent secresy. In this attitude of forced reserve on the rationalist side, an attitude which affected even the argument against the Christian system (since that was supposed to be useful for moralising "the vulgar"), we may see the beginning of the end, as regarded the rationalism of that age. It is very difficult, however, to divine how far the movement was conscious of the unlimited solvent power of its

---

[1] Owen's edition of the *Scepsis Scientifica*, pp. xlii-xlv. See pp. 170, 180, as to Glanvill's apriorism in theology.

method, freely pursued. Mr. Mill has justly censured Berkeley for applying the name Atheist to Hobbes, who always wrote as not merely a Theist but a Christian ; but on due reflection we find some reason for surmising that, even as the Christianism of Hobbes was regarded by the Deists of the time as a mere prudential formality, so his Deism might be regarded by the Atheists in turn as a mere precaution against prosecution. The man who illustrated the vogue of "senseless and insignificant words, " made up of Greek or Latin names," by the fact that in French " our Saviour " was called the *Verbe* but not the *Parole ;* and who wrote : " To say God hath spoken to " man in a dream, is no more than to say man dreamed " that God hath spoken to him," this reasoner was indeed, as Mr. Green has remarked, assailing with "pitiless logic " (" hard and narrow logic " Mr. Green had called it, two sentences earlier) the very theory of revelation ; and to define religion further as growing from the seed of the " fear of invisible powers " was to put the God-idea itself on a " narrow and slippery ledge ", as Mr. Gladstone might say. " It is impossible," says Hobbes,[1] " to make any profound inquiry into natural causes, without being inclined thereby to believe there is one God eternal ; though they cannot have any idea of Him in their mind, answerable to His nature." But the argument goes on to leave the theistic conclusion on all fours with the polytheistic, as a creation of an imaginary entity from a " variety of fancy" ; declaring that thoughtful men " chose rather to confess He is incomprehensible, and " above their understanding, than to define his nature by " ' spirit incorporeal ', and then confess their definition to " be unintelligible ".[2] And in an earlier work he had put, with that keen concision in which he surpasses all other philosophical writers, the fatal rebuttal of all interpretative Theism : " As if it were possible for men that " know not in what manner God seeth, heareth, or

---

[1] *Leviathan*, ch. xi. [2] *Id.*, ch. xii.

"speaketh, to know nevertheless the manner how he intendeth, and predestinateth. A man therefore ought not to examine by reason any point, or draw any consequence out of Scripture by reason, concerning the nature of God Almighty, of which reason is not capable."[1] All which is sufficiently near to modern Agnosticism to enable us to give some credit to a letter of Bentley's, in the last decade of the century, concerning the usual mental attitude of Hobbists. It is an interesting and little-known document. His friend Professor Bernard having suggested an alteration in the line of argument in the *Sermons on Atheism*, Bentley writes:—

"I cannot think that I should do well to balk the "proofs of a Deity, to attack either Theists or Jews. "The Jews do us little hurt; and perhaps to bring their "objections into the pulpit, and the vulgar language, out "of their present obscurity, would not do well: and few "would care to hear or read such discourses. Of all the "parts of my task, that shall be the last that I will "meddle with. And then for Theists you say, they have "books written, but Atheists have only talk. Must "we then pass by the Atheists, against the judgment "and command of my Honble Benefactor, who hath put "them in the very first place as the most dangerous "enemies? Atheism is so much the worse that it is not "buried in books, but is gotten εἰς τὸν βίον; that taverns "and coffee-houses, nay Westminster-hall and the very "churches, are full of it. A sermon therefore must be "*contra malos mores*, not *malos libros*. But are the "Atheists of your mind, that they have no books written "for them? Not one of them but believes Tom Hobbes "to be a rank one; and that his corporeal God is a meer "sham to get his book printed. They understand the "Cabbala well enough: that all that is but juggle; and "that a corporeal infinite God is downright nonsense. I "have said something to this in my first sermon, and I

[1] *De Corpore Politico*, Part ii, ch. 6.

THE ATHEISTIC PHASE.

" know it to be true by the conversation I have had with
" them. There may be some Spinosists, or immaterial
" Fatalists, beyond seas; but not one English Infidel in a
" hundred is any other than a Hobbist; which I know to
" be rank Atheism in the private study and select conver-
" sation of these men; whatever it may appear to be
" abroad . . . . In your last you seem to hint, that the
" astrological notion of our origin is a fancy of my own,
" and that nobody ever believed it. But 'tis your happi-
" ness, that you have not known by conversation what
" monsters of men have been of late days. You know
" the ground of the old ones, that derived us out of the
" soil from mechanism or chance, was that equivocal
" generation of frogs and insects, and plants *sine semine:*
" to that they said when the earth was fresh and vigourous
" that more perfect animals were produced out of her.
" Now, therefore, because the generations of plants and
" insects are reduced to the starry influences, they carry
" in consequence the production of ourselves to the same
" cause. Besides Cardan, Cæsalpinus, and Berigardus,
" &c., do in express words ascribe it to planetary in-
" fluences; and 'tis now the reigning opinion of the most
" learned living Atheists among us; and therefore ought
" not to be past by. You say, "*our fabrick being a portion
" of the world must have a like origin, and not descend from
" the stars, even in the opinion of God's enemies.* This
" arrangement [? argument] is true, if the dispute was
" about the *materia* of human bodies. But now that we
" talk about the *forma* of it, it proves as well that the half
" pound of butter and pudding that we had at dinner,
" because they were portions of the world, are made at
" the same time with it. The γένεσις of animals was
" posterior to that of the stars in the opinion of all man-
" kind: I do not mean the substance of animals, but their
" forms and textures that denominate them what they
" are."[1]

[1] *Museum Criticum:* Cambridge, vol. ii, 1826, pp. 557, 558.

This was written in 1692; and it casts a very interesting light on the thinking of that generation, when the new stirrings of science were making a first ferment in the old physical theories of the universe. The reference to the "astrological notion of our origin", vilipended by Bentley in his third Sermon, is the more interesting when we remember that a cognate theory, which derives life on the planet from astral germs, has in our own day been advanced on theistic grounds, by way of evading the application of the principle of natural causation to biological origins. The theorem of the early Atheists, who had the ample excuse of lacking a basis of sound inductive science for their hypotheses, becomes the refuge of belated Deists, who frame their hypotheses as if their own science did not exist. It is of course not safe to believe Bentley's testimony to anything like its full extent: we shall find him talking of Locke's friend Collins, who was undoubtedly a Deist, as an Atheist concealing his real opinions; and we shall see the reverend doctor in the same connection displaying those qualities of mind and temper which lead us to surmise that had he been born among the needy and illiterate class he would have sought a livelihood and reached distinction as a burglar, if he did not prove his originality by anticipating the invention of garotting. But, ruffian as the eminent emendator was, he must have had some basis for his assertion that in private certain Hobbists avowed themselves Atheists.

Despite the declaration of Ascham in the previous century, it was probably with Hobbes that this thoroughgoing tendency arose in a conscious shape. Almost all ascriptions of Atheism in England before his time are to be looked on with suspicion, as being probably mere theological scurrilities. It sufficed that a man should be doubtful of any detail in the Scriptures, or any item in the creed, to bring upon him the imputation, which at this stage could hardly be said to be dangerous, though it would probably have sufficed in 1593 to destroy Marlowe, had he lived to be arraigned on the evidence that has chanced to be preserved as to his conversation. *The Unmasking of the Politique Atheist, by J. H. [John Hull] Batchelor of Divinitie,* published in 1602, is simply a tract against the Church of Rome, elaborating the simple thesis that whereas Catholics call Protestants Atheists, the truth is the other way about, seeing that " Satan is the " master builder of their [the Catholics'] Church, and " Atheisme the chiefe foundation of their kingdome." Bishop Fotherby's posthumous folio *Atheomastix* (1622) goes further, alike as to bulk and as to matter; but that also yields little evidence of any contemporary atheistic movement. Bishop Fotherby does not profess to have known any Atheists; though he complains—and this is a notable detail, for that time—that the passion for disputing and proving has gone so far that " the Scriptures (with many) " have lost their authority, and are thought onely fit for " the ignorant, and idiote ".[1] And not only does he make out three classes of Atheists, of whom only one " deny " there is a God ", the other two being irreligious and unworshipping believers, but he decides that though the Atheist of the first class may " deny both God and all " Religion, yet he is inwardly inforced to beleeve them, " and to hold (even against his will) many notable points " of Christian Religion ".[2] Similarly Lord Herbert of Cherbury, in his deistical treatise *De Veritate* (1624), argues that there are no real Atheists, but that some men have acquired that reputation by refusing to believe in a God with the attributes of that currently worshipped, holding that it were better to believe in none than in such a one. Herbert himself seems to have known no philosophic Atheists. We are thus far from anything like a body of even privately avowed atheistic opinion; and twenty years later the evidence is still scanty.

In the *Dispute betwixt an Atheist and a Christian; the Atheist being a Flemming, the Christian an Englishman* (1646), the so-called Atheist is a very pronounced Deist.

[1] *Atheomastix*, Pref.   [2] *Id.*, p. 129.

At the outset, on challenge, he declares: "I doe believe "in an universall Providence that governs the things as "well of the greater as of this inferior Globe; and of the "Souls eternity: and after this life in a state of unspeak- "able felicity. And indeed I am not affraid of the "gnashing of the teeth which is spoken shall happen to "the bad after this life in the old law, nor yet of the "trouble of the conscience which in the new Law is "supposed shall be to those of the same Damnable "condition. And indeed I rather think *Moses* to be "inspired with a wit above the rest of the *Egyptians*' "bondmen than with a spirit." Whereupon the Christian becomes piously uncivil; and after a little, despite the Deist's disclaimer, thus impeaches him:[1] "I perceive then "then that you are an Atheist, but a refined one, one of "the new stamp; you believe in God, but not in Christ "his Son, nor the holy Ghost: but according to our "opinion he that denyes the Son and Holy Ghost, "denyes the Father, and therefore is an Atheist". This very "short way with the Deists" would no doubt be popular.

But as time goes on we find signs that the corrosive logic of Hobbes, working in a time of profound disturbance of opinion, had for some intelligences so far eaten through the tissue of religious belief as to leave a very definite scepticism concerning all ideas of deity. In an anonymous work attributed to Sir Charles Wolsely, published in 1669, *The Unreasonablenesse of Atheism made manifest: In a Discourse written by the command of a Person of Honour*, there is a comparatively intelligent attempt to discriminate and trace the development of Atheism in terms of current causes. The author gives six: (1) The attempt "to "bottom all Religion upon Humane Authority", specifying the doctrine of Hobbes alike on politics and on religion; (2) the prevailing mockery of religious practices; (3) "the multiplicity of Oaths that were some late years "past among us: the Taking and Renouncing them,

[1] P. 13.

"Backward and Forward, has been no useless friend to "Atheism"; (4) "the contempt that has been cast upon "the Scriptures, and all supernatural Revelation, has "opened a wide door to Atheism"; (5) nonconformity in worship leading to total abstinence; (6) "the general "revival of, and the great applause that hath of late been "given to such Philosophical Notions as broadly and "directly lead this way. Here the Atheist is most busily "at work, and drives on his greatest Trade." This is substantially plausible; and when such a monumental treatise against Atheism as Cudworth's *Intellectual System of the Universe* (1678) had the effect rather of encouraging Atheists and embarrassing Christians than the contrary, it can hardly have been that such argumentation as Wolsely's availed much to check the tendencies he specified, though it cannot be said that he is nearly the worst apologist of the period. The works of some of his successors are indeed calculated to suggest that, barring such types as Cudworth and Henry More, the brains of the Restoration age had gone over in mass to heresy. One of the drollest anti-atheistic treatises of the seventeenth century is a pamphlet issued in 1685, *The Atheist Unmasked, or, a Confutation of such as deny the Being of a* SUPREAM DEITY, *that governs* HEAVEN *and* EARTH. *By Unanswerable Arguments deduc'd.* "By a Person of Honour." The Person of Honour is visibly little used to composition; and his sentences are as breathless as his argument, which alternately vindicates the truth of the Scriptures against ordinary Deistic criticism, demonstrates the existence of a God as against Atheists, and argues that there are no real Atheists at all. That the honourable author had not gone through much controversy may be gathered from the whole run of his reasonings, of which this, in the original punctuation, is a sample:[1] "And if there be not a God, how comes it to "pass, that the Sea which is agreed to be bigger and "higher than the Land, should contrary to the Nature of

[1] P. 18.

"Water (which is to diffuse itself) be restrained by a low
" sandy shore from overflowing the Earth, which cannot
" be but by that God that has set it, its bounds, and says
" hitherto, shall you come, and no further, and that the
" Sea is higher than the Land, is demonstrable by the
" Springs which under *Aristotles'* favour, have another
" cause then what he asserts "—the true source being, in
the opinion of the Person of Honour, the sea, whose
waters the earth sweetens in their passage through its
crannies: a theory once common, but pronounced by
Thomas Burnet, in 1684, " so gross, and so much against
" Reason and Experience, that none I think of late have
" ventured to make use of it."[1] In 1685, however, the
Person of Honour had no misgivings on the subject.
That deep dialectician avowedly had resolved " to confine
" my discourse into a very narrow compass, for I observe
" the fate of long tracts to be fruitless in a great measure,
" because the price deters most from buying, and the
" length from reading." Even this politic precaution,
however, did not enable the treatise to prevail against the
atheistic tendencies of the age; for at the end of the
century we find the Boyle Lecture in full blast, " for
" proving the Christian Religion against notorious In-
" fidels, viz., Atheists, Deists, Pagans, Jews, and Maho-
" metans; not descending to any Controversies that are
" among Christians themselves "[2]— a truly prudent stipulation, the obvious grounds of which seem to have led the
majority of the lecturers to leave the Jews and Maho-
metans in equal peace, concentrating their energies on
the more intimate enemies, Atheism and Deism.

Bentley led off in 1692, the year after the death of the
pious founder ; and in view of the endowment there can
have been no difficulty in maintaining the apostolical
succession. All that was wanted for a Boyle Lecture on
Atheism was a moderate amount of reading in the existing

---

[1] *Sacred Theory of the Earth*, 6th ed., vol. i, p. 20.
[2] *Epistle Dedicatory* to Bentley's *Eight Sermons against Atheism*.

THE ATHEISTIC PHASE. 89

manuals on the question, and that perfect hatred which casteth out at once candour and courtesy. This last is the characteristic note, though there are exceptions, such as the lectures of Clarke. Perhaps there has never been an evangelically-minded treatise in defence of Christianity against non-Christian criticism that was written without some of the malice which, according to Christian theory, is so unchristian, and which is yet so constant and so vital a part of the Christian consciousness in relation to unbelief; but these polemists of two hundred years ago must make even believers wince to-day by their undisguised, their rabid malignity. Bentley in these matters makes the impression of a man positively neurotic with hate, facing antagonists in the temper of a mad bull, suspicious of the net. No dispassionate person, reading him in contrast with those he assailed, as Hobbes and Collins, could well fail to gather some distaste for the religion which affirmed itself with such snarling fury, and some preference for the contrary way of thought, whose nearest approach to heat is by way of irony, and whose normal tone and temper is that of good breeding, often rising to good feeling. Where the innovators are full of a bright intellectuality and argumentativeness, varying, of course, in quality of output, the defenders of the faith, with a bitter monotony, repeat the traditional arguments against the elusive Atheism which never avows itself, always taking the ancients as the mouthpieces of the moderns; and, with probably not one exception, they impute moral perversity as the basis and motive of the Atheist's opinions. In a fairly extensive study of them, the present writer has not met with more than one or two works which treat the antagonist with amenity and grant him credit for intellectual honesty; and even these are unamiable and ungenial in comparison with many of those they oppose. Sir Charles Wolsely takes it for granted that " ' Twas at this " back Door of the *Will* that *Atheism* first enter'd ";[1] and

---
[1] *Unreasonableness of Atheism*, p. 19.

the "Atheist's Catechism" at the end of his book proceeds thus :—

" Q. Do you believe there is a God?
" A. No : I believe there is None.
" Q. What is the True Ground of your Belief?
" A. Because I have no mind there should be one.
" Q. What other Reason do you give for it ?
" A. Because I never saw him.
" Q. If there is no God, How came this World to be?
" A. It made itself by meer Chance."

And so on, on the plane of the primordial Sunday School teacher. Cudworth himself ends his preface with the avowal: " This labour of ours is not intended only for " the conversion of downright and professed Atheists (of " which there is but little hope, they being sunk into so " great a degree of sottishness;) but for the confirmation " of weak, staggering, and sceptical Theists". Bentley, again, sets out with the customary text about the fool who saith in his heart there is no God, and whose works are corrupt; informing those he undertakes to confute that they are no less wicked than stupid. " There are " some Infidels among us, that not only disbelieve the " Christian Religion, but oppose the assertions of Provi- " dence, of the Immortality of the Soul, of an Universal " Judgment to come, and of any Incorporeal Essence : " and yet to avoid the odious name of Atheists, would " shelter and skreen themselves under a new one of " Deists, which is not quite so obnoxious. But I think " the Text hath cut them short, and precluded this sub- " terfuge; in as much as it hath declared, that all such " wicked Principles are coincident and all one in the issue " with the rankest Atheism."[1] " No Atheist, as such, can " be a true Friend, an affectionate Relation, or a loyal " Subject. The appearance and shew of mutual Amity " among them is wholly owing to the smallness of their " number, and to the obligations of a Faction. 'Tis like

[1] *Sermons*, 5th ed., p. 7.

"the Friendship of Pickpockets and Highwaymen, that
" are said to observe strict Justice among themselves, and
" never to defraud a comrade of his share of the Booty."[1]
The record of the Christian amity in which the learned
preacher lived throughout his life with his fellow acade-
micals enables us to imagine the ethical fervour with
which the verdict would be given out.

A later Boyle lecturer, Mr. John Harris, of the Royal
Society, similarly proceeds from the text that " The
" wicked through the pride of his countenance will not
" seek after God ", " In which words we have an Account
" more particularly by what Methods and Steps Men
" advance to such an exorbitant height of wickedness, as
" to set up for Atheism, and to deny the existence of a
" God ; for there are in them these Three Particulars,"
the preacher goes on, " which I shall consider in their
" Order.

" I. There is the general Character or Qualifications of
" the Person the Psalmist speaks of; which is, That *he is*
" *a wicked Man.* . . .

" II. The particular kind of Wickedness, or the Origin
" from whence the Spirit of Atheism and Irreligion doth
" chiefly proceed ; And *That is Pride.* . . .

" III. Here is the great Charge that is brought against
" this Wicked and Proud Man ; viz., *Wilful Atheism and*
" *Infidelity, He will not seek after God.* . . .

" In discoursing on the two First of these Heads, I
" shall endeavour to show, that *Immorality* and *Pride* are
" the great Causes of the Growth of Atheism amongst
" us. . . ."[2]

It is not to be supposed that attacks like these, delivered ever so regularly by paid champions, could alter
the formed opinions of any man ; but they could do
something less directly effective: they could make the

---

[1] *Id.*, p. 43.
[2] *The Atheistical Objections against the Being of a God*, etc. By John Harris,
M.A., 1698, pp. 1-2.

small group of thoroughgoing thinkers more and more chary of avowing their opinions, especially at the universities, where in such a period the more thoughtful men were likely to seek to be. Indeed, as the hardy and audacious days of the Civil War and the Restoration lapsed further and further from memory, and the spirit of unflinching speculation began to suffer the normal pressure of settled habits and routine administration, the requisite intellectual courage for even an inward resistance to the ordinary assumptions of theism would itself tend to become scarcer. And as the days of crude fanaticism grew more and more remote, and for the austerity and cant of Puritanism there was substituted the licence and ribaldry of the new generation of scoffers, middling people would tend more and more to a medium of prudent religiosity, neither praying much nor neglecting prayer. But this natural tendency to middling activities of mind would at the same time be reinforced by the no less natural reassertion of the power of the Church after the Revolution of 1688. Boyle's lecture was a type of a number of efforts that would be made by religious laymen to check the spontaneous scepticism of the time through organised and endowed propaganda; and William's "Presbyterian" Bishops and university authorities would be apt to be more hostile in a financial way to sceptics than were their Tory predecessors, who would be likely to wink at a man's Hobbism in religious matters provided he were practically Hobbist in his royalism. In one way or the other, then, the bolder freethinking of the latter half of the seventeenth century, unpublished as it had been, must needs be restricted; and the intellectual forces needed for its replacement were not available. For the philosophic question, when all was said, remained one of speculation; and the simple agnosticism to which the unbelievers attained was not a thing to battle for in the open, especially when it was suspected even by the more confident that creeds were good things for "the "vulgar". On the other hand, not only did the new concrete science offer a more fruitful and attractive field for research, but the theistic protestation of some of the leading men of science, though it would not reconvert unbelievers, would discourage those who had looked to that Science itself for leverage in the struggle with superstition. On all grounds, outright Atheism tended to diminish.

CHAPTER III.

THE ANTI-ATHEISTIC PROPAGANDA.

IT was not that there were any new or valid developments in theistic philosophy. The high-water mark of that, for the period, at least as regards elaboration and learning, had been reached in 1678, in Cudworth's *Intellectual System of the Universe*, which supplied the later polemists, Bentley included, with nearly all their arguments, properly so-called. And the most memorable fact in regard to Cudworth's performance is that, since despite its touch of godly insolence it really acknowledged and handled many of the difficulties of Theism, and further assailed those Christian sects whose doctrine created special difficulties, the treatise aroused far more of suspicion than of satisfaction among the orthodox—the inevitable result of any theistic discussion which approaches candour. Shaftesbury has told part of what happened :—

" You know the common Fate of those who dare to
" appear *fair authors*. What was that pious and learned
" Man's Case, who wrote the *Intellectual System of the*
" *Universe ?* I confess it was pleasant enough to consider
" that though the whole World were no less satisfy'd with
" his Capacity and Learning, than with his sincerity in the
" Cause of Deity; yet was he accus'd of giving the
" upper hand to the Atheists, for having only stated their
" reasons and those of their Adversarys fairly together."[1]

So Dryden, in the dedication to the second volume of his translation of the Æneid, remarks that Cudworth " has raised such strong objections against the being of a

[1] *The Moralists*, Part I, Sec. 3 (*Characteristics*, ed. 1733, vol. ii, p. 262).

"God and Providence, that many think he has not
"answered them¹"; and Warburton later scornfully
testifies that "there wanted not County Clergymen to
"lead the Cry, and tell the World that under Pretence of
"defending Revelation, he wrote in the very manner that
"an artful Infidel might naturally be supposed to use in
"writing against it. . . . In a word that he was an
"Atheist in his heart and an Arian in his book. . . .
"Would the reader know the consequence ? . . . The
"silly Calumny was believed; the much injured Author
"grew disgusted; his Ardour slackened; and the rest and
"far greatest Part of the Defence never appeared."[2]

Nor was there anything unaccountable in the facts. Whether or not Cudworth was as some protested a Tritheist—a point on which few persons in these days can claim to have any opinion—he certainly gave, on the one hand, a serious shock to the popular Theism of his day by abandoning the principle of a direct creation of animals by miracle, and on the other hand, a no less serious shock to philosophic Theism by his implicit rejection of the principle of predestination. He "evinces every-"where", as Mosheim notes, "a violent antipathy to "those Christians who suppose all things to be decreed "fatally by God, and considers that, were their opinion "to prevail, it would be impossible to defend religion "against the attacks of those who wish to overthrow it "altogether". That is, he was one of the Theists who save the character of their Deity by negating his Omnipotence. No doubt it was the former position that gave most trouble. To meet the difficulty, raised not only by Atheists but by his own understanding, of conceiving an Omnipotence consciously deciding at every instant on every event in the universe, Cudworth resorted to the old theory of a "plastic Nature", or labour-saving principle, endowed by Deity with the faculty of going on without

---

[1] *Works*, Scott's edit., vol. xiv, p. 170.
[2] *Divine Legation*, vol. ii, *preface*.

his interference. "That everything in Nature should be
"done immediately by God himself, this, as according to
"vulgar apprehension it would render divine Providence
"operose, solicitous, and distractious, and thereby make
"the belief of it to be entertained with greater difficulty,
"and give advantage to Atheists; so, in the judgment of
"the writer *De Mundo* [Aristotle], it is not so decorous
"in respect of God neither that he should . . . . set his
"own hand as it were to every work, and immediately do
"all the meanest and triflingest things himself drudgingly
"without making use of any inferior or subordinate
"instruments. 'If it were not congruous in respect of
"'the state and majesty of Xerxes the Great king of
"'Persia, that he should condescend to do all the
"'meanest offices himself; much less can this be thought
"'decorous in respect of God. But it seems far more
"'august, and becoming of the divine majesty, that a
"'certain power and virtue, derived from him, and
"'passing through the universe, should move the sun
"'and moon, and be the immediate cause of those lower
"'things done here upon earth.'" To which Pagan
plea Cudworth added another, in respect of "that slow
"and gradual process, that is in the generations of things,
"which would seem to be but a vain and idle pomp, or a
"trifling formality, if the agent were omnipotent; as also
"by those ἁμαρτήματα (as Aristotle calls them), those
"errors and bungles, which are committed when the
"matter is inept and contumacious; which argue the
"agent not to be irresistible, and that nature is such a
"thing as is not altogether uncapable (as well as human
"art) of being sometimes frustrated and disappointed, by
"the indisposition of matter. Whereas an omnipotent
"agent, as it could dispatch its work in a moment, so it
"would always do it infallibly and irresistibly; no inepti-
"tude or stubbornness of matter being ever able to hinder
"such a one, or make him bungle or fumble in anything."

[1] *Intellectual System*, Harrison's ed., vol. i, p. 222-223.

We can imagine how Hobbes would have thrust his blade through this hopeless theorem; and how many a Theist, with little enough of Hobbes' power, would wince at a process of reasoning which, on the one hand, deprived him of resort to Deity as an answerer of prayer, and, on the other hand, made Nature itself a kind of underling or apprentice God, albeit an unconscious one, doing the best it could in the Master's absence, and making downright " errors and bungles " in the process. And if any help were wanted to enable such to see the dilemma, it was at length supplied by Bayle, whose keen eye saw at once that in Cudworth's argument, as presented by Le Clerc, the game was up. The difficulty of the constructive Atheists, he noted, had been to account for the rise and development of animal life, which they attributed to an unconscious cause that yet followed a regular plan. But the Plastic Nature of Dr. Cudworth, and the Vital Principle expounded in Dr. Nehemiah Grew's *Cosmologia Sacra* (1701), were in exactly the same case, " and thus they " take away the whole force of this objection against the " Atheists. For if God could communicate such a plastic " power, it follows that it is not inconsistent with the " nature of things that there be such agents. They may " therefore exist of themselves, will the adversary say. . . " One may then equally suppose that matter exists of " itself, and that motive power is essentially proper to it."[1] Le Clerc desperately sought to save the position by arguing that the Plastic Nature or Natures of Cudworth owed all their powers to Deity. Bayle then asked whether they were after all simply passive instruments; to which Le Clerc replied that they were not that either, but were " under God's direction, who conducts them, though we " cannot explain after what manner ".[2] This in turn over-

[1] *Continuation des Pensées diverses* . . . *à l'occasion de la Comète* . . . . *de* 1680, Amsterdam, 1705, tom. i, p. 91.

[2] *Bibliothèque Choisie*, tom. vi, p. 422, cited by Birch in his biographical sketch of Cudworth.

looked the "errors and bungles" admitted by Cudworth, so that the failure of the defence on this point was complete, by the later admission of Warburton.[1]

Thus was Cudworth's three-decked galleon wrecked on the usual rock of personalising Theism. Professed Deists like Charles Blount were found by the religious to be more religious than he, since they argued for a universally controlling Providence consciously deciding every event down to the minutest. In comparison with such Deism, Cudworth's idea of a self-sustaining Nature was for nearly all practical purposes atheistic. Nor was his book even left ultimately with the credit of a storehouse of trustworthy learning; for the copious notes which Mosheim in the next century appended in his Latin translation have more often the effect of controverting than of substantiating the text. Every little while the learned translator has to point out that the learned author is misrepresenting Aristotle, or misconstruing Plato, or putting on slight passages a sense they will not bear, or forgetting that what he charges as an error on Atheists has been maintained by Christians, or flying in the face of mountains of evidence when he maintains monotheism to have been the primordial and prevailing doctrine of antiquity. Where Mosheim gave Cudworth a cordial support was in the insistence on such doctrines as that Deity had made the universe out of nothing. That was expressly asserted in the Scriptures; and Mosheim, a man of uncommon natural sagacity and critical power, unwittingly made signally clear the importance of the demand for a real freedom of thought by solemnly insisting with Cudworth on the written dogma,[2] while judging with acuteness and discrimination on a hundred difficult questions of ancient and modern philosophy. Locke exhibited the same benumbing power of the sacrosanct creed by standing woodenly to the same amazing dogma in his *Essay on the*

[1] Letter to Birch, cited by him.
[2] See his *Dissertation on Creation out of Nothing*, translated in Vol. iii, of Harrison's ed. of Cudworth.

Human Understanding :—" But you will say, Is it not "impossible to admit of the making anything out of "nothing, since we cannot possibly conceive it? I "answer, No; I. Because it is not reasonable to deny the "power of an infinite being because we cannot com- "prehend its operations."[1] In the previous paragraph he had remarked that it was needless to confute the absurdity of maintaining that "you have always been "a thinking being from all eternity", a proposition obviously just as valid as the other by his own tests.

But the greatest instance which the literature of the time affords of the power of the theological mortmain on thought is Sir Isaac Newton's theistic doctrine concerning matter. Known now to have been like Milton an Arian, Newton seems to have been so rooted in a theistic conception of things that his physical philosophy was powerless to rectify his metaphysics. Even as the scholar Cudworth and the philosopher Locke stood to the doctrine of creation of an infinite universe out of nothing, so did the great physicist stand to the position that the "matter" thus created was originally lacking in the very quality under which we now mainly conceive matter, the property of gravity. By the explicit teaching of his own *Principia*, there could be no creation out of nothing, because the substance of Deity was infinite—was everywhere;[2] but he allows the theological doctrine to stand, and to be stated in the name of physics, without a word of contradiction. He has put his doctrine distinctly enough in his Letters to Bentley, written in 1692-1693 (just before his attack of insanity), in answer to queries put by his correspondent on points just before treated of

---

[1] *Essay*, Book iv, ch. 10, § 19.

[2] " Omnipræsens [Deus] est, non per virtutem solam, sed etiam per substantiam, nam virtus sine substantia subsistere non potest. In ipso continentur et moventur universa." (*Principia Mathematica, Scholium generale*, at the end). The proposition goes on: "sed sine mutua passione. Deus nihil patitur ex corporum motibus; illa nullam sentiunt resistentiam ex omnipræsentia Dei;" but this is a mere burking of the dilemma.

by Bentley in his Boyle Lectures on Atheism. "When I "wrote my Treatise about our system," Sir Isaac calmly avows, "I had an eye upon such Principles as might work "with considering Men, for the Belief of a Deity; and "nothing can rejoice me more than to find it useful for "that Purpose." And the foregoneness of his conclusions is further made plain in a passage of the second letter: "You sometimes speak of Gravity as essential and "inherent to Matter. Pray do not ascribe that Notion to "me; for the Cause of Gravity is what I do not pretend "to know, and therefore would take more time to con- "sider of it."[1] And in the third letter the negative position is thus developed: "It is inconceivable that "inanimate brute Matter should, without the Mediation "of something else, which is not material, operate upon "and affect other Matter without mutual Contact, as it "must be, if Gravitation in the Sense of Epicurus be "essential and inherent in it. And this is one reason "why I desired you would not ascribe innate Gravity to "me. That Gravity should be innate, inherent and "essential to matter, so that one Body may act upon "another at a distance through a *Vacuum*, without the "Mediation of anything else, by and through which their "Action and Force may be conveyed from one to another, "is to me so great an Absurdity, that I believe no man "who has in philosophical Matters a competent Faculty "of thinking, can ever fall into it. Gravity must be caused "by an Agent acting constantly according to certain "Laws; but whether this Agent be material or imma- "terial, I have left to the Consideration of my Readers."[2]

This language must have one of two meanings. Either Newton meant by *Vacuum* the mere absence of non-ethereal or tangible matter, or he used the word in the strict and theoretic sense. In the latter case he might be arguing against the possibility of gravity holding good

---

[1] *Four Letters from Sir Isaac Newton to Dr. Bentley*, ed. 1756, p. 20
[2] *Id.*, pp. 25-26

between the planets on the theory of there being absolute vacuum beyond the atmosphere: that is, he would be contending that an absolute vacuum is impossible or inconceivable; though he would doubtless refuse to put his doctrine on the same grounds with that of Descartes. And as Bentley in his Sermons, following the ancient Theists and the Cambridge Platonist More, unhesitatingly assumed an alternation of matter and vacuum in varying degrees throughout all space,[1] it might conceivably be in Newton's thought to contemn that conception. But in view not only of the context but of his attitude to Bentley as a theistic propagandist, we cannot conclude that he was bent on showing Bentley to be a grossly absurd reasoner. We are therefore forced back to the other interpretation, that by *Vacuum* he meant merely space devoid of tangible matter, and that he was thus declaring it to be absurd to imagine the attribute of gravity to have originally belonged to matter. His doctrine here coincides exactly with that of his opponent Leibnitz, who later maintained "that the attraction properly so called of bodies is a miraculous thing, not being explicable by their nature".[2] That is, there was at one time tangible matter devoid of gravity—a proposition which the physicists of to-day would dismiss as unthinkable, and as being further wholly irrelevant to physical science. *Tantum religio*. Even in Newton's own day, Toland could reach the view that motion necessarily belongs to the definition of matter, and still hold by the notion of a "guiding intelligence".[3] But the hypothesis of which Laplace had no need in forming the great theory that absorbs and engulfs that of Newton, the earlier astronomer *had* need of, not for his theory, but for his psychological satisfaction, for the imposition on his theory of a hallucination from which he could not deliver

[1] *Sermons against Atheism* (1692), 5th edit., p. 253.
[2] *Correspondence with Clarke*, third letter of Leibnitz, end.
[3] Pünjer's *History of the Christian Philosophy of Religion*, Eng. trans., p. 327.

himself. *Hypotheses non fingo*, he put down as his maxim. It is the supreme self-deception in literary history. The physicist, with his frail physique sustaining his unique mathematical faculty, and with a brain so finely balanced as to be capable of temporary overthrow, had from his youth up stayed his spirit so completely on an emotional hypothesis that he could not take a ratiocinative step save in its name. When we learn to know men's minds as bodily functions, the case of Newton no less than the case of Pascal will probably serve to light up the knowledge by its peculiar vividness, somewhat as the genius of the men has here and there lit up the obscurities of surrounding Nature.

But, however that may be, we can be sure that the psychological fallacy even of Newton cannot have availed much to reconvert from anti-theism those minds which had taken such a bent. His mere authority could not be greater than that of the *orbis terrarum*, which they had already set aside. Whatever might be the difficulties of explaining natural processes without the theistic hypothesis, they were obviously as nothing (to men who had critically looked at theism) in comparison with the colossal and perpetual paralogism of asserting that Deity was omnipresent and omnipotent, and at the same time separating it from Nature and Man. The atheists, besides, could set authority against authority, since the professedly theistic Descartes was logically on their side. In 1714 we find Clarke protesting that "the "universal prevelancy of Cartes's (*sic*) absurd notions, "teaching that matter is necessarily infinite and necessarily external, and ascribing all things to mere "mechanic laws of motion, exclusive of final causes, and "of all will, and intelligence, and divine Providence from "the Government of the world hath incredibly blinded "the eyes of common reason".[1] In the following year

[1] Clarke's Answer to Butler's Fifth Letter. See Henry More's *Divine Dialogues*, Dial. I, as to the vogue of Descartes at that time (1668) in England.

Clarke was pointing out that the philosophy of Leibnitz "tended to banish God from the world",[1] while Leibnitz contended that the mathematical principles relied on by Newton were the same as those of the materialists.[2] Finally, it was matter of common talk that the great astronomer Halley, while accepting Newton's physics, was none the less an "infidel"; and the fact was cited by some freethinkers, including Garth, in their own support.[3] So that, as we have already said, it was no form of argument that finally availed in that age to check the open development of opinion on atheistic lines. It was the threefold force of, (a) above all, the principle of organised ostracism, operating against a small body of men, to many of whom ostracism meant ruin; (b) the opening of a new field of fruitful study by the development of natural science, which would in general attract above all the men of atheistic bent, and give them a firmer standing-ground than that of speculative or constructive Atheism, which had always hitherto made the mistake of leaving the impregnable position of resistance to the hollow explanatory formulas and insoluble contradictions of Theism in order to offer fanciful explanatory formulas of its own; and (c) the relative remoteness of the cosmological problem as beside the concrete and partly documentary problem of Deism *versus* Christian Trinitarianism, which could engage, on the heretical side, a far greater number of intelligences than could take the step of Atheism, and which could disquiet on the orthodox side a great number of intelligences that felt quite secure on the subject of the existence of Deity.

In short, the philosophic spirit of Atheism was not destroyed, or even essentially altered. It was simply silenced and disguised, mainly by social pressure. Men continued to relate themselves to Nature on atheistic

---
[1] Clarke's Answer to Leibnitz's First Letter, *end*.
[2] Leibnitz's Second Letter, par. 1.
[3] Berkeley, *Defence of Freethinking in Mathematics*, par. vii, and Stock's Memoir of Berkeley.

lines; but they ceased to proclaim their Atheism; and at length, perhaps, even to recognise it, in virtue of the dependence of all logical consciousness on clear expression. Indeed the very faculty of abstruse science seemed to dwindle in England for two generations after Newton, so that it was the irreligious French philosophers of the latter half of the century that first competently took up and developed Newton's principles and methods;[1] a fact which swiftly disposes of the propaganda based on the religiosity of Boyle and Newton. And so distinct is the heredity of modern physics from the avowedly and the virtually atheistic thought of the seventeenth century, that the physical science of to-day is still found doing in its own name what the early Atheists did in the name of Atheism—striving after formulas that shall explain the known in terms of the unknown, that is, of the ultimate nature of matter, with the old results of perpetual uncertainty and flux of opinion. Mr. Stallo has sufficiently shown as much in his *Concepts and Theories of Modern Physics*. If that body of quasi-metaphysical science were avowedly atheistic, it would be open to theistic attack very much as was the old Atheism. What it does is for the most part to carry on an essentially atheistic argument without recognising the theistic hypothesis at all; and if its professors, as such, occasionally assume to have quashed Theism in terms of physical science, it is found, by those who care to make the necessary analysis, that the assumption rests upon no proper logical process. The non-theistic physicist, by keeping clear of all thoroughgoing and above-board handling of the prevailing religious opinions, has lapsed into an unscientific frame of mind on the main problem involved. For the refutation of Theism is only partially a process of reasoning in or from physics; and in so far as it is so, the argument from physics is properly a step in the argument from moral and humanist science, from psychology and anthropology.

[1] This is explicitly avowed by Brewster, *Memoirs of Newton*, vol. i, ch. xiii.

Standing alone, the argument from physical science merely forces Theism to transform itself, as we have seen recently in the case of Dr. Romanes, who in a stage of physiological decay found for a second time mental solace in a set of arguments which even in that state of health would hardly have been possible to him had he added anthropology and hierology to his stock of sciences. The true criticism of Theism, as Strauss said of Dogma in general, is its history, which shows it to be simply primitive science gone astray, morally vitiated by emotionalism, anchylosed by ignorance, and paralysed intellectually by pecuniary interest. Technically speaking, religion is just an economic differentiation of science; and the fitting answer of either the speculative physicist or the scientific sociologist to the theologian who presses on him the theistic abracadabra, would be that of the comic paper's man on the beach who rejects a proffered tract with the remark: "No, thanks, I write 'em myself". The physicist works at his insoluble ultimate problems with fresh intelligence, and on that score at least can turn his back on the hypnotics and hirelings of faith: the sociologist, who is the potentially true moralist, works at his relatively feasible problems from a point of view in which all religion is a kind of social disease.

But to return to our seventeenth century ground: the frank discussion of the popular creed, never (for forcible reasons) carried on openly from a standpoint of naturalistic Atheism, passed into the hands of a type or succession of men disposed and trained only to humanist or literary studies, and therefore apt to lack an important part of the psychological preparation for the thoroughgoing study of religious systems; while, by reason of the inchoate state in which Christianity had kept the sciences of hierology and anthropology, they lacked much of the proper basis for their work as humanists. But these relative defects left them practically in touch with their time, inasmuch as they remained Deists, thus satisfying ordinary common-sense standards and escaping the worst pressure of traditional prejudice. They had enough in common with their average educated contemporaries to make converts and to set up discussions, as distinct from persecutions. To a certain extent they may even have made a common cause with the Unitarians, who seem to have become newly active, step for step with the Deists, towards the end of the seventeenth century, and who were first argumentatively opposed by orthodox divines about the same period.

It is thus finally clear, then, that though an atheistic movement had preceded the main period of the deistic, the latter did not derive from the former any more than it did from Socinianism, but was an independent contemporary development of the critical spirit on a lower or easier intellectual plane. And in the study of its rise and its dissipation we shall accordingly get a broader view of the nature of the social forces that make for ecclesiasticism and make arduous the way of rational thought.

CHAPTER IV.

THE PIONEER DEISTS.

THE literary history of English Deism begins with Lord Herbert of Cherbury, whose first treatise *De Veritate prout distinguitur a revelatione, a verisimili, a possibili, et a falso,* was published at Paris in 1624. That work, taken with those which Herbert published later, *De causis errorum* and *De religione laici,* and the *De religione gentilium,* not completely published till 1663, and read in the light of his unfinished Autobiography, is a human document of uncommon psychological interest. To know the manner of man, and the manner of his life, who first of his nation came out in the open to disavow the principle of revelation, is to realise anew the part played by character and circumstance in the development of ideas. The circumstances are primarily noteworthy. Herbert evidently came by his opinions first in France, where in any of the years 1608-1624 he would be in the midst of just such a revulsion against the religious temper as took place in England after the Civil War, though as yet it had not gone so far. Men had seen fanaticism work havoc unspeakable during a whole generation, raising its head even after apparent collapse to strike down Henry IV as it had struck down Henri III; and they saw the plague ready to break forth afresh at any stimulus. Herbert, with all his turn for fighting, perfectly appreciated the wisdom of President Jannin, who " thought better to have a peace " which had two religions than a war that had none ";[1] and he must have heard many such epigrams from public men in his diplomatic and military experience on the

[1] Herbert's *Autobiography,* Murray's reprint, p. 82.

Continent. At the time of his going to Paris he seems to have been orthodox enough, being wont to give his Sundays "wholly to devotion",[1] though willing at need to make an exception for a duel.

His *De Veritate*, then, may be taken to represent, thus early, the effect on minds at once hardy and reflective of the spectacle of warring fanaticisms, all claiming supernatural leading, and drawing counsels of mutual extermination from the same set of sacred books. A quaint mixture of passion and philosophy, vanity and veneration, he had all the courage needed to sustain him against long odds, and the turn for reverie that was needed to reach a moral estimate of the religious spirit and performance of his time. A less hardily pugnacious man, and a less self-esteeming one, would have shrunk from giving such a challenge as he did to the fanatical intelligence of his age. In accounting for his act, he has made two notable demands on our credence. He affirms that after finishing his book in France he showed it to Grotius, who had come thither on escaping from prison in Holland, and also to the theologian Tilenus, "who, after they had perused it, "and given it more commendations than is fit for me to "repeat, exhorted me earnestly to print and publish it".[2] If any such recommendation were given by the scholars to the soldier, it can hardly have been "after perusal". And Herbert proceeds to avow that, though "it did not a "little animate me that the two great persons above "mentioned did so highly value it, yet as I knew it would "meet with much opposition, I did consider whether "it was not better for me to suppress it. Being then "doubtful in my chamber, one fair day in summer, my "casement being opened towards the South, the sun "shining clear, and no wind stirring, I took my book, *De* "*Veritate*, in my hand, and kneeling on my knees, de-"voutly said these words—

"'O Thou eternal God, author of the light which now

[1] *Id.* pp. 72-74. [2] *Id.* p. 93.

"'shines upon me, and giver of all inward illuminations,
"'I do beseech Thee, of thy infinite goodness, to pardon
"'a greater request than a sinner ought to make; I am
"'not satisfied enough whether I shall publish this book
"'*De Veritate;* if it be for Thy glory, I beseech Thee
"'give me some sign from heaven; if not, I shall
"'suppress it.'
"I had no sooner spoken these words, but a loud
"though yet gentle noise came from the heavens (for it
"was like nothing on earth), which did so comfort and
"cheer me that I took my petition as granted, and that
"I had the sign I demanded; whereupon I resolved to
"print my book. This, how strange soever it may seem,
"I protest before the Eternal God is true, neither am
"I any way superstitiously deceived herein, since I did
"not only clearly hear the noise, but in the serenest sky
"that ever I saw, being without all cloud, did to my
"thinking see the place from whence it came."

This is justifiably cited by Herbert's critics as one of the curiosities of philosophical history. Going about to discredit the conception of revelation in general, he affirms that a kind of revelation was made to himself, to induce him to publish his treatise. There can be no doubt, however, of his good faith, whatever we may think of the quality of his testimony. The pioneers of the attack on revelationism must be allowed to exhibit a measure of the unreason they combat. Herbert was as devout a Deist as ever lived; and, while he could see that in all written revelations so-called there was a family trait of barbarism unmistakably human, his own normal faith came so near hallucination as to pass easily into it in an emergency.

But with the unreason there crop up in Herbert's works germs of all the rational arguments against revelationism. As these: that all alleged revelations are on the same footing, and that a layman must either take on authority what lies nearest, without question, or learn all languages, in order to study all; that the multiplicity of sects under each is a proof of their valuelessness for their professed purpose; that there is nothing in morals established by any which is not better established by unaided reason; and that the failure of every revelation to persuade more than a fraction of mankind negates the idea of omnipotent purpose. Thus at the very outset of the deistic propaganda there were laid down positions which the defenders of Christianity could not meet, save by the two expedients of showing that part of the argument against Christianity tells equally against Deism, and of burking the argument from the inconsistency of their special system with the premiss of a benevolent Omnipotence, by the *argumentum ad ignorantiam*, which is equally good—and bad—for all creeds whatever. So with Herbert's point of the immorality of the Christian doctrine of forgiveness for faith. He supplemented that protest of common-sense morality with an adumbration of the higher verdict of humane science that all wrongdoing is a product of innate bias and circumstance. But his thesis on this head went no further than an amusingly *naif* plea for his own failings of temper and appetite, which he considered to deserve great leniency of treatment because they were so visibly connatural, while he stood for future rewards and punishments as regarded his virtues and other men's sins. To this, as to his other arguments, the Christian answer was obvious. Though Christian ethics could only be defended in the customary manner by falsifying the facts as to the evangelical and Pauline doctrine, Herbert's principles could be shown to "encourage "vice" as much as the doctrine of faith did. And that is, in fine, the substance of Leland's answer to Herbert in the next century, composed as it was in the light of Butler's *Analogy* and all the previous apologetics. For the truth of Christianity there was no plausible argument, but the Christian had always his *tu quoque*.

Broadly speaking, the controversy after Herbert turns on the development of his positions, good and bad. The

Deists always made the mistake of claiming a clearness and satisfactoriness for the "religion of nature" which could no more be made out than the cognate claims for Christianity; and any intelligent atheistic antagonist could have pointed out—what, of course, the Christians were not free to say—that on the Deist's own principles Christianity and all the other creeds were as strictly "natural" as pure Deism. In a manner the Deists turned a somersault in the course of their argument, for while they claimed a primary and true innate perception of the existence of Deity and of the dictates of natural morality, they had to discredit the dogmas and fables of Christian and other systems as being human inventions or perversions. Thus they were virtually arguing that *their* doctrine was the true "revelation", and that the so-called revelations were false pretences. To this end Herbert had argued for a primordial monotheism among the Gentiles, a delusion the more excusable in the soldier and diplomatist, because it was cherished in the next generation by the scholarly Cudworth; but one none the less open to attack from Christians who regarded Cudworth with suspicion as much too Platonic in his Christianity. Thus, both in the last resort and on the face of the case, the Deists, like the Atheists, instead of doing what querulous piety then as now accused all freethinkers of doing, namely, destroying without replacing, actually put themselves philosophically in the wrong by their zeal for putting some theorem in the place of that which they overthrew. Tindal, arguing in Butler's day, saw well enough the nullity of the protest. "When any Notion," he writes, "in Defence of which People have little to say, " is attacked, they usually cry, *Why will you pull down,* " *except you build up?* When in Reality, Error must be " remov'd in Order to make way for Truth: You must " pull down one before you can build up the other."[1] Yet, in point of fact, he was all the while laying himself

[1] *Christianity as Old as the Creation*, 1730, p. 421.

open to fatal criticism by putting a positive and dogmatic Deism in the place of Christianity from the start. What was valid in his book was just the powerful destructive criticism; and though the very profession of Deism was socially in their favour, whatever polemic success the Deists attained all along was reached by minimising positive Deism as much as possible, and making the dispute turn on the concrete issues of Christian legend and Christian practice.

How far Herbert prepared an audience for Hobbes it is now very hard to say; but perhaps the post-Jacobean movement of Freethought was never more natively energetic, or even relatively more successful, than in the generation which read the new works of Herbert and Hobbes together. The demoralised and discredited Church could make no tolerable show of answer;[1] and the power of character in Herbert, backed by his rank, and the power of intellect in Hobbes, backed by his patrons, sufficed alike to outface any menace of orthodoxy. The Restoration Parliament might pass and revise statutes against heresy, but the heretics could feel secure enough behind a profession of Deism. Baxter, in 1671, replying tardily to Herbert's *De Veritate*, declares that " infidels are grown " so numerous and audacious, and look so big and talk so " loud, that any one may see they are not silenced in " their speaking-places or hampered by the Five-Mile " Act". In such circumstances, Cudworth's armada against Atheism would have been felt to be a waste of energy, even if it had not been suspected of supporting a superior form of heresy. Within the Church itself, apart from the too Platonic philosophising of Cudworth and More, there were stirrings of common sense which boded ill

---

[1] Answers were, however, published by Halyburton and Baxter. Dr. Hunt makes a slip in stating (*Religious Thought in England*, i, 276) concerning Baxter's *Unreasonableness of Infidelity* (1655), that " he had as yet no infidels before him except the Anabaptists". But Baxter's answer to Herbert (*More Reasons for the Christian Religion and No Reason against It*) was not published till 1671 (*Works*, vol. 23).

for the integrity of the faith. Thomas Burnet's *Archæologia Philosophia* (1692) courageously revived the ancient esoteric surmise that the Mosaic account of the Creation was mainly allegorical, a suggestion which was not perfectly accommodated to the ecclesiastical mind by Burnet's adherence to the view that creation *had* taken place about the time specified by the chronologies. And it is not unlikely that the vogue attained later by his *Sacred Theory of the Earth* was as much due to heretical sympathy with his views on Genesis as to orthodox sympathy with his rationalistic orthodoxy, which is established by his posthumous treatise *De Fide* (1727). He was indeed made to figure at one time—unjustly enough—as an extreme Freethinker, in a ballad whose contemporary popularity entitles it to notice here as a sign of its time. It has been reprinted in more than one serious culture-history, and may be allowed a place here, with a note of its occasion. Dean Sherlock, of St. Paul's, had published in 1693 a *Vindication of the Holy and ever blessed Trinity*, in which the Socinians were met, in a fashion characteristic of the spirit of the time, with a rationalistic explanation of the mystery in question; whereupon Bishop (then Prebendary) South published a volume of *Animadversions* in which the Dean was wittily but severely handled as a Tritheist, the Three Persons of his demonstration being simply Three Gods. "I cannot see," said South in his most unclerical manner, "any new Advantage "he has got over the Socinians, unless it be that "he thinks his Three Gods will be too hard for their "One". Sherlock duly replied, and South rejoined, the Unitarians and Deists looking on with much enjoyment. Burnet's *Archæologia* happening to be published while the inter-clerical fray was raging, he was grouped with Sherlock and South in the ballad referred to, the author of which, we are told, had a number of "presents" made to him by the nobility and gentry.[1]

[1] *Memoir of Dr. South*, prefixed to his *Posthumous Works*, 1717, p. 130.

It went to the tune of a familiar song, " A Soldier and a Sailor " :—

> " A Dean and Prebendary
> Had once a new Vagary,
> And were at doubtful strife, Sir,
> Who led the better Life, Sir,
>   And was the better Man,
>   And was the better Man.
>
> " The Dean he said that truly
> Since Bluff was so unruly,
> He'd prove it to his face, Sir,
> That he had the most grace, Sir,
>   And so the fight began, etc.
>
> " When Preb replied like thunder,
> And roar'd out 'twas no wonder,
> Since Gods the Dean had Three, Sir
> And more by Two than he, Sir,
>   For he had got but one, etc.
>
> " Now whilst these Two were raging,
> And in Disputes engaging,
> The Master of the Charter
> Said both had caught a Tartar,
>   For Gods, Sir, there were none, etc.
>
> " That all the books of Moses,
> Were nothing but supposes;
> That he deserved Rebuke, Sir,
> Who wrote the Pentateuch, Sir,
>   'Twas nothing but a Sham, etc.
>
> " That as for Father Adam,
> With Mrs. Eve his Madam,
> And what the Serpent spoke, Sir,
> 'Twas nothing but a Joke, Sir,
>   And well-invented Flam, etc.
>
> " That in this Battle-Royal
> As none would take Denial,
> The Dame for which they strove, Sir,
> Could neither of them love, Sir,
>   Since all had giv'n Offence, etc.

"She therefore slyly waiting,
Left all Three Fools a-prating
And being in a Fright, Sir,
Religion took her Flight, Sir,
   And ne'er was heard of since
   And ne'er was heard of since."

But religion, as thus conceived, was found to be not so easily exiled, being held by stronger ties than any theory of the Trinity; and the regulation formula for the same reason held its ground, Burnet doing his part to reinstate it, in the choice Latin for which he was celebrated. Half a century later, we find Archbishop Herring writing: "I "abhor every tendency to the Trinity controversy. The "manner in which it is always managed, is the disgrace "and ruin of Christianity."[1] His Grace was needlessly apprehensive. The dogma of the Trinity will stand, in the pure Athanasian form, as long as the Church stands. But two hundred years ago the Church had not so fully tested its power of resisting rational criticism, and the virtue of its vested interests ; and when its doctrines were openly attacked it took terrified measures of defence.

The fullest, or at least most various, utterance of the humanist Freethought of the seventeenth century is to be found in the works of Charles Blount, son of Sir Henry Blount, author of *A Voyage to the Levant*, six forgotten comedies, a satire entitled *The Exchange Walk*, and *An Epistle in Praise of Tobacco and Coffee*. Father and son seem to have co-operated in the *Anima Mundi* (1678), in which the Deist position is rather led up to by discursive learning than aggressively maintained. In *Diana of the Ephesians* (1680), however, the attack on all clericalism and revelationism is so direct that only the standing of Blount's family can explain the audacity of its publication; and in the same year he struck one of the most practically effective blows delivered during the whole Deistic controversy, in his annotated translation of the first two books of

---

[1] *Letters of Archbishop Herring to Duncombe*, 1777, p. 134.

the *Life of Apollonius of Tyana*, which was actually proceeded against and condemned to be destroyed. The importance of the production lay in the annotations, which are so much bulkier than the text as to swell the whole to 243 folio pages, and in the clear implication that the life of Jesus is properly to be understood as only that of a wonder-working teacher of the type of Apollonius, though his cult chanced to survive in the struggle of systems throughout the Roman Empire. Here there is brought to bear on the religious problem, albeit with a certain dilettantist laxity, much more of intelligent learning than was possessed by Herbert, whose acquirements in that kind had to be extensively eked out, like his Latin, by his industrious drudge, Thomas Masters. And this remains Blount's most considerable treatise. The seizure of his book was a warning too weighty to be ignored; and henceforth his activity ran to a warfare against all fettering of the press, and particularly against Catholicism, as the great exemplar of intellectual tyranny. Much might have been expected from him in the reign of William, whose advent he unambiguously welcomed as made in right of conquest of the bad king by the good. But the abnormality of mind and temperament which, like the exuberant physical courage of Herbert, made Blount one of the first to speak out openly against the popular creed, brought about his death. He loved his dead wife's sister, and characteristically made out the reasonableness of marrying her in a close discussion[1] of the Levitical text; but she refused him, and the friend who prefixed the unsatisfying sketch of his life to his collected works testifies that it was on that ground that Blount committed suicide. It would seem as if something of overbalance and extraordinariness were needed to constitute the pioneers of critical reason in an age of fanaticism tempered only by trimming. What came of the profession of Deism by a more average nature was

[1] *Oracles of Reason*, 1695. p. 137.

seen in the case of Blount's friend and editor, Charles Gildon, who was reconverted to orthodoxy by the very elementary though vehement argumentation of Leslie's *Short Way with the Deists* (1697), a work which Blount could readily have confuted from his larger stores of knowledge. But character as well as knowledge was needed to sustain a heretic in those days, when the spirit of civil war could still flame out in acts of proscription that made even loyal statesmanship a career of hazard.

CHAPTER V.

THE HERESY OF LOCKE AND NEWTON.

How adventurous were the pioneer Deists may be learned by comparing their course with that of some men of high capacity who privately shared their heresies. Two of the greatest names of the reigns of William and of Anne were Newton and Locke. Newton, as we have seen, championed Theism to the uttermost; but it is made certain by his then unpublished papers that he rejected the doctrine of the Trinity. So far, however, was he from venturing to avow his heresy that he dared not even allow the printing of an anonymous French translation of his letter to Locke, *An Historical Account of Two Notable Corruptions of Scripture*, dealing with the texts 1 John v, 7, and 1 Timothy iii, 16. After entrusting the manuscript to Locke for translation, he wrote entreating him "to "stop the translation and impression of the papers as "soon as you can, for I desire to suppress them".[1] Locke, like Newton, a sickly subject in infancy and a debile man always, shows the same timidity in a less degree, having indeed less of positive heresy to conceal. In one of his Latin letters to Limborch, written in Holland in 1685, he avows, *àpropos* of the discussion aroused by the *Histoire Critique* of Father Simon, that he has had doubts and difficulties over the Scriptures. "If "all things in the sacred books are equally to be held as "inspired, without any discretion, certainly a large "handle is given to philosophers for doubting our faith "and sincerity. If, on the contrary, some are to be taken "for purely human writings, how shall the divine authority

[1] Brewster's *Memoirs of Sir Isaac Newton*, vol. ii, p. 325.

"of the scriptures stand, without which the Christian
"religion collapses? What shall be the criterion? What
"the measure? . . . I who everywhere seek the truth
"only, as much as I can lay hold of, whether I find it
"among the orthodox or the heterodox, consider both
"sides." And after citing certain historical passages in
the Gospels and Acts, he confesses that these and many
others "certainly seem in every way to call the infalli-
"bility and inspiration of the Holy Scripture in doubt;
"whence I beg that you will not refuse to tell me what
"you think in the matter; for indeed many points which
"occur in the canonical books, long before my reading of
"this treatise, kept me anxious and doubtful; and you
"will make me most grateful if you will take away my
"scruple".[1] Professor Fowler, citing this letter, decides
that "from the character of his theological writings, com-
"posed during the latter years of his life, it would appear
"that these scruples were afterwards either removed or
"set aside".[2] We must adopt the latter explanation.
There is nothing in the Limborch correspondence to show
that the scruples were "removed"; and, since Locke's
later writings do not remove such scruples for others, we
must consider him to have merely overridden them, con-
structing for himself a notion of Christianity which took
no account of the bearing of his early objections. Nay
more, there is sufficient reason to believe that, like Newton,
he was a Unitarian, though like Newton he never spoke
a plain word on the matter.

Part of the evidence lies in the manner of his controversy with Stillingfleet. We have seen what very short
work he made of the difficulty about the dogma of the
creation of the universe out of nothing. It seems hard
that a philosopher who would thus sacrifice all for Holy
Writ should be charged by a bishop with virtual Atheism,
but so it was. Already in 1697 Locke writes to Moly-

---

[1] *Some Familiar Letters between Mr. Locke and Several of his Friends*, 1708, pp. 302-304.
[2] *Locke*, p. 49.

neux: "A man of no small name, as you know Dr. "S[tillingfleet] is, has been pleased to declare against "my doctrine of no innate ideas, from the pulpit in "the *Temple*, and, as I have been told, charged it with "little less than Atheism".[1] And the Christian philosopher adds this commentary: "Though the Dr. be a "great man, yet that would not much fright me, because "I am told, that he is not always obstinate against "opinions which he has condemned more publickly than "in an harangue to a sundays auditory. But that 'tis "possible he may be firm here, because 'tis also said, he "never quits his aversion to any tenent he has once "declared against, till change of times bringing change of "interest, and fashionable opinions open his eyes and his "heart, and then he kindly embraces what before deserved "his aversion and censure."

That side-light is valuable; and yet, on scrutiny, it would be hard to say whether it is the Bishop or Locke who lies most open to challenge on the' score of straightforwardness. Their discussion arose out of the fact that Toland, in his *Christianity not Mysterious* (1696), grounded himself in part on the doctrine of Locke as to clear and other ideas. "I was far enough," writes Stillingfleet with unwitting candour, "from condemning your way of Ideas, "till I found it made the only ground of Certainty, and "made use of to overthrow the Mysteries of our Faith. ".... This was it which made me look more narrowly "into it. . . . ."[2] That is to say, the Bishop did not attack Locke's doctrine as being erroneous in itself, but as being found to damage Christian dogma. With such an antagonist Locke had of course capital openings; but his own position is really no better than the Bishop's. Stillingfleet puts the point forcibly enough at the beginning of his second Answer :—

"Suppose I had *born* a little *too hard upon you* in

[1] *Familiar Letters*, p. 175.
[2] *The Bishop of Worcester's Answer to Mr. Locke's Letter, &c.*, 1697, p. 132.

"joyning *your* Words and *anothers Intentions* together;
" had it not been an easie and effectual way of clearing
" your self, to have declared to the World, that you
" owned the *Doctrine of the Trinity*, as it hath been
" Received in the Christian Church, and is by ours in the
" *Creeds and Articles of Religion*? This had stopt the
" Mouths of the Clamorous, and had removed the
" Suspicions of the Doubtfull, and would have given full
" Satisfaction to all reasonable Men. But when you so
" carefully avoid doing this, all other Arts and Evasions
" do but leave the Matter more suspicious among the
" most Intelligent and Impartial Readers. This I
" mention, not that you need be afraid of *the Inquisition*,
" or that I intend to charge you with Heresie in denying
" *the Trinity*; but my present Design is to shew, That
" your mind is so entangled and set fast by your *Notion* of
" *Ideas*, that you know not what to make of the Doctrines
" of the *Trinity* and *Incarnation*; because you have no
" *Idea* of *One Nature* and *three Persons*, nor of *two Natures*
" and *one Person*; as will fully appear afterwards." It
was perfectly true. Of course the profane could say that
the Bishop could no more than Locke have an "Idea"
on the subject in hand; but there was the difference that
Locke knew his incapacity in the matter, while the
Bishop perhaps did not know his. In any case, we can
readily gather from Locke's way of answering the Bishop,
and from his anonymous work (1695) on *The Reasonableness of Christianity* (which would have served the Bishop's
purpose admirably had he known it to be Locke's) that
the philosopher in his own mind set the doctrine of
the Trinity aside as gratuitous and unintelligible, and
that he was practically an Arian or a Socinian. As
here in the *Second Vindication* of the treatise :—

" What was sufficient to make a man a Christian in
" our Saviour's time, is sufficient still—the taking him for
" our King and Lord, ordained so by God. What was
" necessary to be believed by all Christians in our
" Saviour's time, as an indispensable duty which they

"owed to their Lord and Master, was the believing all "divine revelation as far as each could understand it; "and just so it is still, neither more nor less. . . No man "has a right to prescribe to me my faith, or magisterially "to impose his opinions or interpretations on me; nor is "it material to anyone what mine are, any further than "they carry their own evidence with them".[1] And an extremely latitudinarian principle is laid down in the original treatise :—

"There be many truths in the Bible which a good "Christian may be wholly ignorant of, and so not believe; "which perhaps some lay great stress on, and call funda- "mental articles, because they are the distinguishing "points of their communion."[2]

This is simply a paraphrase of the doctrine laid down by Hobbes forty years before,[3] that no Christian could as such be asked to do more than was stipulated for in the texts, " Whosoever shall confess with his mouth the Lord Jesus, and believe in his heart that God raised him from the dead, shall be saved ";[4] and " Whosoever believeth that Jesus is the Christ, is born of God ".[5] It was certainly true, as Locke protested in his reply to Stillingfleet, that he had taken no part whatever in the controversy between Trinitarians and Unitarians. He had indeed scrupulously held his tongue on that in the *Essay*. But his words in the anonymous treatise are those of a man who in his heart entirely took the Socinian side; and Locke's argumentation about matters of faith not being matters of knowledge was distinctly of the nature of that verbal trifling which in others he con- fessedly resented above all things.

---

[1] *Works*, edit. 1823, vol. vii, pp. 358-359
[2] *The Reasonableness of Christianity*, 1695, p. 292.
[3] *De Corpore Politico*, Part ii, ch. 6. Mr. Stephen (*English Thought*, vol. i, p. 96) traces the doctrine to the *Naked Gospel* of Arthur Bury (1690), but not to Hobbes.
[4] *Romans*, x, 9.
[5] 1 *John*, v, 1.

Thus there emerges the instructive fact that the two leading English thinkers of the year 1700 whose names figured on the side of orthodoxy against both Deism and Atheism were not orthodox at all, but concealed Unitarians, who differed from the Deists only in taking a more sympathetic view of the Christian sacred books. No names counted for more as such, and the names were employed under a deep delusion as to the men's real opinions, a delusion due, it must be said, to their dissimulation. We need not now concern ourselves to blame them: our business is rather to assimilate the lesson of their course. That they were both unrobust men, and constitutionally timid, is a large part of it. And the rest is this: that specifically religious emotion is not only, as we are so often reminded by religious writers, in opposition to the intellectual temper, but is to some extent the corruptress of that. To say this is not to denounce religious emotion either; for we can very well see that in Newton and Locke, as in Pascal, and more recently in Dr. Romanes, that it may be itself a pathological symptom. People think of Newton the mathematician and of Locke the metaphysician as pure intellect; but we know Newton, who at birth was barely viable, to have been anæmic, nervous, querulous, and suspicious of his fellows; we know him to have fallen at one time (1692-93) into absolute insanity, and to have been thereafter conscious of shaken powers,[1] and we know Locke to have fought a battle with lung disease all through his life. It is hard to kick against these pricks. For Newton, "voyaging through strange seas of thought alone," his Theism, above all after the terrifying stroke of his long spell of madness, was a psychological support against temperamental weakness; for Locke, a belief in Christianity was a support against not only physical weakness but the sense of the injustice and imperfection around

---

[1] See Brewster's *Memoirs of Newton*, vol. ii, ch. xvii, and p. 175. Brewster vainly belittles the evidence.

him. The incurable malevolence of theologians, the stupid intolerance of sects, the barbarism and the blundering of legislators, would have weighed too heavily on him to leave him any tranquillity had he not the religious basis for an optimism on which, albeit inconsistently, he could rest his spirit.[1] But the intellectual result was disastrous. His prudent philosophy, finally accommodated in name if not in spirit to the reigning irrationalism, had no great ameliorative effect on life and thought, with all its popularity; and his attitude on religion not only discouraged that exact historical study which was as necessary there as in the physical sciences, where he welcomed it, but finally even made for the "enthusiasm" and hysteria which he distrusted and disparaged. His doctrine that the understanding is "the "most elevated faculty of the soul", and is "employed "with a greater and more constant delight than any of "the other",[2] is not agreeable to the pious ear; and his insistence that Scripture should be read with an eye to its general bearing, and not on the fanatic's principle of the mysterious validity of any sentence in the text,[3] is in the same case. But when the religious world learned that the scriptural studies of his closing years "produced in "him a very lively and sincere piety", and a "more "noble and elevated idea of the Christian religion than "he had before"; that "if his strength would have "allowed him to begin new works it is probable that he "would have written some, in order to inspire others "with the same grand and sublime idea"; that when he thought upon "the method found out for the salva-"tion of mankind", he "could not forbear crying out, "'O the depth of the riches of the goodness and "'knowledge of God'";[4] and that Dr. Watts was

---

[1] Since writing this sentence, I find that a similar remark is better made by Professor Fowler in his *Locke*, p. 162.
[2] *Epistle to the Reader*, prefixed to the *Essay*, par. 1.
[3] *Reasonableness of Christianity*, 1695, p. 291. (*Works*, vii, 152.)
[4] See the *Life* in Des Maiseaux' edition, 17.

inspired by these facts to write an Ode, containing the lines,

> "Reason at length submits to wear
> The wings of faith, and lo! they rear
> Her chariot high, and nobly bear
> The prophet of the skies "—

when the successors of the Puritans learned these things they might well feel that philosophy had been worsted by faith.

If any further light is needed on Locke's attitude to the popular religion, it is to be found in the narrowness of his historical knowledge. He had, as Professor Fraser well says, a "languid historical imagination";[1] and his study of Christian origins never went beyond the most elementary inquiry. At all times, indeed, he read little, so that Mr. Lewes[2] is entitled to conclude that he had studied neither Hobbes nor Spinoza—an extraordinary thing to be predicable of such a man in that age. But hardly less extraordinary is his attitude on the question of the historical aspect of miracles. The actuality of the Gospel miracles was one of his two main grounds for accepting Christianity; yet we find him writing to Limborch in 1692 :—" I desire to be made more certain (*certiorem fieri* "*cupio*) concerning miracles after the times of the "apostles. I am not sufficiently versed in ecclesiastical "history to know what I may rightly set forth con- "cerning them (*ut quid de iis statuam norim*). There- "fore I earnestly ask you, for it behoves me to know, "whether miracles were wrought in the Christian church "after the time of the apostles; by what authors and "by what testimony preserved in memory; and whether "in the reign of Constantine they long continued ; and "who was the Thaumaturgus (*quis fuit ille Thaumaturgus*), "and what was done by him, whose so specious title has "come down to us. I do not ask concerning the miracles

---

[1] *Locke*, p. 261.
[2] *History of Philosophy*, 4th ed., ii, 242.

"which are catalogued by the ecclesiastical writers, but
"whether it rests on the authority of worthy historians
"that there were real miracles, whether they were
"wrought seldom or often, and how long that gift was
"allowed to the church."[1] The *Reasonableness of
Christianity* was being planned in this state of information
and critical preparation.

As little critical or original was he on moral problems.
Professor Fowler has remarked on "the inadequate con-
"ception he has formed to himself of the grounds and
"nature of Moral Philosophy";[2] and has noted, though
not in that connection, how the charter of Carolina,
which Locke, as Ashley's secretary, had a hand in drawing up, provided, on the one hand, that "no man was to
"be permitted to be a freeman of Carolina unless he
"acknowledged a God, and agreed that God was to be
"publicly and solemnly worshipped"; and, on the other
hand, that "every freeman of Carolina should have abso-
"lute power and authority over his negro slaves, of what
"opinion or religion soever".[3] We must not look on that
matter as we should if it belonged to our own time; but
we are free to say that it shows Locke's satisfaction over
the Christian moral system to have no great moral
significance.

The end of the inquiry is that the religious element in
Locke, whatever it might do for him in the way of solace,
affected his intellectual processes distinctly for the worse.
In a serene mood, and in the society of a congenial intelligence, his happiness lay in the sense of loyalty to truth:
witness the oft-quoted sentence in his letter, written in
old age (1703), to his young friend Anthony Collins:—
"Believe it, my good friend, to love truth for truth's sake
"is the principal part of human perfection in this world
"and the seed-plot of all other virtues; and, if I mistake
"not, you have as much of it as I ever met with in any-

---

[1] *Familiar Letters*, pp. 338-339.
[2] *Locke*, p. 76.
[3] *Id.*, p. 23.

"body." Yet at this very time he was in the way of edifying Dr. Watts; a few years before he had hedged as we have seen on the question of irrational dogmas; and when writing to Limborch in response to a request for his idea of a demonstration of the unity of God, he had stipulated that his correspondent should not give any copy of the letter to anyone whatever, and should promise to burn it when called upon to do so.[1] The age of Philistine fanaticism was too strong for the weak-chested truth-lover.

It is only just to remember how formidable were the dangers from which Locke and Newton recoiled. In the very year of Stillingfleet's attack on the *Essay*, an appeal was made to the King by the House of Commons to use his personal influence to discourage "vice, prophaneness, "and irreligion," and, in particular, antitrinitarianism. "We do further," said the virtuous legislators, "in all "humility beseech your majesty, that your majesty would "give such effectual orders as to your royal wisdom shall "seem fit, for the suppressing all pernicious books and "pamphlets, which contain in them impious doctrines "against the Holy Trinity, and other fundamental doc- "trines of our faith, tending to the subversion of the "Christian Religion; and that the authors and publishers "thereof may be discountenanced and punished. And "we do also most humbly beseech your majesty, that "your said proclamation may be ordered to be read at "least four times in the year in all churches and chapels, "immediately after divine service; and at the Assizes and "Quarter-Sessions of the Peace, just before the charge is "given."

And the king graciously responded, winding up thus his black-letter proclamation of 24th February, 1697:—

"And whereas several wicked and prophane persons "have presumed to print and publish several pernicious "books and pamphlets, which contain in them impious

[1] *Familiar Letters*, p. 412

"doctrines against the Holy Trinity and other funda-
"mental articles of our faith, tending to the subversion
"of the Christian Religion; therefore for the punishing
"the authors and publishers thereof, and for the prevent-
"ing such impious books and pamphlets being published
"for the future, we do hereby strictly charge and prohibit
"all persons, that they do not presume to write, print or
"publish any such pernicious books or pamphlets under
"the pain of incurring our high displeasure, and of being
"punished according to the utmost severity of the law.
"And we do hereby strictly charge and require all our
"loving subjects to discover and apprehend such person
"and persons whom they shall know to be the authors or
"publishers of any such books or pamphlets, and to bring
"them before some justice of peace or chief magistrate,
"in order that they may be proceeded against according to
"law."[1]

Nor was the matter left to the personal influence of the King. The Act 9 and 10 William III, which is the corner-stone of our still-subsisting blasphemy laws, provides that "If any person, having been educated in or "at any time having made profession of the Christian "Religion within this realm, shall by writing, printing. "teaching, or advised speaking, deny any one of the "Persons in the Holy Trinity to be God, or shall assert "or maintain there are more Gods than one, or shall "deny the Christian Religion to be true, or the Holy "Scriptures of the Old and New Testament to be of "divine authority," he shall on conviction of a first offence be adjudged incapable in law to hold any office or employment, ecclesiastical, civil, or military; and on a second offence be pronounced incapable to sue or plead in any court of law, or to make any deed of gift; and shall suffer three years' imprisonment without bail.

Under this statute, Newton would have been deprived

[1] The Address and the Proclamation are prefixed to the *Account of the Societies for Reformation of Manners*, 5th ed., 1701.

of his Fellowship, or, later, of his Mastership of the Mint, and Locke of his Commissionership of the Board of Trade, had they been proved from their writings to be Unitarians. Other men had been struck at. To say nothing of the destruction of Blount's translation of the Life of Apollonius, Locke had before his eyes the case of Toland, who in his *Christianity not Mysterious* had applied Locke's own principles with a certain measure of thoroughness, and so had the effect of giving point to the plea that no man could be asked to believe propositions he did not understand. Toland was the type of temperamental frankness and propagandist imprudence, a perfect contrast to the reticence and caution of Locke, and so a predestined fighter in the deistical campaign. And when, in Dublin, where discreet dissimulation had been cultivated in a double degree, he went about propounding his views and challenging other people's, the terrified Molyneux wrote to Locke, whose name Toland had used, explaining that Toland was a man to be repudiated; to which view Locke more than assented. Soon Toland and his book were "presented" by a Dublin Grand Jury, "not one of which, I am "persuaded," wrote Molyneux, "ever read one leaf in "*Christianity not Mysterious*. . . . . The dissenters here "were the chief promoters of this matter."[1] And so Toland had to fare forth on his restless course, his foible of vanity and his instability of thought serving alike to keep him always a pioneer in the wilderness, while men no more orthodox than he, but with a turn for secresy, stayed snug and undisturbed in their sinecures.

[1] *Familiar Letters*, p. 228.

CHAPTER VI.

THE PROFESSIONAL DEFENCE.

IT thus begins to appear that in the deistic crisis, as in the Reformation crisis, the course of average opinion and action was shaped by all manner of considerations apart from truth. Broadly speaking, the defence of orthodoxy was a hired defence, not in the sense that men were expressly employed all round to write up religion, but that religion was written up by men retained in its service. Christians have been wont to find an odd solace in the belief that their faith, with some twenty thousand salaried exponents, substantially triumphed in England over the criticism of some dozen unsalaried Deists, every one of whom risked at least odium and ostracism by his action. The supposed result of the struggle, after a warfare of a hundred years, is held to illustrate the supernatural sustainment of the Church by its Founder. Those who hold to the materialistic view that Providence is on the side of the biggest battalions must be glad that at least this once they are in a manner agreed with the other party. For one who believes that ideas prosper, commercially speaking, in the ratio of the facilities for their acceptance, there is nothing surprising in the fact that England in the year 1800 was roughly about as orthodox as in the year 1700. The facilities for the growth of rational views at any time are to be estimated in terms of the conditions: the amount of general education, constituting the intellectual soil; the competition of other intellectual interests; and the degree of organisation of hostile forces. Now, in the England of 1800, proportionally to population, there was not more culture than in the England of 1700. The population had

[1] The Ac Societies for R... mainly in the lower industrial strata; and

there was no educational machinery at all fit to give these even an elementary culture. On the other hand, the organised resistance to the critical moment had been very fully developed, in respect of a tolerably steady promotion of clerical interests, especially in the latter half of the century. Thus, while the revivalism of Wesley and Whitfield could best appeal to the new ignorant industrial populations, the machinery for forming opinion among the middle classes was relatively ample. At the same time there had gradually arisen a body of intellectual interests which in large part took the place of those which had occupied educated people in the first part of the century—interests economic, political and literary. The leading contemporary names at the beginning of the century, in the intellectual life, were such as Newton and Locke. The leading contemporary names at the end of the century, in the intellectual life, were such as Smith and Burke. For disputes about God and the nature of ideas and abstract political principles, there had been substituted, in the eye of the ordinary intelligent person, disputes about practical politics—this before as well as after the French Revolution. The new industrial development and the new imperial development had alike wrought for this. The charge that England cared little about ideas begins to be possible only in the latter half of the century. In the first, she showed at least as much interest in ideas as any other nation. What happened was the steady rise of commercialism and industrialism, involving a constant increase in the number of people with strictly practical interests; and such people would in natural course turn to concrete politics and emotional religion rather than to critical and quasi-scholarly discussion.

Whatever might be said by partisans, the critical ferment had never ceased among the thinking; but when heads were counted it would doubtless seem that the battle had gone against them. This, we say, was in the circumstances a matter of course. Opinion, such as it was, was made among the majority more and more by the clergy, as the Church recovered her lost social status. Such an episode as the Sacheverell Trial had shown that within two generations of the Restoration, when she had been at her nadir in point of credit, she had enormously developed her political power; and when Walpole, learning his lesson as an Opportunist, decided to keep on good terms with her, there began the reconquest of her intellectual influence. But the process was substantially one of subsidised propaganda, of which the effect was reaped in the form of factitious opinion among mediocre people, as in our own day systematic advertisement makes its effect by mere quantity of impression on the largest accessible number of persons. There was neither philosophical nor "spiritual" development, but there was gain to organised orthodoxy, in the production of what may be termed a respectable fanaticism, or well-dressed prejudice in favour of church-going, the one "orthodoxy" that can really subsist among people who do any reflection whatever. For there was no statable doctrinal agreement anywhere. The Christians were divided into Trinitarian and Unitarian. Among the Trinitarians, when any attempt was made at ratiocination, somebody was sure to raise the charge of Tritheism; and the Tritheist would retort a charge of "enthusiasm" or of Catholicism. The Unitarians, in turn, were challenged by the non-Christian Deists; and the Deists in turn, whether or not known to be Christian, charged each other with misconception and misrepresentation of Deity. Thus the systems of Newton and Leibnitz, and of Leibnitz and Clarke, were reciprocally hostile, each seeing in the other a sort of Atheism or a degradation of Deity, or else Pantheism.

Reviewing the controversy, it is impossible not to feel, from the work of Stillingfleet onward, that if rationalism could have been put on anything like a similar financial and legal footing with churchism, Deism would have become the opinion of the great majority of the middle classes, among whom "enthusiasm" was still felt to be something rebellious, regicidal, and "vulgar" in the old sense of the term. In spite of the legal penalties upon any denial of the Trinity, it is clear that Deism was not less common, and far more paraded, in upper class and educated society than Agnosticism is to-day, and this in varying degrees through a period of some seventy years. All the while, however, the Church kept up a constant professional warfare, meeting every deistical treatise with a dozen replies, so that many more people would always hear of the dispute from clerical than would hear of it from heretical voices. And whereas in the earlier days of the controversy (the days of unsettled polity), the assailants were able to find many open-minded and candid listeners, latterly every reading man or woman might be supposed to have learned the regulation parries to the deistic thrusts; and thus the mere habit of formal rebuttal would create the species of orthodoxy that best served the church's turn.

It would be a crude misconception, of course, to suppose that the orthodox polemists in general wrote with tongue in cheek, in conscious falsehood. That is not how self-interest shapes opinion in any field of dispute. More often than not, orthodox championship would be a simple matter of knowing on which side one's bread was buttered, and of seeing that, whatever the truth might be, there was plenty to be said on the side of faith. Of course there were some disinterested champions, both lay and clerical. The editors of Addison's *Evidences of the Christian Religion* made much of the fact that Boyle, Locke, Newton and Addison, were all laymen, and all therefore disinterested in their zeal for Christianity. The plea is an admission that clerical advocates were not so disinterested. As regards Newton and Locke, as we have seen, it was delusive; but apart from that it was valid enough. Boyle, described as "the most exact Searcher into the Works of "Nature that any age hath known",[1] was in reality a

---

[1] Addison's *Evidences*, ed., 1763, pref., p. v.

"singular mixture of science and credulity, who left a
"parcel of red earth to Locke and his literary executors
"with directions for turning it into gold," a performance
which Locke would hopefully have undertaken.[1] Boyle
was no doubt disinterested enough. His wealth, however, served to buy the pens and tongues of others.
The Boyle Lecture is his best remembered subsidy; but
his funeral sermon tells of many more.

"He was at the Charge of the Impression of the New
"Testament into the *Malayan* Language, which he sent
"over all the *East-Indies*. He gave a noble Reward to
"him that translated Grotius's incomparable Book of the
"*Truth of the Christian Religion* into *Arabick*, and was at
"the Charge of a whole Impression, which he took care
"to order to be distributed in all Countries where the
"Language is understood. He was resolved to have
"carried on the Impression of the New Testament in the
"Turkish Language; but the Company thought it became
"them to be the Doers of it, and so suffer'd him only to
"give a large share towards it. He was at seven hundred
"Pounds charge in the Edition of the *Irish* Bible, which
"he ordered to be distributed in *Ireland*, and he contri-
"buted largely both to the Impression of the *Welsh* Bible,
"and of the *Irish* Bible in *Scotland*. He gave during his
"Life three hundred Pounds to advance the design of
"propagating the Christian Religion in *America*; and as
"soon as he heard that the *East-India* Company were
"entertaining propositions for the like design in the *East*,
"he presently sent an hundred Pounds for a Beginning
"and an Example, but intended to carry it much further,
"when it should be set on foot to purpose. He had
"designed, tho' some Accidents did upon great considera-
"tion divert him from settling it during his Life, but not
"from ordering it by his Will, that a liberal Provision
"should be made for one, who should in a very few well-

---

[1] Prof. Fowler's *Locke*, pp. 68-69. See Newton's letter to Locke, in Lord King's *Life of Locke*, 1829, p. 220.

" digested Sermons, every year set forth the Truth of the
" Christian Religion, in general, without descending to
" the Sub-divisions amongst Christians; and who should
" be changed every third Year, that so this noble Study
" and Employment might pass through many Hands, by
" which means many might become Masters of the
" Argument."

It would be tedious, if it were necessary, to trace out the many similar subsidies to religious propaganda in that age; but it will probably be taken for granted that they were numerous.[1] And for everyone that was openly avowed, such as the Boyle Lecture, and such as the stimulus so conscientiously acknowledged by Waterland on the title page of his " *EIGHT SERMONS preach'd at* " *the Cathedral Church of St. Paul in defense of the Divinity* " *of OUR LORD JESUS CHRIST*; *upon the Encourage-* " *ment given by the LADY MOYER*,[2] *and on the* " *appointment of the Ld. BISHOP of LONDON* " (1720), there would be a multitude of temporary benefactions. To these there would be nothing comparable on the deistic side, save in such support as may have been privately given to poor champions like Toland, who had in any case sufficiently shown their sincerity by choosing to be free lances when they might easily had had preferment in the Church. For there can be no reasonable doubt that, as was repeatedly complained by Christian polemists, there were many deistical clergymen. It would be absurd to suppose that in a keen controversy which lasted through two generations at the hands of a hundred writers, and was followed by many thousands of disputing readers, every man who happened to hold a church benefice was satisfied of the truth of the Church's case. We have seen what Locke privately thought of the character of Stillingfleet; and we know, many of us, what

---

[1] A short list, including courses of lectures among the Dissenters, is given by Farrar, *Critical History of Freethought*, note 49, p. 658.

[2] This benefaction subsisted till 1773. Note to Reid's ed. of Mosheim, *end*.

we think of some bishops and many parsons in our own day, in the matter of genuineness of conviction. It would stand to reason, were there not plenty of evidence, that in an age of admittedly low political morality, the age of Marlborough's treacheries, and Bolingbroke's championship of the Church, and Walpole's maintenance of the laws against dissent, many of the clergy, high and low, were dissemblers in the current controversies. One of the most earnest and powerful of all the deistical treatises, Tindal's *Christianity as old as the Creation* (1730), was the work of one who had grown grey as a university Fellow in forced conformities, having been first an Anglican under Charles II, a Catholic under James II, and again an Anglican under William. There must have been others of similar experience, if of less ratiocinative power,[1] who shared Tindal's final sentiments without avowing them.

It has indeed been in later times bitterly complained of the whole body of divines who set themselves to answer the Deists that they show nothing of the true spirit of religion, and might as well have taken their stand with those they opposed. That is the religious way of seeing the fact above suggested, that not intellectual conviction but income and professional habit inspired a large part of the defence. And sometimes it is so futile, so blankly unplausible, that it is a little difficult to believe in the seriousness of the defender. Dr. Stackhouse, for instance, author of a *Complete Body of Divinity*, published in 1732 a *Defence of the Christian Religion from the several Objections of Modern Antiscripturists*, which does the Deists the service of putting their main objections in a condensed and forcible fashion, and answering them with such consummate inefficiency as to make the treatise almost a Freethinkers' handbook. In one of the reviews of the

---

[1] Locke said of Tindal's Essay *Of the Powers of the Magistrate and the Rights of Mankind in matters of Religion* (1697) that it "maintains the cause of impartial and universal liberty of conscience with such uncommon strength, as will hardly be met with in any other books". (Publisher's preface to Tindal's *Four Discourses*—anonymous—1709).

time the objections are quoted verbatim and the answers summed up so as to make their pointlessness perfectly apparent; and yet the reviewer gravely affects in concluding to rejoice that "the Book is like to prove not only " *(sic)* a *Monument* of the Poison which has been vended " from the Press in this profane age, but a *Repertory* " likewise of what the ablest men among us have, at the " same time, done to defend our common Christianity ".[1] The reviewer can hardly have been serious; but we must conclude Dr. Stackhouse to have been so, and to have represented that large wing of the orthodox host which was stedfast in the degree of the density of its understanding.

A very different type was the Rev. Arthur Ashley Sykes, rector of Rayleigh in Essex, the antagonist of Middleton, who published *an Essay upon the Truth of the Christian Religion* in reply to Collins's *Discourse of the Grounds and Reasons of Christianity*, of a nature not at all likely to give general satisfaction on his own side, being not only entirely courteous and candid to the other, but critical of orthodoxy. Its preface pleaded " that the cause of Christianity " may not be deemed indefensible or false, because some, " who have meant well, have ill defended it," and " that " the ridiculous opinions of its professors may not be " imputed to Christianity itself . . . . Since Divinity " has been made a science, and systematical opinions have " been received and embraced, in such a manner that it " has not been safe to contradict them, the burden of vin- " dicating Christianity has been very much encreased. Its " friends have been much embarrassed through fear of " speaking against *local Truths;* and its adversaries have " so successfully attacked those weaknesses, that Chris- " tianity itself has been deemed indefensible, when in " reality the follies of Christians alone have been so . . . " Whereas, were Christians left to their full liberty to " defend the doctrines of Christ and his Apostles . . .

[1] *Historia Litteraria*, vol. iii, 1732, p. 91.

"which is all that Christians, *as such*, are obliged to "defend .... I do not see which way their cause "could receive any damage, nor how Infidelity could make "any converts."

The critical method by which this position is maintained is to a large extent such as would have been called rationalistic in Germany at the close of the century; though Sykes adheres to the main dogmas. "There does "not appear," he says, "to be reason sufficient to make "us reject the accounts we have of the resurrection of "Jesus; and therefore we may conclude that fact to be "true;" but as regards much of the argument from prophecy he makes very swift work. "There is no one "thing," he declares, "that has made the New Testament "the subject of ridicule to Jews and Infidels, so much as "the absurd inferences which Christians usually have "drawn from passages which visibly contain not one tittle "of what is pretended .... To see the most glaring "and eminent follies and weaknesses of men sanctified by "divine words, and vended as important truths, or put "upon the world as the Revelation of God, is entirely to "alienate men's minds from truth." So he readily allows to Collins that the quasi-prediction about a Virgin conceiving a son was not a prediction at all; and reasons that the citation in the gospels was a mere "accommodation "of the words of the prophet to the case in hand", a sort of appropriate historical quotation, as it were, like Cromwell's saying he had "fulfilled" a passage in a Psalm, but no more. And so with other passages. The Apostles "used a style and phraseology which was then common "among the Jews, and understood by them as easily as "our European phraseology is understood by us."[1]

This is perhaps the high-water mark at once of candour and of compromise on the part of the defence; and as such it was of course not maintained. Neither its purport nor its temper could possibly please the faithful; though

[1] I quote from the review in the *New Memoirs of Literature*, 1725, vol. ii, pp. 81-103.

it gives the impression of a much more sincere belief than that of many disputants who conceded nothing. A community which paid on the whole well to be defended against unbelief felt it had a right to a little more zeal. The acceptable tone was this:—" When a Toland or a " Woolston, in Defiance of common Sense, Decency and " Piety, endeavours to poison the Minds of Men with his " pernicious and blasphemous Notions . . . . . I believe " any one may be allowed, and is even sometimes obliged, " to call things by their proper Names ; and that the words " *Calumny, Lye, Imposture, Extravagance, Impertinence, and* " *Nonsense*, may be employ'd without the least Violation " of good Manners, and that regard which is owing to " Mankind, or the Infringement of any Christian Vertue."[1] This was said in answer to a reviewer's suggestion that argument is more convincing than abuse ; and here, of course, we all recognise a sincere expression of the religious spirit.

The same will readily be allowed in the case of Berkeley, whose papers on the Freethought question in the *Guardian* are among the most vainly virulent of the attacks made on the Deists. Berkeley's nature seems here transformed. He outgoes the bitterness of Swift as far as passion can outgo a misanthropy that attacks individuals only because individuals happen to cross its path. It was either Berkeley or Steele who wrote that " if ever man deserved " to be denied the common benefits of air and water, it is " the Author of *A Discourse of Freethinking* "[2]—that is, Anthony Collins, whom Locke loved,[3] and held, as we

[1] Letter to the Author of the *Present State of the Republick of Letters,* 1733. vol. vi, p. 202.
[2] *Guardian,* No. 3, end.
[3] There is another notable testimony to Collins' character, that of Sir James Dalrymple (d. 1751), given in the *Autobiography* of Dr. Alexander Carlyle (p. 210) :—" One day we were talking of the deistical controversy, " and of the progress of deism, when he [Dalrymple] told me that he knew " Collins, the author of one of the shrewdest books against revealed reli- " gion. He said he was one of the very best men he had ever known, and " practised every Christian virtue without believing the Gospel ; and added,

have seen, to have as much of disinterested love of truth as any man he had known. It may have been Steele who penned the piece of savagery just quoted, as it was Steele who wrote of Freethinkers, probably in his cups:—" I " would not have persecution so far disgraced, as to wish " these vermin might be animadverted on by any legal " penalties."¹ But it was Berkeley who wrote:—" It is " my opinion that free-thinkers should be treated as a set " of poor ignorant creatures, that have not sense to discuss " the excellency of religion;"² and again:—" If a person " who exerts himself in the modern way of free-thinking " be not a stupid idolater, it is undeniable that he contri- " butes all he can to making other men so, either by " ignorance or design; which lays him under the dilemma, " I will not say of being a fool or a knave, but of incurring " the contempt or detestation of mankind;"³ and yet again:—" For my own part I shall omit no endeavours to " render their [freethinkers'] persons as despicable, and " their practices as odious, in the eye of the world, as they " deserve". And eight years later, in his *Essay towards Preventing the Ruin of Great Britain* (1721), we have the same angry conviction that all unbelievers are wicked men. Berkeley bitterly complains that " a cold indiffer- " ence for the national religion, and indeed for all matters " of faith and Divine worship, is thought good sense;" and he protests in so many words that " the public safety " requireth that the avowed contemners of all religion " should be severely chastised;" asking " why blasphemy " against God should not be inquired into⁴ and punished " with the same rigour as treason against the King."

" that though he [C.] had swam ashore on a plank—for he was sure he " must be in heaven—yet it was not for other people to throw themselves " into the sea at a venture. This proved him [D.] to be a sincere though " liberal-minded Christian."

¹ *Tatler*, No. 135.
² *Guardian*, No. 55.
³ *Id.*, No. 88, end.
⁴ In the *Discourse to Magistrates* (1736) Berkeley speaks of an extraordinary " fraternity of blasphemers" in Dublin, calling themselves " blasters".

That is the invariable tone of Berkeley when he comes to close quarters with unbelief; and the result is that *The Minute Philosopher* is a sadly spiteful performance, in which a puppet or two are set up and knocked about by way of discrediting the work and influence of Herbert, Hobbes, Blount, and Toland. Intermittently conscious of the unfitness of his frame of mind on the subject, Berkeley begins one of his *Guardian* papers with the assurance that he is not going to "object ill designs" to his adversaries, as polemical writers are apt to do. It is the promise of the passionate man that this time he will not lose his temper; and it has the value which such pledges are usually found to possess. Berkeley cannot discuss Freethinkers without attacking their characters: even Spinoza he furiously asperses as a "weak and "wicked writer".[1] The outcome is that the subtlest intelligence on the Christian side in that day contributed to the defence of the faith, apart from a metaphysic which finally does nothing for it, less of intelligent argument than any other combatant of any standing. Beyond all question, the truth is that where Berkeley's mind is under the specific influence of religious feeling it produces nothing of the slightest intellectual value. On any question of pure reasoning he is extraordinarily acute and suggestive; and on sociological questions apart from his creed he is one of the most original thinkers of his time; but in him religion was a passion; and when the point of evangelical faith is touched, the thinker of the *Querist* and the *Analyst* becomes a hysterical priest. The entire outcome of the *Analyst* is implied in the 62nd of the concluding queries: "Whether mysteries may not "with better right be allowed of in Divine faith than in "human science"; or, as he puts it in the succeeding *Defence of Freethinking in Mathematics*, "Is it not a "proper way to abate the pride and discredit the pre-

His wild account of their doings is hardly credible; but neither Mr. Lecky nor Mr. Stephen seems to have investigated the subject.

[1] *Minute Philosopher*, Dial. vii, § 29.

"tensions of those who insist upon clear ideas in point of "faith, if it be shown that they do without them even in "science?" We have here an adroit and original employment of the weapon resorted to later by Butler in the *Analogy;* but as a plea for the "mysterious" over which Berkeley was so exercised, it is finally even more futile than the argument of Butler. That because you accept the mathematical doctrine of fluxions on the credit of Sir Isaac Newton you should accept all the Christian mysteries on the credit of Jesus Christ, is a plea which merely sets a thinking man to the task of rationalising the doctrine of fluxions without altering his attitude to the Gospels. The position of Berkeley, quietly considered, is just a little ridiculous. He seems to have supposed that if you could but infect the sceptic with one attack of credulity, by getting him to accept some one proposition without understanding it, you could triumphantly proceed to demand his assent to any religious dogma you liked.

To this singular position Berkeley came in virtue of his remarkable combination of great intellectual power with an emotionalism that was, in the strict sense of the term, morbid. It is the case of Newton and Locke with a certain difference. Where Newton was affected by latent neurosis, and Locke by physical debility, Berkeley was the victim of hypochondria;[1] and his passionate clinging to his evangelical creed is simply the expression of that side of his temperament. But the keen intelligence could not be content so to efface itself in the process as to leave the act of faith apparently devoid of rational sanction ; and so we get the elaborate but passionate argument to show that religious faith is on all fours with accepted processes of scientific thought. He held by the Gospel and argued for it as he did for tar water, and with about as much of permanent success. With an ordinary reader, seeking common-sense evidences for his creed, Berkeley must

---

[1] Stock's Memoir, *end.*

have counted for much less than an average defender of the faith like Waterland, whose ripe absurdities[1] would not strike the ordinary intelligence then as they do now; or like Sherlock, who could "try the witnesses" and clear the character of the twelve apostles from suspicion. What would be most popular in Berkeley's work was just the worst part of it, the virulent aspersions and the angry demands for the punishment of audacious infidels. And even in the matter of malice he would be less effective than some men of another type, as thick of skin as he was tender, and gifted with the Old Bailey manner and spirit, which his subtle intelligence could never put on, with all its stress of nervous bitterness. To see round the defence, we must study that Old Bailey side, as represented and typified by one of the most notorious controversialists of the time.

[1] See these well set forth by Mr. Stephen, *English Thought*, vol. i, pp. 257-260.

CHAPTER VII.

BENTLEY AND ANTHONY COLLINS.

Among the details supplied by the writers of our own day who have professed to sketch or write the history of the deistic movement, one of the more familiar is to the effect that Anthony Collins, the friend of Locke, and author of *A Discourse of Freethinking* and other treatises, was crushingly answered, as regards the *Discourse*, by the celebrated Richard Bentley, D.D., who convicted him of fallacy and ignorance in general, and of grossly bad scholarship in particular. That is the academic legend. Professor Jebb, who really studies the controversies on which he passes judgment, has unfortunately not examined this one in his admirable monograph on Bentley. Others have passed judgments without much examination. Mr. A. Storey Farrar, in his so-called *Critical History of Freethought* (1862), pronounces that the *Discourse of Freethinking* was "refuted entirely by Bentley in the *Phileleu-*" *"therus Lipsiensis;"* and Mr. Leslie Stephen, from his different point of view, writes in his own way that " Poor " Collins's scholarship is slashed and torn, till pity, if pity " were a possible emotion towards a Deist, might have " touched some of his opponents. It is a case in which it " is impossible to avoid the hackneyed allusion to the " fourth-form schoolboy."[1] To call a man "poor" is notoriously one of the easiest ways to discredit him; and the fact that Mr. Stephen offers no illustration of the "slashing" process is only the more suggestive of the hopelessness of the case.

Nor is Mr. Stephen the only nominal rationalist who

[1] *History of English Thought in the Eighteenth Century*, vol. i., p. 207.

gives Collins up. Mr. Mark Pattison, in a famous essay, brackets Bentley's *Remarks* with Butler's *Analogy*, as one of the very few apologetic treatises of that age which can be said to have been completely successful. "Coarse, " arrogant, and abusive, with all Bentley's worst faults of " style and temper, this masterly critique is decisive."[1] But he goes on: " Not, of course, of the deistical con- " troversy, on which the critic avoids entering;" and he again observes that "Bentley does not attempt to reply to " the argument of the *Discourse on Freethinking*", which leaves us in some perplexity as to the nature of Mr. Pattison's critical principles. When he further describes Collins's treatise (a book of 178 pages) as "a small " tract", we are led to surmise imperfect study of the facts. The "decisiveness" of Bentley's remarks appears to have consisted, in Mr. Pattison's opinion, in convicting Collins of a variety of mistranslations and errors con- cerning the classics. Collins, he says, "flounders hope- " lessly (in Bentley's *Remarks*) among the authorities he " has invoked. Like the necromancer's apprentice, he is " worried by the fiends he has summoned, but cannot " lay; and Bentley, on whose nod they wait, is there like " another Cornelius Agrippa, hounding them. Collins's " mistakes, mistranslations, misconceptions, and dis- " tortions are so monstrous that it is difficult for us now, " forgetful how low classical learning had sunk, to believe " that they are mistakes and not wilful errors. It is rare " sport to Bentley, this rat-hunting in an old rick; and " he lays about him in high glee, braining an authority at " every blow. .... The Remarks of *Phileleutherus* " *Lipsiensis*, unfinished though they are, and trifling as " was the book that gave occasion to them, are perhaps " the best of all Bentley's performances. They have all " the merits of the *Phalaris* dissertation, with the ad- " vantage of a far nobler subject. They show how " Bentley's exact appreciation of the value of terms could,

[1] *Essays and Reviews*, ninth edition, p. 307.

"when he chose to apply it to that purpose serve him
"as a key to the philosophical ideas of past times, no
"less than to those of poetical metaphor."

This unstinted estimate is one of the many which serve to stir up curiosity as to the value at some points of the honor paid to Bentley's memory in our universities. The breadth and independence of his scholarship no student will dispute who has studied his dissertations; but to those of us who realise—what, indeed, his eulogists do not venture to deny—that his emendations of Milton are the most monumental example of pedantic insanity in all literature, displaying such blindness to the values of terms and of "poetic metaphor" as would argue mere imbecility in any other man, and that his emendations of Horace are more often than not presumptuous follies, it is highly interesting to know that he is held to have succeeded marvellously where it is impossible to check him, in putting sense into passages of unintelligible Greek. However that may be, a study of his critical treatment of Collins leaves us only more dubious than before. The reader will perhaps forgive a brief excursion over a few samples of his method, to the end of realising what kind of argumentation it was that aroused orthodox academic enthusiasm in that day, and has retained its traditional esteem in our own.

One of Bentley's most cocksure flings at Collins's scholarship is made in the following passage:—[1]

"But now a specimen of his (Collins's) learning again,
"which he sprinkles by the way. *It was universally believ'd,*
"says he, *among ordinary people, that the Gods themselves*
"*came down from Heaven, and eat of the repasts which the*
"*Priests had prepar'd for them at the people's expense.* And
"again, in the next page, *that the Gods came down to eat*
"*upon earth.* Now, did not I guess right, and for all his
"fine panegyric upon the *Ilias* of *Homer*, he was little or
"not at all acquainted with that poem? For if he were,

[1] *Remarks*, Part I., p. 26.

"he would have learnt from thence, that, in the Heathen
"notion, the Gods could not *eat upon Earth*, nor devour
"human *Repasts*:
"Οὐ γὰρ σῖτον ἔδουσ', οὐ πίνουσ' αἴθοπα οἶνον
"Τοὔνεκ' ἀναίμονές εἰσι, καὶ ἀθάνατοι καλέονται.[1]
"Whence, therefore, had our learned author this bold
"assertion of *universal belief*? Even from *Bel and the
"Dragon;* and what *his mother* once taught him there, he
"ascribes to Paganism in common. The real matter is
"no more than this. When a Heathen Priest slew a
"victim, he had no more of it for his share than Law and
"Custom allow'd, scarce worth the custom of butchering;
"the Entrals and most useless Parts were burnt on the
"Altar, and the best of the victim was carried home to
"the Sacrificer's house, to be feasted upon by his Family
"and Friends; and if the Priest was invited, too, as a
"Guest, it was a Work of Supererogation. Nor did the
"most credulous believe that Gods came down and
"devour'd *Flesh;* nor was any such *Repast* set apart for
"them. If any victuals was *(sic)* so set, either in Temples
"or in the open Streets, it was well known that the
"sweepers of the Fanes got the first, and the Poor of the
"Town the latter. All they believed in relation to the
"Gods, besides the Piety and the Prayers, was only that
"the Steam of the burnt sacrifice ascended up to Heaven,
"and delighted, or (if you will), fed the Gods. This
"*Homer* would have told him, too, that *Libation* and *Steam*
"was the only share the Gods had in any offering:
"Λοιβῆς τε κνίσσης τε· τὸ γὰρ λάχομεν γέρας ἡμεῖς[2]
"Whence *Aristophanes,* in his Play, call'd *The Birds,* makes
"a City to be built in the air, on purpose to stop all inter-
"course between Heaven and Earth, *that no smoke from
"Sacrifices should ascend to the Gods;* and presently *Pro-
"metheus* is introduc'd, bringing the news, *That the Gods
"were almost starv'd, having not had one particle of* steam
"*since* Nephelococcygia *was built.* 'Tis true, indeed, there

[1] *Iliad,* v, 341. 342. [2] *Iliad,* iv, 49.

"was another Notion,[1] that the Gods often came down
"from Heaven in Human Shape, to inquire into the actions
"of men, and so, like Strangers and Pilgrims were unawares
"entertain'd, and (seemingly) eat and drank with their
"Hosts. But this is nothing to the *Priests*, nor to the
"assertion of the Author, who no doubt will anon be
"found a most suitable Interpreter of *Solomon* and the
"*Prophets;* after he has been so miserably impos'd on by
"that silly and spurious Book, *Bel and the Dragon*."

To realise fully the character of this typical criticism, we must first quote Collins's actual preliminary words, which Dr. Bentley had carefully ignored. In the Discourse, the passage cited begins: "But one of the "commonest miracles among them, and which was uni- "versally believed among ordinary people, was," etc. By this it might reasonably be supposed that every educated man who read Collins's treatise would know the practice to which he was referring; and the question arises, had Dr. Bentley ever read or heard of a Roman *Lectisternium?* He cites one passage from the Iliad, and one from the Odyssey, to prove that in "the heathen Notion" the Gods could not eat upon earth; and we must suppose that Mr. Pattison and Mr. Stephen thought the thesis and the proof sound and scientific, since this is the first particularised attack in Bentley's first pamphlet[2] on Collins's scholarship upon a concrete issue, and the learned rector and historian must at least have read so far. Yet every professed scholar might be supposed to be well aware that one of the commonest of Roman religious practices, for at least two centuries before the Christian era, was the holding of *Lectisternia*, or functions in which the statues or figures of Gods were placed at table and served with food, senators and others sharing in the banquet. The unlearned reader may find the main details collected in such an exoteric treatise as Ramsay's *Roman Antiquities*,[3] where the conclusion come to is that "it would appear that as early as

---

[1] *Odyssey*, xvii, 485.   [2] P. 26.   [3] Edition 1851, p. 345.

" B.C. 191, *Lectisternia* formed part of the ordinary worship
" of certain Gods, and were going on during the greater
" part of the year." This, of course, was what Collins
was thinking of; and Bentley's parade of details about the
procedure in private sacrifices would be wholly beside the
case even if it were accurate, which it is not.

The only way in which Collins's statement can honestly
be called in question is by raising a doubt whether the
pagan multitude in Rome really believed that the Gods
partook of the banquet set before them. As to this,
however, little doubt can be left in the mind of anyone
who reads Livy's statement[1] that at the Lectisternium
in the Year of the City 574 (B.C. 178), when there was
an earthquake, " the heads of the Gods who were on their
" couches turned away, and the robe (lana) and coverings
" of Jupiter fell off ". If such a story found general
currency among the educated, the popular belief in the
consumption of viands by the divine statues would follow
as a matter of course. As to this one point, we may cite,
in preference to other witnesses, Dr. Bentley himself.
For the learned Doctor had actually written, in his third
Sermon against Atheism,[2] of " the gross idolatry of the
" [ancient] vulgar (for the philosophers are not concerned
" in it), that believed the very statues of gold and silver
" and other materials to be God, and terminated their
" prayers in those images; as I might show from many
" passages of scripture, from the apologies of the primitive
" Christians, and the heathen writers themselves ". And
this was the pundit who twenty years later was to
maintain that throughout the Pagan world the Gods were
held incapable either of partaking of food or of coming to
earth, save in cases which were " nothing to the priests ".

The " decisive " expert is not even trustworthy as to
the evidence of the Iliad and the Odyssey, on which he so
absurdly stakes the whole question of " the heathen

[1] B. xi, c. 59.
[2] *Eight Sermons preached at the Honourable Robert Boyle's Lecture, in the First Year*, 1692. By Richard Bentley, M.A. Fifth edition, 1724, p. 51.

"notion". He quotes the passages which suit himself, but he says not a word of such as these :—

Αἰεὶ γὰρ τὸ πάρος γε θεοὶ φαίνονται ἐναργεῖς
Ἡμῖν, εὖτ' ἔρδωμεν ἀγακλειτὰς ἑκατόμβας·
Δαίνυνταί τε παρ' ἄμμι καθήμενοι, ἔνθα περ ἡμεῖς.[1]

"For indeed, always heretofore the Gods appear manifest
"unto us when we offer up glorious hecatombs; and they
"feast sitting together with us, wheresoever we be."

Ζεὺς γὰρ ἐς Ὠκεανὸν μετ' ἀμύμονας Αἰθιοπῆας
Χθιζὸς ἔβη κατὰ δαῖτα, θεοὶ δ' ἅμα πάντες ἕποντο.
Δωδεκάτῃ δέ τοι αὖτις ἐλεύσεται Οὔλυμπόνδε.[2]

"For yesterday went Zeus to Oceanus, among the
"excellent Ethiopians, to a feast, and all the Gods
"followed him; but on the twelfth day he will return to
"Olympus."

Such passages evidently point to a conception at least as common as that of the undescending Gods who received only odours of sacrifice; the latter idea being obviously a late sophistication of the early and always popular conception of the deities as having the appetites no less than the form of men, in terms of the primitive Hebrew tale told in the eighteenth chapter of Genesis, where "the Lord" figures as one of three men, who talk and eat with Abraham as fellow creatures. Modern scholarship indeed surmises[3] that the institution of the Lectisternium was borrowed by the Romans from the Greeks; and these archaic passages in Homer may be taken as clues to early Greek phases of the practice, being rather more to the point than some cited allusions to the bed of Venus,[4] which do not imply any banqueting.

Either Bentley remembered these familiar Homeric passages or he did not. If he did not, his parade of

[1] *Odyssey*, vii, 201-203.
[2] *Iliad*, i, 423-425. *Cf. Odyssey*, i, 26.
[3] *Cf.* Marquardt and Mommsen, *Handbuch der Römischen Alterthümer*, 1878, Band vi, S. 81; and Preller, *Römische Mythologie*, S. 133, ff.
[4] *E.g.*, Pausanias, viii, 47; Theocritus, xv., 127.

omniscient learning was the merest browbeating. If he did, his argument was piously dishonest. Here we may conclude that, though he had little enough notion of being honest in a religious quarrel, he wrote in oblivious ignorance, attempting no conscientious study before making up his mind, but snatching at any quotations that occurred to him for his purpose. Of the whole matter of ancient sacrifices, on which he affects perfect knowledge, he displays the most astonishing ignorance, vending the vague reminiscences of an undergraduate, and overlooking details that many undergraduates would remember. He writes as if all Greek sacrifices were of single animals by single persons or families, as if there were no such things as hecatombs and chiliombs; and he is absolutely wrong in stating that the priests get nothing worth mentioning. Unprejudiced modern investigation shows that in post-Homeric times we have, "chiefly from inscriptions, a " vast number of details and regulations regarding the " disposal of sacrifices," most of which "define the " portion which is the perquisite of the priest (θεσμοιρία: " γερη: ἱερώσυνα). This differed in different worships; " frequently it is the legs and skin, sometimes the tongue " and shoulder. . . . The thighs, flanks, and left side of " the shoulder are mentioned."[1] It may be said that many of the inscriptions here founded on were not available to Bentley; but he had only to turn to Archbishop Potter's *Archæologia Græca*, published in 1697-98, to find at least one inscription, that "on a pillar " in the Anaceum, which testified that of the sacrificed " oxen, ' one part should be reserved for the games, and " ' of the other two one should be given to the priests, " ' another to the parasitoi ' ".[2] And the same quietly vigilant scholar would have reminded Bentley that in the Homeridian Hymn to Apollo, the God "promises the " Cretans, whom he had chosen to be his priests, that

[1] Smith's *Dictionary of Greek and Roman Antiquities*, 3rd ed., art. *Sacrificium* (ii, 585).
[2] *Archæologia Græca*, Book ii, ch. 3.

"they should have a maintenance out of the sacrifices".[1] But Potter was a loyal seeker for knowledge, and a kindly keeper of its stores; whereas to Bentley, learning was rather a fenced demesne, where he might play the Beadle in the interests of the Church, and in the gratification of his own passion for the cudgel.

As for his snorting reference to *Bel and the Dragon*, it can only be taken to express the view that because the book is spurious, that is, uncanonical, it has no evidential value as to ancient practices. This is an argument which Bentley would not have dreamt of using in any non-religious discussion, since, even for a scholar who discriminates between "inspired" and "uninspired" documents, the latter are still evidence as to the beliefs entertained at the time of their writing. It is difficult to believe that Mr. Pattison would have disputed this, or to understand how, knowing as he must have done the almost universal range, down till modern times, of the primitive superstition as to the supernatural consumption of votive food, he could have accepted Bentley's handling of the passage in Collins as "decisive" of anything but the ignorance or the bad faith of the critic. On this alternative it is of course not altogether easy to decide. It seems scarcely credible that Bentley, with his immense range, not only of reading but of recollection, could have been unaware of, or could even have forgotten, such explicit passages in Homer and the well-known facts as to the Roman *Lectisternia*. If, however, he had not forgotten them, his audacity in writing as he did must be held to exceed even his normal practice, for he must have known that dozens of his or of Collins's readers would recall the passages in point. He had laid himself open to a retort far more effectual and triumphant than any of his own attacks, so that of the alternative explanations of knavery and ignorance, the former is at this point the less tenable. We are almost driven, then, to conclude that the braggart scholar, going about to

---

[1] Hom. Hymn to (the Delian) Apollo, *end*.

trounce an amateur for bad scholarship, had himself lost all recollection of some of the best-known facts in regard to one of the ancient practices on which he professed to write with absolute knowledge, and had thus made a far worse blunder than any he imputed. And we seem to be further constrained to conclude that Mr. Pattison and Mr. Stephen, who pronounced Bentley's treatise so decisive in point of scholarly interpretation of antiquity, had either read the discussion with the same oblivion or ignorance of the essential facts, or had pronounced their panegyrics after merely skimming Bentley's pages, and perhaps without checking them by those of Collins at all. The University itself had in 1715 publicly thanked its learned pugilist for his performance, "praying him, in the name of the "University, to finish what remains of so useful a work". The learned body had evidently no misgivings; whence, perhaps, Mr. Pattison's traditional confidence.

In any case, it would be hard to find in Bentley's "Remarks" any criticism more to the purpose than that above examined, or to find a solitary passage which entitles us to ascribe to it, as Mr. Pattison does, a nobility of subject raising it "far" above the Phalaris dissertation. Such a verdict one must be content to put aside as inexplicable. Bentley not only does not enter into the deistical controversy (which, by the way, was not the special subject of Collins's *Discourse*, as Mr. Pattison seems to have supposed); he does not even discuss on its merits Collin's theory that "Free-thinking" had always been the source of whatever good thinking had been done in the world; and he burkes all the more serious of Collins's propositions as to the lack of good evidence for the orthodox creed. Again and again he falsifies his author. He charges[1] Collins with imbecility in saying, on the authority of Grabe and Mills, "that no canon was "made till about sixty years after the death of Christ". A canon, says Bentley, is "an entire collection of the

[1] P. 59.

"Sacred Writings, to be a *Rule, Standard,* and *System* to
"Christianity. Now, according to those doctors and the
"plain matter of fact, all the books of the New Testament
"were not written till above sixty years after the death of
"Christ. What sense is there in this complaint then,
"that the books were not collected before they were
"made?" In reality, Collins had simply translated
Grabe[1] as saying "that the Canon of Scripture was not
"made while the Apostles were alive ; no not . . . when
"Clemens wrote his Epistle to the Corinthians . . . ,"
and Mills as saying[2] that "There was no collection made
"of any books of scripture, *whether Epistles or Gospels,* till
"above three-score years after the death of Christ. Not
"of the Epistles certainly. . . . Nor of the four Gospels,
"the reading of which in the churches was then deter-
"mined and agreed on, as I shall show presently." Of
both passages, which he has accurately translated, Collins
gives the Latin originals in his footnotes. Thus Bentley
first falsely represents that Mills had declared some of the
books to be non-existent before A.C. 96, whereas Mills
not only says no such thing, but implies that they were
then existent ; so that Collins is held up to ridicule as a
blockhead for simply reciting the words of his orthodox
authorities. If there was any absurdity in the matter, it
was on the part of these eminent divines, and as the
absurdity could only be made out against Collins by
falsifying their views, Bentley promptly did so.

Of the same sort is his tactic in regard to Collins's
remark that the great charge of maintaining such
numbers of priests "is a burden upon society, which was
"never felt upon any other occasion". Bentley
demands :[3] "But what news does he tell us ? *That the
supporting of Priests is a burden unknown before Christianity ?*"
And he proceeds to exclaim, in his incomparable manner,
over the ignorance which could assert such a thing.
Collins had of course made no such statement. His

[1] P. 85.   [2] P. 86.   [3] *Remarks,* Part ii, p. 14.

words, "upon any other occasion," mean "from any "other cause", as is made clear by the context:[1] "For "I suppose it will be allowed me that the revenues "belonging to the orders of *Priests*, *Monks*, and *Fryars*, "in *Popish Countries*, are a greater tax upon the subject, "and have introduc'd a greater degree of poverty than "has ever been felt from any lay-tyrants or conquerors". The very supposition that Collins could have meant to deny that pre-Christian priesthoods were burdensome is a piece of rascality, for part of his previous argument had consisted in showing that all priesthoods were burdensome; and Bentley, with characteristic candour, had actually contradicted him on that score, as we have seen.

Such are a few samples of the procedure which Mr. Pattison has pleasantly described as "braining an "authority at every blow". It is a mere alternation of arrogant error and insolent irrelevance. When by chance Bentley does score a point, it lies in detecting a misprint or a mistranslation that has no bearing on the essentials of Collins's argument, which consists in showing grounds for an attitude of critical scepticism towards the Christian creed, books, and ecclesiastical claims. One of the minor points that has been most magnified is the translation of *idiotis evangelistis*, in Collins's *Discourse*, by "idiot "evangelists", an oversight which was at once exclaimed against by every educated reader, and which it needed only the commonest scholarship to detect. Other critics took the translation rather as an unseemly levity than as a blunder. In all probability it was a mere printer's error, soon altered of the author's own accord,[2] for, in the

[1] *Discourse*, p. 114.
[2] Mr. Stephen makes some amends for endorsing without inquiry Bentley's judgment of "poor Collins", by taking the trouble (Notes to ch. iv., Work cited, i, 274) to clear Collins of a charge falsely and maliciously made against him by Bentley's biographer, Bishop Monk—of having *reprinted* the Discourse with corrections, so to make Bentley's criticisms seems untrue. The pious calumny was worsened in the congenial hands of De Quincey. Mr. Stephen points out that the Dutch reprint mentioned by Monk was at least the fourth edition, and that it *refers to Bentley's*

copy in the hands of the present writer, which is dated 1713, and so purports to be still of the first edition, it is already corrected by the simple substitution of the Latin words cited, *idiotis evangelistis*; while the printer's error of " Zozimus " for " Zosimus ", also exclaimed against by Bentley (and noted by Mr. Pattison with a pitying smile),[1] is uncorrected. This last oversight seems to be regarded by Mr. Pattison as justifying Bentley's assertion that the author of the *Discourse* discussed the Old Testament without Hebrew, and Zosimus and Plutarch without Greek, though Collins had actually cited his passage from Zosimus in the Greek, and though not one per cent of the clergy who weekly enounced the Scriptures from the pulpit in Bentley's day, as now, had the least pretension to be Hebrew scholars. It is one of the stock theorems of modern Christian scholarship that no one is entitled to reject the New Testament without a good knowledge of Greek, though all are entitled to believe it without knowing one Greek letter from another, and though all Christians are free to reject the Koran without having so much as seen a letter of Arabic.

Beyond discovering misprints, Bentley rarely does more than declaim furiously over a loose or free translation, such as the rendering of Horace's *terrores magicos* by " panic fears ", and Virgil's *metus omnes et inexorabile fatum* by " all kinds of fears, even of death itself ", the last a freedom of the most innocent kind, seeing that in the classics *fatum* is more often used in the sense of death than in any other, and that in all probability " death " is the implication the poet meant to convey, rather than " destiny and divination ", as Bentley insists. Bentley

---

work. But he has not noticed that the second edition, printed in London from the types of the first, corrects the *idiotis* passage, but not the " Zozimus", whereas if Collins were proceeding on Bentley's corrections he would have noted the latter misprint also.

[1] Though Bentley himself, to judge from this treatise, is as much given to bad spelling as to bad grammar, writing "plages" for "plagues", "shrew'd" for "shrewd", "two" for "too", and so on.

himself feels free to translate *strepitum Acherontis avari* by "the terrible noise and rumour of Acheron",[1] which is tolerably loose; and paraphrases *sive tu vatem, sive tu omen audieris* thus:[2] "If you hear a lunatic or fanatic in the "streets fortelling some mischiefs; if a word is spoken "accidentally in your hearing which may be interpreted "Ominous," explaining that "the *Vates*, or *Divini*, were "mad fellows, bawling in the Streets and Rodes; and "their Predictions might be contemn'd, but must necessarily be heard, if you came that way". That is, because Horace in a satire speaks[3] of stopping in his walk to listen to the *divini*, we are to decide that there were no *divini* or *vates* save those who declaimed in the streets, and that these were either "lunatics" or "fanatics".

On hardly any matter of general judgment is Bentley more nearly right than Collins, and on many he is much less so. He had, indeed, in virtue of his scholarly insight, dimly divined that Homer was no such masterpiece of knowledge as Collins, like most men of that time, had been taught to believe; though Bentley's own acceptance of the commonplace that Homer wrote the Iliad for men and the Odyssey for women[4] was just as much of a conventional fallacy. But, taken as a general answer to Collins's soundly philosophic plea for freedom of thought on all subjects, and to Collins's claim that all progress in thought has been made by setting aside authority in a greater or less degree—to these theses the reply furnished by the *Remarks* is simply a tissue of shallow scurrility. Bentley brazenly affirms that nobody was then opposing freedom of thought or speech, which was notoriously false. His whole reply is thus a paralogism, and Mr. Stephen's endorsement of it as against Collins is only one of his too frequent capitulations to the orthodox view of things. We have a decisive test on this head in Mr. Stephen's comment on the passage in which,

[1] *Remarks*, p. 44.
[2] P. 36.
[3] *Sat.* vi, 114.
[4] *Remarks*, Part i, p. 18.

in answer to Collins's remarks on the decline of superstition under the play of freethought, Bentley retorts that heterodoxy in religion had nothing to do with the matter. Let us cite Mr. Stephen's words:—

"'The Devil,' says Collins truly, 'is entirely banished "'the United Provinces, where freethinking is in the "'greatest perfection; whereas all round about that "'commonwealth, he appears in various shapes, some- "'times in his own, and sometimes in the shape of an "'old black gentleman, sometimes in that of a dead man, "'sometimes in that of a cat.'[1] To this Bentley replies, "with infinite scorn, that the honour of routing the "devil belonged, not to the sect of Freethinkers, but to "the Royal Society, the Boyles, and the Newtons. "*Nothing could be more true*, and apparently conclusive."[2]

That "nothing could be more true" is one of the too many propositions which breed in a reader a distrust of Mr. Stephen's authority. He has not paid proper heed to Bentley's words; and he has given and can give no proof for his sweeping endorsement of them. To begin with, Bentley, in the passage in hand, does not discuss simple belief in apparitions of the Devil. He is not dealing with Collins's words on that head, cited by Mr. Stephen; he passes over also the reference to Holland altogether; his remarks have no relevance to that; he attempts only to answer Collins's further proposition[3] that, from the time of the late revolution, "upon the "*Liberty* given and taken to *think freely*, the Devil's "power visibly declined, and *England* as well as the "*United Provinces* ceased to be any part of his Christian "territories. Let the *Priests* give such an instance of "their success against the Devil anywhere." It is to this that Bentley answers by attributing the decline of the belief in demoniac possession and witchcraft, first, by implication, partly to the good sense of the clergy; next,

[1] *Discourse*, p. 28.
[2] *History of English Thought in the Eighteenth Century*, 2nd ed., vol. i., p. 206.
[3] P. 30.

to the cultivation of "learning" since the Reformation; and thirdly, to "the Royal Society and College of Physicians: to the Boyles and Newtons, the Sydenhams and Ratcliffs".[1] There could be no more striking challenge to the common notion that Bentley is a clear and close reasoner. He does not give these answers as parts of a cumulative speculation: he knocks down each one with the others, or, at least, the first two with the last. And not one of the explanations, either singly or in combination with the others, is true. The pretence of Bentley, as Lipsiensis, that in England he observed "fewer of the clergy give in to particular stories "of that kind than of the Commonality or Gentry", deserves no credit. The statement, again, that "in the "dark times before the Reformation, not because they "were Popish, but because unlearned," there was a proneness to belief in diabolical powers, is disposed of in the very pages under notice in Collins, where it is pointed out that Bishop Jewel, a very learned man, affirmed a great increase of witchcraft in his own day; and that later, King James, also a learned man, affirmed the same thing still more emphatically. And if the assertion of Bentley had been true, it is negated by his own concluding statement above cited.

Now, the work of the Royal Society and of students like Sydenham no doubt tended indirectly to promote scepticism about witchcraft; but it is a complete blunder to give to that the whole credit. Even on that very point, the statement is no confutation of Collins, who never pretended (as Bentley makes him out to have done, and as Mr. Stephen strangely assumes he did), that the men who practised "freedom of thought" were all freethinkers in the sense of deists. He could have answered that the History of the Royal Society itself attributed the progress made in its studies to the "free way of reasoning" which its members had from the first employed; that the very

[1] *Remarks*, p. 33.

formation of the Royal Society was by way of a conscious reaction against all religious discussion; and that a number of its members had been freethinkers in religion. But even if all that were waived, it would still be untrue that it was the Newtons and Boyles, the Sydenhams and Ratcliffs, who had done all the work, as Mr. Stephen decides.

A glance at the culture history of the time will yield the proof. Hobbes expresses the most thorough-going contempt for popular superstitions in his *Leviathan*, published in 1651, when the Royal Society had only begun to exist in germ; and that treatise had already a wide popularity at a time when the Royal Society was still in the stage of sending out queries as to "whether "diamonds and other precious stones grow again after "three or four years, in the same places whither they "have been digged out?"[1] Further, there is a wholesale disparagement of popular superstitions of the kind under notice in Sir Thomas Browne's *Inquiries into Vulgar and Common Errors*, published in 1646, before there was even a germ of the Royal Society in existence; and that Browne was merely going with a strengthening stream of tendency is made pretty clear by the passage in the earlier written *Religio Medici* (circa 1633), in which he affirmed his own belief in witches, and wrote that "They "that doubt of these do not only deny them, but spirits, "and are obliquely, and upon consequence, a sort, not of "infidels, but of Atheists".[2] In fine, the true account of the matter is that given by Buckle,[3] of whom Mr. Stephen has made light, but of whom, here and elsewhere, he has something to learn. As Buckle puts it, the scientific movement was "partly cause, and partly effect, of the "increasing incredulity of the age".

As to the writers whom Bentley names, they can have

[1] Sprat's *History of the Royal Society*, 1667, p. 158.
[2] *Works*, Bohn edition, ii, 366.
[3] *Introduction to the History of Civilisation in England*, current edition, vol. i, pp. 363, 364.

contributed only very indirectly, if at all, to the discredit of the belief in witchcraft. It is true that Boyle was a thorough-going freethinker in science, and that he wrote *The Sceptical Chemist*; but on all matters of religious belief his mind remained hypnotised by faith. He expressly justifies credulity on the score of ignorance:[1] and, so far from calling in question the existence of a devil or the possibility of witchcraft, he expressly argued for the probable existence of grades of spirits,[2] and urged that revelation should be accepted in respect of statements not understood.[3] It is indeed sufficiently idle to pretend that men who stood blindly to the authority of the Scriptures, which abundantly affirm the reality of witchcraft and the occurrence of demoniacal possession, did more than Freethinkers to discredit these insanities. Boyle is one of the historic examples of a genius for physical science going with the most childish orthodoxy in religion, and a total incapacity for new views in moral science. It was part of his faith that " The howlings of " the damned as well sound forth His (God's) praises as " do the hallelujahs of the saints. . . . . Hell's darkness " doth as well contribute to God's glory as heaven's " eternal splendour; as shadows, judiciously placed, do " no less praise the painter than do the livelier and " brighter colours."[4] This. in the generation of Locke, who, equally bent with his friend on retaining Christian theism, caught at the principle of conditional immortality, rather than blacken his faith with Boyle's horrible dogma that God was glorified by the howls of hell. Boyle's case really suggests that religion is one of the forms of insanity that are apt to correlate with genius. In any case, his was a different thing from the orthodoxy of

---

[1] *Discourse of Things above Reason, and Advices in Judging of Things said to Transcend Reason*, 1681.
[2] *Discourse* cited, p. 84.
[3] *Ibid*, p. 93.
[4] *Some Motives and Incentives to the Love of God*, 5th ed., "much corrected," 1670, p. 87.

Bentley, who, in this very matter of the alleged decline of superstition, had after all to leave room for belief in witchcraft, as a biblical tenet expressly maintained by law,[1] even while pretending that Christian philosophy has done what Freethinkers claimed to be doing.

It only remains to point out, to those who regard Bentley as infallible in matters of classic lore, that his reputation on that head has been much magnified, and that there is a very solid *per contra*. It is now commonly supposed, by reason of Mr. Dyce's uncritical partisanship, and of Macaulay's loose rhetoric and the frequent endorsement of it by scholars, that in the famous *Phalaris* controversy all the right was on Bentley's side, and all the wrong on the other, though somehow his contemporaries mostly took another view. In point of fact, Bentley made many blunders; and young Charles Boyle, his foremost adversary, did not make the blunder, now usually attributed to him, of maintaining the genuineness of the "Epistles of Phalaris". He had never maintained that, having on the contrary given some good reasons for doubting it; and he did but assail a number of Bentley's worst arguments when Bentley fell upon his as if he had really maintained it. Professor Jebb is almost the only modern writer who has correctly stated the case; and while Professor Jebb, in the opinion of some of us, gives an unduly favourable account of Bentley's management of the controversy, he points out not a few of Bentley's blunders, and one or two of his dishonesties. As thus:—

" Bentley's retort (as to 'common' words being prosaic)
" is a mere quibble, turning on the ambiguity of 'common'
" as meaning either 'vulgar' or 'simple'—*but illustrates*
" *his readiness*. Once, *as if in contempt for his adversary's*
" *understanding*, he has indulged in a notable sophism.
" Boyle had argued that the *name* tragedy cannot have
" existed before the *thing*. Bentley rejoins:—' 'Tis a pro-
" ' position *false in itself that things themselves must be, before*

[1] *Remarks*, Part i, p. 33.

"'*the names by which they are called.* For we have many
"' new tunes in music made every day, which never existed
"' before; yet several of them are called by *names* that
"' were formerly in use. . . And I humbly conceive
"' that Mr. Hobbes's book, which he called the *Leviathan*,
"' is not quite as ancient as its name is in Hebrew.' But
" the name of which Boyle spoke was descriptive, not
" merely appellative. Bentley's reasoning would have
" been relevant only if Boyle had argued that, since a
" tragedy is called the *Agamemnon*, tragedy must have
" existed before Agamemnon lived."[1]

The unspeakable sophism here exposed is not the only thing of the kind in Bentley's *Dissertation*, and it may help some readers to understand his method of answering Collins. For the rest, Professor Jebb points out:—

" That an emendation which he (Bentley) proposed in
" Isæus rested on a confusion between two different classes
" of choruses; that he had certainly misconstrued a passage
" in the life of Pythagoras by Iamblichus; that the *Minos*,
" on which he relies as Plato's work, was spurious; that,
" in one of the Letters of Phalaris, he had defended a false
" reading by false grammar. . . Bentley was demon-
" strably wrong in asserting that no writings bearing the
" name of Æsop were extant in the time of Aristophanes.
" In one place Bentley accuses Boyle of having adopted
" a wrong reading in one of the Letters, and thereby made
" nonsense of the passage. Now, Boyle's reading, though
" not the best, happens to be capable of yielding the very
" sense which Bentley required."[2]

Professor Jebb writes as if Boyle and his colleagues had overlooked all Bentley's blunders, but in reality they pointed out a number, and repelled a good many of his attacks, as for instance, that in which he derided Boyle for making the Phalaris of the Letters to be born at " Astypalæa, a town in Crete,"—a localisation justified by the text, and now admitted to be so by Professor Jebb.

[1] *Bentley*, pp. 69, 70.   [2] *Ibid.*, pp. 75, 76.

If Bentley could fall into so many blunders in a case in which he had special reason for caution—for many of those cited are made in his second and expanded Dissertation—it becomes intelligible enough that when grown older in arrogance he could handle such a book as that of Collins with a recklessness heightened in the degree of his rage against the new heresy. Against its doctrine he must have felt himself powerless, his one resource against the Deists having been to make out that they were Atheists, and to revile them accordingly. His cue, therefore, was to make a tremendous display of contempt for deistic scholarship, and he proceeded as we have seen.

We can imagine how Bentley would have comported himself over his own errors had he been able to detect them in the *Discourse of Freethinking*, and how learnedly Mr. Pattison and Mr. Stephen would have nodded approval, and smiled at the pitiable ignorance of "poor "Collins", themselves blind all the while to blunders of Bentley's in the case of some of which, as Mr. Stephen would say, "it is impossible to avoid the allusion to the fourth-form schoolboy"—or, at least, to Macaulay's.

CHAPTER VIII.

BUTLER AND AFTER BUTLER.

Whatever may have been the influence of the polemic of Bentley, there would seem, according to most accounts, to be no question that a real influence was exercised by that of Bishop Butler. Writing of him, Sir James Stephen speaks of English Deism as having been "so decisively "defeated in controversy that it had to be reimported "from the continent before it could take any fresh hold "on the English mind."[1] And yet it is impossible to trace any such impression in our polemical literature for a long time after Butler's death. One of the earliest expressions of such an opinion, so far as the present writer has noticed, is in a weekly sheet in the old manner of the *Spectator*, dated as late as 1792, in which an apologist speaks of the "mighty performance of Bishop Butler".[2] Mr. Gladstone writes that "until the present century, "and indeed until more than half of it had passed "away, Butler, as represented by his most conspicuous "production, had no censors; that is to say, none of "any note".[3] That is true; but it would be equally true if for "censors" we said either "eulogists" or "critics". In the last century Butler seems hardly to have been publicly discussed at all. Dr. Kippis in his memoir (1804) states that the Charge to the Clergy of the Durham Diocese was the only one of Butler's publications "which ever produced him a direct literary "antagonist". A later biographer has found one contemporary pamphlet, by one Bott, in which the *Analogy*

---

[1] *Horæ Sabbaticæ*, 2nd series, p. 281.
[2] *The Looker-On : a Periodical Paper*, Nov. 10, 1792, p. 17.
[3] *Studies Subsidiary to the Works of Bishop Butler*, ch. iii, begin.

was attacked. Mr. Stephen mentions that he has seen an anonymous pamphlet, dated 1737, criticising the sixth chapter; but this, on examination, turns out to be that ascribed to Bott. Dr. Halifax[1] further traces a criticism of a passage of Butler in Dr. Arthur Ashley Sykes's *Scripture Doctrine of Redemption*. Nothing further has been adduced. All this, of course, is no proof that the *Analogy* was not attentively read on its appearance (1736). A review published shortly afterwards cites a private critique by one who declared that "Never were "there so many *Cures for Deism* as at present; and yet "never did that disease rage wider or more furiously. "Scarce a weak Mind can stand its Shock, and thousands "of such continually fall before it"; but asserts that Butler's treatise "has in a few Days made its Way "throughout the Kingdom; some hundreds of them being "already vended. Which to me, notwithstanding what "has been above hinted, is a happy Indication, that "Unbelief is not so prevalent and universal as some are "apt to fear, and others to wish for."[2] This moderate claim cannot well be disputed, seeing that the book reached a second edition within the year. Still, there is nothing to show that Butler's work made any such impression on its issue as it has made since. The review just mentioned, after favourably analysing the *Analogy* through three monthly numbers, winds up with this temperate panegyric:[3]—"If the Reverend Author had made his "Periods somewhat shorter, his Paragraphs more numer-"ous, and distinguished the Bounds and Connections of "the several Parts of his Arguments more obviously, in "Condescension to the Capacities of ordinary Readers, "and in respect of Method and Diction, had made it as "intelligible to those, as it deserves to be understood, it "would have merited the Preference above, and been "more generally useful than, almost any Discourse in our

[1] Ed. of Butler's Works, 1824, p. 54.
[2] *Present State of the Republick of Letters*, July, 1736, pp. 24, 26, vol. xviii.
[3] Vol. cited, p 281.

"Language, upon this Subject; as it is, one cannot easily exceed in Commendation." Certainly the reviewer has come short of excess.

The common notion, then, that Butler's treatise in a manner closed the deistic controversy, by confuting the Deists on their own ground, is a delusion, arising partly, perhaps, from Mill's remark that "the argument "of Butler's *Analogy* is from its own point of view "conclusive: the Christian religion is open to no "objections, either moral or intellectual, which do not "apply at least equally to Deism; the morality of the "Gospels is far higher and better than that which shows "itself in the order of Nature. . . ."[1] This estimate, to begin with, is inaccurate so far as it goes; and it does not take into account the whole of the case. It is clearly not true that Deism is open to the same *intellectual* objections as Christianity, for one of the main Christian perplexities is the multitude of explicit narrative and other contradictions in the sacred books, to which there is nothing analogous in extra-human Nature. Nor is it true, further, that the moral objections to Christianity apply equally to Deism; for the Deist did not profess to find his moral principles in the "order of Nature" but in his own mind; and in terms of his intuitions, which he held to be divinely implanted, he condemned the Christian morals. But even if Butler's argument had been as logically valid as Mill makes out, it would not follow that it sufficed to non-plus the Deists. These had been for a generation exposing the insoluble difficulties of Christianity; and if Butler did show them difficulties in their own creed which they had not before recognised, they might all the same continue the campaign just as the Christians had done. And it is a significant fact in culture-history that there is no sign of Butler having in any way impressed the intelligence of the notable Deists of the latter part of the century, French or English, some

[1] *Three Essays on Religion*, p. 214.

of them men of higher reasoning power than the Deists to whom Butler's book was a reply. There is no reference to him in Hume, in Adam Smith, or in the Autobiography of Gibbon; and the present writer does not recall any in Voltaire. We must conclude that the later Deists did not feel that he had shaken their position; and as a matter of fact the *Analogy* is in more ways than one wanting in the conclusiveness with which Mill credited it.

It is needless here to go to any length in an analysis of Butler's familiar argument, which is admittedly a colligation or fusion of a number of the best pleas that had been used on the orthodox side in the Deistic controversy. Its two main limbs are the argument from general probability, which is substituted for the frequent pretence on the Christian side to "demonstrate" the truth of its doctrine, and the older argument used by Origen, from the analogy between the perplexities of the Bible, considered as a divine revelation, and those of Nature, considered as under divine government. We have seen that Berkeley had already employed the latter argument independently against the deistic mathematicians; and in the same year (1734) an anonymous Scotch pamphleteer had with similar ingenuity argued that the erroneous accounts of the laws of Nature in the Bible were exactly analogous to the errors of perception set up by the bodily senses.[1] What Butler did was to make the theorem at once more practical and more plausible. Beyond comparison, the *Analogy* is the most prudent and weighty performance on the clerical side in the whole dispute, up to its appearance; and it has thus sufficiently deserved its long celebrity. Yet it must have been felt by critical readers in its own day, as now, singularly ill-fitted to set up conviction in any man who had learned on the ordinary lines to doubt the supernaturalness of the Christian books

---

[1] *The Philosophy of Divine Revelation no argument of imposture.* Edinburgh, 1734. Reviewed in the *Republick of Letters*, vol. xv., 1735. Farrar mentions also a treatise of 1733, by Dr. Peter Browne, on *Things Divine and Natural conceived of by Analogy.*

and the truth of their doctrine. The recent defence of the *Analogy* by Mr. Gladstone leaves absolutely uncured the central flaw of the treatise, to wit, its failure to show any valid reason for rejecting, say, the Koran while accepting the Bible, or for the converse. If the moral barbarism of great parts of the Old Testament could be defended only by the plea that we must not presume to criticise God's procedure, the Old Testament is so far on all fours with the Koran, which can be and is defended in exactly that fashion. Butler here stultifies his case, since by his own statement the conformity of the Old Testament to the normal sense of probability is the thing to be proved: and the veto he lays on human criticism the moment the defence becomes difficult is the destruction of his own pretence of rational justification. The process of showing that the history of the Koran and of Islam does not satisfy certain conditions which are satisfied by the history of the Gospel and of early Christianity[1] is wholly beside the case, for these conditions are in no way bound up with the *a priori* conception of a revelation; and the argument might be just as easily turned the other way, making out the circumstances of the rise of Islam to be those most agreeable to the notion of divine intervention, and those of the rise of Christianity to be accordingly repugnant to it. It might be forcibly argued that a religion which could succeed without miracles was *ipso facto* more likely to be divine than one which made its way by a claim to miracles, the genuineness of which would inevitably be denied.

Even if Deists did not raise these arguments, however, they would feel that Butler's reasoning was rather an appeal for a truce on public grounds than a vindication of his creed. We cannot tell how far it led any readers of that generation to the Atheism which is the logical way out of the position. There is no overt trace of such a

[1] *Analogy*, Part ii, ch. 7.

movement till the posthumous publication of Hume's *Dialogues on Natural Religion* (1779); and there is no reference there to Butler. Some influence in the way of making Deists less Deistic the *Analogy* must have had, but apparently not in its own generation. Mr. Gladstone is indignant[1] that Mr. Stephen should interpret Mill's account[2] of its effect on his father to have meant that it led him to Atheism. We have, however, the further evidence of Mackintosh that "Atheists might make use" of Butler's answer to the Deists, "and have done so".[3] But this testimony also carries us to the end of the last and the beginning of this century: as regards Butler's own period there is none. And the conclusion forced upon us is this: that so long as there lasted the disinterested concern for truth which inspired the first Deists, the critical movement went on unaffected by Butler's negative reasoning. The Deists, indeed, were at a level of conviction at which they could hardly appreciate the difficulties of their own case. All alike, Christian and non-Christian, had been so long wont to take their Theism as a matter of course that the suggestion of difficulties by an avowed Theist was apt to have the air of sophistry. "Common men," said Butler, "are capable of being convinced upon real evidence, that "there is a God who governs the world; and they feel "themselves to be of a moral nature, and accountable "creatures."[4] "Quite so," the Deist would reply; "and on that side there is nothing to dispute about. But it is the want of real evidence for your written system, and its repugnance to our moral nature, that makes us reject it." Butler's argument at best claimed only a decided "probability" on the Christian side, inasmuch as, despite obvious objections and difficulties, "the proof "is not lost in these difficulties, or destroyed by these "objections". Such language is far removed even from

---

[1] *Studies Subsidiary*, p. 55.
[2] *Autobiography*, p. 38.
[3] *Life of Mackintosh*, 2nd ed., 1836, vol. ii, p. 454.
[4] *Analogy*, Part ii, ch. 6.

the compromising tactic of Sykes, and much more from the indignant certitude of the earlier apologists, who would never admit that "difficulties" existed save in so far as they were invented by ill-meaning men; and the Deists had presented to them by Butler himself[1] a form of rejoinder which to most of them would seem as forcible as the rebuttal. They would argue, he suggested, "that "it is a poor thing to solve difficulties in revelation by " saying that there are the same in natural religion; when " what is wanting is to clear both of them of these their " common, as well as other their respective difficulties; " but that is a strange way indeed of convincing men of " the obligations of religion, to show them that they have " as little reason for their worldly pursuits; and a strange " way of vindicating the justice and goodness of the Author " of Nature, and of removing the objectious against both, " to which the system of religion lies open, to show that " the like objections lie against natural providence; a way " of answering objections against religion without so much " as pretending to make out that the system of it, or the " particular things in it objected against, are reasonable." And, despite Butler's profession of repelling such an answer, we may fairly say that his case in truth was a "poor thing" as compared with the historic claim to supernatural certitude, and indeed with the very substance of the claim. As the later Irrationalists scornfully put it, the method of Butler made out that "there are three " chances to one for revelation, and only two against it."[2] And as there must still have been hot pietists of the old sort, to whom Butler's qualified way of pleading would be distasteful,[3] we may surmise that their dissatisfaction would have some effect in keeping his treatise in the background rather than in the foreground during his generation.

[1] Part ii, ch. 8, *beginning*.
[2] *Tracts for the Times*, No. 86, cited by Pattison.
[3] Byrom's *Journal*, March, 1737 (cited by Pattison) mentions that some readers thought Butler "a little too little vigorous," and " wished he would have spoke more earnestly."

What it really signifies for us, in fine, is just the widespread feeling among intelligent people that the Christian system had been seriously shaken. The admissions made by Butler would in a previous age have brought on him a charge of heresy from the orthodox; and we can see that they were forced from him by the discussion all around, in society as well as in books. He is most candid towards the close of his work: the most uncandid, portion, it has been pointed out, is the first chapter, which is aloof from the main scheme, and which we may surmise to have been written earlier in life than the rest. Its singular argument that a future life is much more likely than not, and that there is nothing in Nature " to " afford us even the slightest presumption that animals " ever lose their living powers ", looks like a youthfully hasty retort to a saying of Saint Evremont, whose writings where much in vogue in England in Butler's younger days:—" I have an opinion that you will not " approve of. I believe it notwithstanding to be true " enough. It is, That no Person has ever well appre- " hended, by the sole Lights of Humane Reason, whether " the Soul be Immortal, or subject to Corruption. It is " our Interest to believe its Immortality, but it is not " easie to conceive it."[1] There can be little doubt that St. Evremont's opinion would seem to most thinking men much the more reasonable; and if Butler had reasoned throughout in that vein, he would have impressed few.

But the moderate method of his subsequent pleadings was exactly what would best appeal to a later age, when once more, after a long period of torpor in the universities, the old problem was energetically forced forward, and a new generation took it up. And this is what historically happened. To begin with, the answers to the Deists, singly and collectively, entirely failed to

---

[1] Essay, *Man that desires to know all things is ignorant of himself*, in *Miscellaneous Essays by Monsieur St. Evremont, translated out of French.* (? By Dryden), London, 1692, p. 281.

discredit them. Ten years after Bentley's attack on the *Discourse of Freethinking*, Collins produced his *Discourse of the Grounds and Reasons of the Christian Religion* (1723), which elicited thirty-five separate replies;[1] and which he followed up by a still more effective work, *The Scheme of Literal Prophecy Considered* (1727). Then came Tindal, who is said to have been answered in more than a hundred treatises, on which Butler drew largely for his *Analogy*. Still the tide flowed. The deistic movement not only went on after the *Analogy* and the *Minute Philosopher*, but went on with signs of fresh earnestness. The later writers, as Chubb and Morgan, while less learned than the earlier, as Toland and Collins, show more moral warmth, and seem to have made quite as many converts. The random and indeed ribald attack on miracles by Woolston (1727) is followed up by the finished and masterly argument of Hume (1749); while the clear effect of Middleton's *Free Inquiry* on the same subject is to lead up towards the discredit of all miracle stories on historico-critical grounds. And while the criticism was thus active and progressive, the Church, with all its systematic defence, showed many symptoms of decline in its hold of the people. The motive for Butler's famous Charge to his clergy on " External Religion " (1751) was that he had " observed with deep concern the great " and growing neglect of serious piety in the kingdom " ; and his Charge, taken as a supplement to his *Analogy*, amounts to something like a confession of the failure of faith. The crowning stroke was that it was sharply attacked as tending, by its insistence on mere externals and ceremonial, to promote Romanism. Finally, the encomiastic verses written by way of epitaph at his death (1752) credit him with piety, benevolence, and eloquence, but say nothing of him as a defender of the faith. The first trace I have noted of his later high reputation is in a

---

[1] The list is given in the preface to Collins's *Scheme of Literal Prophecy Considered*.

hostile anonymous pamphlet, *Thoughts on Miracles*, by a Deist, dated 1767, in which the *Analogy* is spoken of as " this much admired performance of Bishop Butler's ".

Notably enough, the decline in the deistic propaganda coincides with the period of deepest intellectual torpor in orthodoxy, as represented by the universities. And here it may be surmised that the flagging of the attack was in part due to a common feeling among educated readers that the main part of the Deists' case was proved, and that the orthodox side was in large measure insincere. Professor Cairns tells us that the Deistic movement " failed " intellectually through exhaustion ", this in face of the fact that the two most influential thinkers of the latter part of the century, Hume and Smith, and the greatest historian, Gibbon, were Deists (unless Hume were at heart an Atheist); and that there is no orthodox name of anything like equal weight to set against them. Johnson and Burke, the one devoid of philosophical bias and the other philosophical only in seeming, are typical of the state of religion. Dr. Cairns seems to have supposed that because after the publication of Bolingbroke's *Philosophical Works* (1754) there was a lack of fresh deistic literature, there was by consequence a lack of the opinion. The truth was that the matter had been thrashed out so far as that generation could grasp it; and the library of the deistic writers was in all readers' hands. Whatever of exhaustion there was, entered equally into the whole speculative thought of the time, into its science[1] and into its orthodoxy. In that sense there was indeed an arrest of progressive thought for a generation. " The mode of free-" thinking," writes the orthdox Gray in 1750, " has given " place to the mode of not thinking at all."[2] Walpole's policy of political stability had ended in developing a war of political parties behind which the Hanoverian dynasty stood unchallenged; and " barbarous and absurd " faction ", as Hume described it, became the main mental

---

[1] See above, p. 104.
[2] Letter xxxi, in Mason's Memoir.

interest. Gibbon and Smith have shown us the state of things in the universities, where a student could do anything he pleased, except be known to read any sceptical philosophy.

It may be well to sum up the forces or conditions of inertia. As before noted, the energy of the nation had begun to drain off in non-intellectual directions—in new industry, in conquest, in war, in extending commerce. The active forces of Deism had been drawn from two quarters, the scholarly class and the educated upper class. But (1) the educated upper class was more and more solicited to the pursuits of politics, travel, fashionable society, and, above all, war. The period of maximum activity in the deistic controversy was between 1713, the date of the Peace of Utrecht, and 1743, the date of the new embroilment of England with France. The first date is that of Collins's *Discourse of Freethinking;* and the last notable treatise in the controversy, save those of Bolingbroke, posthumously published, and the later writings of Hume, is Dodwell's *Christianity not Founded on Argument* (1743), which is a vigorous application, on dubiously orthodox lines, of the thesis thrown out later as a sarcasm by Hume, that faith has nothing to do with argument. From 1743 to 1748 there is war with France, with the rebellion of 1745 added ; and war is resumed in 1756, going on simultaneously in India, North America, the Continent, and the high seas, and employing at least 100,000 men ; this being the period of Pitt's most energetic action, in which the nation put out more military strength and enterprise than at any previous period; which is equivalent to saying that its available intellectual energy was greatly reduced. And when the Peace of Paris was signed in 1763, the "barbarous "and absurd faction" entered on its wildest period, that of Bute and Wilkes, the period of rapidly changing ministries, of the Letters of Junius, and of the long quarrel with the Colonies, ending in the War of Independence, which runs simultaneously with manifold fresh war in Europe, lasting till 1783.

(2.) This, too, is the period of rapidly extending industry, invention, commerce, and agriculture. Seven hundred enclosure Acts were passed between 1760 and 1774.[1] James Watt patented his steam engine in 1769; Hargreaves the spinning-jenny in 1770; Arkwright the water-frame in 1771; Crompton the mule in 1779; and Cartwright the power-loom in 1785. Between 1760 and 1784 the manufacture of iron was revolutionised, and the output quadrupled; and the population, which before 1751 had never increased more than 3 per cent in ten years, increased 6 per cent in each of the next three decades, and 9 per cent between 1781 and 1791. The great mass of this new industrial life was either illiterate or little cultured; and the rest was necessarily much occupied with its own lore. Smith's *Wealth of Nations* (1776) is the sign and expression of manifold previous economic discussion. The lack of "interest in ideas" which from that time forward is chargeable to English life, means that the ideas which engrossed English attention were of a strictly practical kind, the more intellectual interests of the past having been thus superseded.

(3.) All the while, there steadily operated the force of ostracism as against the scholarly class. In 1713, Collins found it prudent to take flight to Holland; and, though the menace of arrest was not in his case repeated, there was plenty of terrorism in other cases and other kinds. In 1720 Woolston was fined £100, sentenced to a year's imprisonment, and ordered to find £2,000 security for his good behaviour afterwards. Not being able to pay the fine, he remained in prison till his death, in 1733. In 1756 Jacob Ilive, for denying in a pamphlet the truth of revealed religion, was sentenced to be put in the pillory thrice, and to be kept at hard labour for three years. In 1763 Peter Annet, then seventy years of age, and visibly of unsound mind, was sentenced to be pilloried twice, and to undergo a year's hard labor, for ridiculing the Penta-

---

[1] Gibbins, *Industrial History of England*, p. 153.

teuch. Apart from these cases of special vengeance there was in constant operation the lesser machinery of persecution and slander. Bishop Hare,[1] writing in 1716, in a treatise which has still[2] a wide application, gives a vivid notion of the stifling pressure brought to bear upon all independent thought among the clergy. Writing as "a Presbyter of the Church of England" on *The Difficulties and Discouragements which attend the Study of the Scriptures in the way of Private Judgment: Represented in a Letter to a Young Clergyman*, he grimly advises the student to leave the study of the Scriptures alone, because its proper prosecution involves long labour, and in the end he will not be free to publish any results worth mentioning without being presented as a heretic. "A profound and "laborious study of the Scriptures will not make you at all "more orthodox;"[3] it will only hurt the public by disturbing the peace of the Church, and further himself, by getting him ostracised. There were at that moment two excellent clergymen of umblemished character, Whiston and Dr. Clarke, both champions of the faith against the Freethinkers; but on the score of technical heresy on the point of the Trinity they were alike habitually defamed by churchmen. "Whatever therefore you do, be orthodox: "Orthodoxy will cover a multitude of sins; but a cloud of "virtues cannot cover the want of the minutest particle of "orthodoxy.[4] You and your children will not be burnt

---

[1] There is a mystery, noticed by Mr. Stephen, in regard to Bishop Hare's authorship. He is said to be the author of *The Clergyman's Thanks to Philelentherus for his Remarks on a late Discourse of Freethinking: In a letter to Dr. Bentley* (1713), which is an extravagant and uncritical eulogy of Bentley's attack on Collins. Yet the treatise cited above, published in 1716, also anonymously, is one of the most damaging criticisms ever passed on Church orthodoxy from within, and was censured by Convocation. It certainly seems impossible that the same man should have written the two treatises.

[2] M. Renan used almost identical language of the state of things even in France a generation ago.

[3] Reprint in vol. iv. of *The Pillars of Priestcraft and Orthodoxy Shaken*, 1768, p. 17.

[4] P. 35.

"indeed; but you may be as effectually ruined as if you
"were. You may be excommunicated, and in virtue of
"that be thrown into jail, to rot there, while your family
"are starving." And the result of this habitual odium on
all free-thinking, in the Presbyter's opinion, is that the
more intelligent of the clergy are in the habit of keeping
their serious opinions to themselves, and pursuing other
studies. "For name me any one of the men most famed
"for learning in this or the last age who have seriously
"turned themselves to the study of the Scriptures. . .
"Who are the men that have excelled most (excepting
"always Sir Isaac Newton) in philosophy, astronomy,
"and mathematicks? Have they not been clergymen?
"And was not their skill in these sciences the effect of
"their great and constant application to them? . . .
"To be plain, the one thing that turned them [from
"Scriptural study] was the want of *liberty*, which *in this
"study only* is denied men. They found it was dangerous
"to examine impartially and speak freely; that they must
"write without liberty, or with no safety; that it would
"be expected of them to strain all their wit and learning
"to patronize and palliate gross errors, instead of exposing
"or mending of them. . . . The consequence of which,
"besides the improvements made in arts and sciences, has
"been that many of them have separately made more good
"emendations, and happily explained more difficulties, in
"the smallest Pagan writer than they have done, take
"them all together, in two hundred years upon the whole
"body of the Scriptures. . . . Follow such ex-
"amples. . . . Spend ten or twelve years upon
"Horace or Terence. To illustrate a billet-doux or a
"drunken catch; to explain an obscene jest; to make a
"happy emendation on a passage that a modest man
"would blush at, will do you more credit, and be of
"greater service to you, than the most useful employment
"of your time upon the Scriptures."[1]

Convocation solemnly censured this pamphlet for

[1] Pp. 47, 50.

treating "of things sacred in a ludicrous and prophane "manner", and otherwise offending; but its general truth is not to be disputed. And the situation being broadly as here described, the Church held in its very organisation a certain security for the ultimate slackening of the supply of critical Freethought literature. In the universities the only efficient machinery was that for repressing thought. When "the unhappy Middleton", as the happy Mr. Pattison calls him, published anonymously a letter to Waterland criticising the more absurd parts of that theologian's *Vindication of Scripture* (a reply to Tindal), he was threatened with a deprivation of all his preferments at Cambridge, and had to publish a disclaimer: and after all he was nearly deprived of his Librarianship.[1] With heresy thus promptly repressed in the schools and in the Church, and with the ten thousand hired priests regularly at work, whatever might happen to religious conviction, there was a fair probability that the production of heretical literature would gradually slacken even if the free laity were not increasingly drawn away to other pursuits. Dr. Cairns narrates that "The Church "of England, though sadly feeble and worldly, ... "rose above her disputes, Arian and Bangorian, and "presented a united front to the enemy, from Leslie on "the extreme right, himself a Nonjuror, to Middleton on "the extreme left, almost excommunicated as a Free-"thinker".[2] When Christians can take comfort in such frontal developments as these there is no more to be said. Leslie was one of the most childish, as he was one of the first, of the anti-Deists. Middleton was actually a Freethinker, who held that it would be "criminal and "immoral" to overthrow Christianity even if it were known to be an imposture, because some "traditional "religion or other" was a necessity to the multitude.[3]

[1] *The Comedian* or *Philosophical Enquirer*, May, 1732, p. 32.
[2] *Unbelief in the Eighteenth Century*, p. 116.
[3] See Middleton's positions fully set forth by Mr. Stephen, *English Thought*, vol. i, pp. 253-272.

Such were some of the conformists behind the "united front"; such some of the realities behind the mask of English Christianity in the latter half of last century. If it could not stand by faith, it could stand by finance.

Yet withal, so far as there remained an educated and leisured public caring for serious thought, it is plain that deistic opinions never died out between the time of Hobbes and the outbreak of the French Revolution, when for a time all rationalism was put to silence. The polished anti-clerical satire of Shaftesbury (a kind of previous incarnation of Matthew Arnold, alike as to amenity, finish, and measure of departure from orthodoxy), kept its vogue with the other good writing belonging to the age of Anne; and the social tone under George III was far from conforming to the King's views. Burke's "Who now reads Bolingbroke?" might have been met by the challenge, "Who now reads anything rationally serious on religious matters?" As a matter of fact, the philosophy of Bolingbroke was everywhere familiar in the classic verse of his pupil, Pope, the professed foe of Freethinkers; and even the prose of Bolingbroke was a good deal more read in upper class society about 1780 than Butler's. The Life of Hannah More shows that society as far from being religious as Burke was from being metaphysical; and of a cousin "fond of Bolingbroke "and Hume" she writes: "He is much too fashionable in his principles, though I believe very correct in his conduct". Of Maclaine's reply to Soame Jenyns she writes that "the Deists will triumph" over it, "and exclaim, 'see "'how these Christians disagree'"."[1] Were there no other evidence, the reception given to Voltaire, in England as elsewhere, sufficiently showed that the temper of educated society was rationalistic, and that it only needed a fresh and attractive seizure of the old subject to secure a wide and interested audience. And the vogue of

---

[1] Letter of April, 1777: *Life*, abridged ed., p. 36.

Priestley's Unitarianism testified no less to the permanence of much of the deistic work.

One important difference, however, can be already noted before the great political convulsion. In the period of religious indifference among the educated class there had grown up, as we have seen, a new England of manufacturers, artizans, and miners; and in that new world, in which the middle strata tended to grow out of the lower, there was a new field for that "enthusiasm" which the whole first half of the century, from Locke to Bolingbroke, held in such cold contempt. The Wesleyan movement worked largely in virgin soil, that of a population which in a century had nearly doubled, chiefly in the proletariat, without anything approaching to a proportional provision for education of any kind. Here was the opportunity of religion. On the new area of toiling ignorance was reared a new popular fanaticism, carefully alienated by its leaders from politics; and the new hard-working middle class, relatively little more deeply instructed, found its religio-literary ministration from congenial writers, from Johnson and Cowper, religious through hypochondria; from Hannah More, like them a constant sufferer; and from sententious poets like Young and rhapsodists like Hervey. For such a generation, the old Deists were really too hard reading: it read the old miscellanies, the *Spectator*, the *Tatler*, the *Guardian*, as it read the later *Rambler* and the *Mirror*, and as it read the Augustan poetry in general. Voltaire and Hume, and probably Gibbon and Montesquieu, were left to the intellectual minority. And whether or not these new influences were capable of forcing themselves down to the general public in time, the process was abruptly stopped for a whole generation by the event which really divides the last century from this—the French Revolution.

CHAPTER IX.

THE MORAL AND INTELLECTUAL OUTCOME.

IT may be worth while, by way of completing our notion of the deistic movement, to consider its relation to the general moral and intellectual life. Such opponents as Berkeley habitually spoke of it as a phase or correlative of moral corruption; and a good deal of the language even of Butler tends to support the impression set up with such vivacious malice by Berkeley's dialogues. And no doubt freethinking went to some extent hand-in-hand with libertinism in the fashionable life of the period, putting grave men like Butler in fear of a general growth of license. But it is clear enough to a dispassionate eye that the libertinism was not a whit the worse or the more general for the freethinking. We have seen the moral practice of the German Protestantism around Luther; and we get some idea of upper-class life in sixteenth-century England from the evidence led in the trials of Anne Boleyn and Catherine Howard, to say nothing of the normal charges against the monks and nuns. It may have been that some libertines of the hardier sort were pleased to feel that the moralities urged against them had no sacrosanct foundation; but such a sentiment rather made against hypocrisy than for vice; and they certainly had plenty of comradeship from professed believers. The day of George I and George II did not owe its vices to the works of the Deists.

Nothing can be clearer, to begin with, than the fact that the "dissolution of morals" was avowed before Deism was anything more than the half-avowed opinion of a small minority. The "Societies for Reformation "of Manners" which were formed in the closing years of the seventeenth century, and which propose with customary Christian wisdom to effect their purpose by repressive laws, complain bitterly of an almost universal habit of blasphemous swearing among the lower orders, and of endless drunkenness and open debauchery in all orders. These disorders clearly can have had nothing to do with the study of deistic literature, which had barely begun to exist, and which, in any case, could not be read by the majority of those concerned. To couple street-swearing with rationalistic writing as alike forms of "irreligion", is a procedure not calling for serious discussion. The reformers claimed, besides, that in a few years' time, by causing many thousands of swearers and thousands more of lewd persons to be imprisoned, fined, or whipped, and by rooting out hundreds of disorderly houses, they greatly purified the morals of London.[1] If that be true, the Deism of the first half of the eighteenth century flourished in a partly reformed society; and if the street-walkers made head again, it can hardly have been through the study of Toland and Collins.

Where there was most obvious need for reformation, apart from the vice and misery of the lower classes, was in the old matter of ill-will and incivism among fellow-citizens. The main historical impeachment of Christianity is that, though put forward at all times as an influence for mutual good-will, it has in all ages greatly multiplied the permanent grounds of hate. The tendency was never clearer than at the end of the seventeenth century, when for a hundred and fifty years Europe had been torn by a series of wars of creed, of which the special English share was two civil wars and two revolutions. That religion was doing anything to cure what religion had wrought, there is no evidence whatever[2]; rather the enmity between Church and Dissent was taking on the colour and temper of the older enmity

[1] *Account of the Societies for the Reformation of Manners*, 5th ed., 1701, p. 18.
[2] The subject will be found fully treated by Dr. Hunt, *Religious Thought in England*, vol. ii, ch. 7.

between Protestant and Romanist. "I think there is no "nation under heaven," wrote the translator of Locke's first Letter on Toleration in 1689, "in which so much "has already been said upon toleration as ours; but yet "certainly there is no people that stand in more need "of having something farther both said and done "amongst them in this point than we do." What was done was the practicable minimum of what was desired; and in the next reign the ill-will between Church and Dissent was more rancorous than ever. In this atmosphere of rabid religious malice the Deists played a purely civilising part. No controversial writer of that or any other time surpasses Collins in imperturbable amenity; and even the intermittently ribald Woolston is a good-natured polemist compared with most of the orthodox combatants. In the preface to his *Scheme of Literal Prophecy Considered* (1727), Collins, referring to the multitude of replies to his *Discourse of the Grounds and Reasons of the Christian Religion*, mentions with satisfaction that "several of them are written with a temper, moderation, "and politeness unusual in Theological Controversies, "and becoming good, pious, and learned men," but confesses that most of them are "written in the common "abusive strain, and that two or three of these hardly "admit of any parallel". The savage *rictus* of Bentley, the shouting passion of Leslie, the feverish malice of Berkeley, are the prevailing types of temper on the side of the religion of love: the more likeable men on that side, as Sykes and Clarke and Whiston, are with hardly an exception themselves charged with heresy.

In so far as the orthodox tone in the controversy gradually rose, (through Butler and Leland to Paley, it is clear that the Deists deserve the credit. Their movement it was that put English theological controversy in the way of becoming, at least occasionally a matter of decent and worthy comparison of views; even as it was owing to them that theological thought passed from evangelical delirium, and frantic wrangles over insane shibboleths, to the beginnings of critical and ethical investigation. The manner and matter of most of the orthodox defence against the Deists show how fatal the religious habit of mind had been to all intellectual virtue. From the writers' fashion of paltering with objections to their sacred books, we can infer the amount of bad faith that had been brought to bear on the older doctrinal discussions among the sects. For one fair specimen of the "sincere fanatic", such as Cartwright, there are a hundred conscious jugglers with texts, playing the partisan over formulas like so many Guelphs and Ghibelines of the internecine world of the south; and when we scrutinise even such a type as Cartwright we seem to see clear traces of a willed passion, a factitious fervour, inflating and sustaining itself by a muster of bullying dicta, in the secret consciousness that they are only words, which will not be translated into acts. The more closely we look, the more elusive seems that ideal sincerity with which so many fanatics, slaying and slain, have been haloed by a mistaken posterity. Even downright persecution is as a rule more of a brutal persistence in a quarrel, a dogged refusal to seem to give in, than a conscientious procedure in what is felt to be a necessary course of repression, like the punishment of crime. In Sir Thomas More, the finest Catholic mind of his age, the spirit of persecution emerges as plain physical passion against upstart ignorance, not at all as a paternal concern for the saving of souls; and where he stands thus revealed, it would be idle to credit the violence of more typically violent men to a pure zeal for truth. On due reflection it is seen to be a delusion to suppose, as Mr. Buckle would have had us do, that the typical Inquisitor of the past was a passionless spiritual surgeon, calmly excising what he felt to be corrupt tissue from the body social.

It would of course be unfair to place these flawed zealots of a past time *in vacuo*, with the tacit assumption that because we detect their intellectual vice our own age is free of it. In truth, we can the better realise their mixedness from a study of their congeners among ourselves, with their blend of the spirit of faction and the mere gregariousness of the tribe in stupid cruelty. The temper in question is far from deserving the name of sincere conviction. But while intellectual goodness is thus slow to develop, it is clear that a religious atmosphere is, of all, the most unfavourable to it. In that mental climate, the naturally conscientious man, who would under a saner culture practise a quiet self-criticism, is moved to a strictly hysterical exercise of prayer, which frustrates its own object, and leaves the seeker newly deluded. It was into a world where such religion was the only off-set to the tempers of cynical egoism and virulent faction that the Deists came with a new dialectic, a new tone, a new problem; and the resulting detection of the elements of the orthodox intelligence is tolerably complete. Mr. Pattison has remarked on the brazenness of Bentley's contention, in his attack on Collins, that the fat prizes of the Church, pointed to by the Freethinkers as the stultification of its primary records, were the proper means of attracting ability to the Church; and the same critic has concisely noted for us, concerning the opponents of the Deists, "the astonishing want of candour in their reason-"ing, their blindness to real difficulty, the ill-concealed "determination to find a particular verdict, the rise of "their style in passion in the same proportion as their "argument fails in strength";[1] whereon he fitly quotes Butler's " It is as easy to close the eyes of the mind as " those of the body ".[2] Butler knew whereof he spake.

If society was evil and ugly under the religious regimen before the coming of reasoning Deism, it was bound to present the same features when the stir of active Deism was over, and the endowed creed held nearly undisturbed possession of the fallow ground of the new industrial life. There seems indeed to have been nearly as much retrogression in life, in the midst of the industrial expansion,

[1] *Essays and Reviews*, p. 304. [2] *Sermon X.*

as there was in the mental life outside of it. Hannah More's letters present a picture of rural life, high and low, which could hardly be matched anywhere else in Europe. Writing to Wilberforce from Cheddar in 1789, she describes the "rich poor wretches" of her neighbourhood as "ignorant as the beasts that perish, intoxicated every "day before dinner, and plunged in such vices as make " me begin to think London a virtuous place "; while the clergyman is "intoxicated about six times a week, and " very frequently prevented from preaching by black eyes, " honestly earned by fighting ".[1] Writing from Cowslip Green in 1795, she tells that of the members of her new Sunday School " several of the grown-up youths had been " tried at the last assizes; three were the children of a " person lately condemned to be hanged; many thieves; "all ignorant, profane, vicious, beyond belief! Of this " banditti we have enlisted one hundred and seventy."[2] It was the England of Burke's rhetoric, the Christian England which towered in alien righteousness beside "infidel and anarchic France". Whatever of reforming effort was at work was nearly all Nonconformist, and as such was vilified and resisted by the State clergy: bishop-befriended Hannah More herself was ecclesiastically prosecuted for setting up a village school; and the Dissenters were excluded as completely as possible from the higher culture by being debarred the Universities. The religion of institutions, with its "united front", resisting rational criticism by machinery, had finally identified itself with resistance to every species of progress, making popular ignorance, orthodoxy, abject loyalty, capital punishment, and negro slavery the main planks of its programme.

While, however, the movement of reason had thus failed to conquer clericalism in England, it had profoundly affected intellectual life in countries where that life was on the increase. The literary and popular

[1] *Life*, as cited, pp. 112-113. [2] *Id.*, p. 153.

rationalism of France, the scholarly rationalism of Germany, alike trace back to the generation of English Deists. The orthodox Professor Dorner has admitted that their movement, "by clearing away dead matter, "prepared the way for a reconstruction of theology from "the very depths of the heart's belief, and also subjected "man's nature to stricter observation".[1] "This, how- "ever," writes Professor Cheyne, "as it appears to me, "is a very inadequate description of the facts. It was "not merely a new constructive stage of German theo- "retic theology, and a keener psychological investigation, "for which Deism helped to prepare the way, but also a "great movement which has in our own day become in a "strict sense internationally concerned with the literary "and historical criticism of the Scriptures."[2] The latter statement is within the truth. Even in the midst of the ruling obscurantism in England at the close of the century, with the panic of reaction against the French Revolution darkening the whole intellectual air, the historical thought of Gibbon and the philosophical thought of Hume were at work, shaping the tendencies of a new age; and when at length reaction was trodden underfoot by new forces only partially intellectual, the new movement of reason which entered by the breach was in strict truth an evolution from the positions of the pioneers of a hundred years before. A clerical culture-historian has sketched with unusual judgment the process of the eighteenth century movement, in a page which may here be transcribed:—

"The philosophy of Locke, which attempted to lay a "basis for knowledge in psychology, coincided with "where it did not create [the] general attempt to appeal "on every subject to ultimate principles of reason. The "tone in truth marked the age, and, acting in every

---

[1] *History of Protestant Theology,* Eng. trans., vol. ii, p. 77.
[2] *Founders of Old Testament Criticism,* 1893, pp. 1-2. Compare Lechler, *Geschichte des englischen Deismus,* S. 448, as to the epoch-making effect of the translation of Tindal's chief work into German in 1741.

"region of thought, affected alike the orthodox and the
"unbelieving. .... The principal phases belonging to
"[the] period of the maturity of Deism .... are four:
"(1) An examination of the first principles of religion,
"on its dogmatic or theological side, with a view of
"asserting the supremacy of reason to interpret all
"mysteries, and defending absolute toleration of free-
"thought. This tendency is seen in Toland and Collins.

"(2) An examination of religion on the ethical side
"occurs, with the object of asserting the supremacy of
"natural ethics as a rule of conduct, and denying the
"motive of reward or punishment implied in dependent
"morality. This is seen in Lord Shaftesbury.

"After the attack has thus been opened against
"revealed religion, by creating prepossessions against
"mystery in dogma and the existence of religious motives
"in morals, there follows a direct approach against the
"outworks of it by an attack on evidences.

"(3) In an examination, critical rather than philo-
"sophical, of the prophecies of the Old Testament by
"Collins, and of the miracles of the New by Woolston.

"The Deist next approaches as it were within the
"fortress, and advances against the doctrines of revealed
"religion; and we find accordingly,

"(4) A general view of natural religion, in which the
"various differences, speculative, moral, and critical, are
"combined, as in Tindal; or with a more especial
"reference to the Old Testament, as in Morgan, and the
"New, as in Chubb, the aim of each being constructive
"as well as destructive. ...."

It has only to be added to this that the philosophy of Hume repels Berkeley's, which grew out of resentment of the scientific Atheism seen here and there behind the Freethought movement; that Kant similarly grows out of Hume; that Bolingbroke developed the elements of agnosticism in Hobbes, while like him professing Theism; that the theistic physics of Newton, a reaction against the naturalistic method of Descartes, in turn bred the reaction of Laplace; and that thus alike the transcendental and the naturalistic strains in modern thought affiliate with those of preceding ages. Needless to say, the dynamics of religion are the same all along, through all modifications of dogma.

PART III.
MODERN THOUGHT.

CHAPTER I.

THE TRANSITION.

BEGUN, in a sense, by amateurs, the English rationalism of the eighteenth century passed into the hands of two masters, one in philosophy and one in history, to wit, Hume and Gibbon. Between them these writers laid a large part of the recognised foundation of nineteenth-century thought, the rest being mainly the work of French men of science and German scholars, all alike acting in large part on the stimulus of the movement begun by the physicists and the Deists of a century before. The fundamental weaknesses of the pioneers were apriorism and inexactitude: the advance made by their successors was in terms of inward analysis and outward research. Hume's first and greatest work (1739) was "an attempt " to introduce the experimental method of reasoning into " moral subjects ". On the historical side he was masterly only where his gift for the "experimental method" had free play, as in his *Natural History of Religion* (1757), which once for all shifts the religious problem from the ground of the *à priori* to that of psychology and anthropology. To this work Gibbon's was broadly complementary. Where the earlier Deists had tested Christian claims by general common sense and general comparison of documents, Gibbon established the type of exact modern research by undertaking to trace within a great historic period what Christianity had actually been. And the gradual impact of the work of these two writers alone, with the aid of the light artillery of Voltaire, would conceivably have re-established rationalism in England in a generation on a wider scale and on a firmer basis than ever, but for the shock of the French Revolution. As it was, French and English free thought was in abundant play when the shock came. The preface to a volume of *Essays on the Evidence and Influence of Christianity*, published at Bath in 1790, declares that "the rapid progress "of infidelity appears to be the natural and necessary "consequence of prevailing dissipation"; and in one of the essays it is "readily granted that the number of "those who do not believe is great". Nowhere is there any support to Burke's pretence of a decay of scepticism. Even after the Terror and the Anglo-French war had dug deep the channels of reaction, we find a defender of the faith describing the *Monthly Magazine* as "a work which, "without avowing it, is pretty evidently devoted to the "cause of infidelity".[1]

As we have, seen, however, there was a fresh element of resistance at work in England, even before the French Revolution. The new ignorant industrial world was going freshly through the old process of fanatic-culture from the superstitious study of the Sacred Book, thus reproducing types of mind which abounded in the latter part of the sixteenth and the first half of the seventeenth century. "It is curious," writes Hannah More of her Sunday scholars, with but a vague perception of the bearing of her words, "It is curious to see the ignorant and undisciplined "mind falling into the same errors, and deviating into "the same eccentricities, with philosophers and divines. "Some of our poor youths, who did not know their letters "when we took them in hand, have fallen into some of "the peculiarities of William Law, without ever having "heard that there was such a man in the world; and I "fear they judge unfavourably of my zeal, because I have "refused to publish a severe edict against the sin of "wearing flowers, which would be ridiculous in me who "so passionately love them. I find it necessary, in some "instances, to encourage cheerfulness, as certain austerities "are insisted on by some of them, which are rather of a

---

[1] *The Gospel Its Own Witness*, by Andrew Fuller, 2nd edit., 1800, p. 128.

"serious nature."[1] In this society she proposes to enable a maimed young collier "to add writing and arithmetic "to his religious knowledge ", and thereafter " to set him "up as a schoolmaster for the sons of farmers and trades- "men on week-days, and for the poor people on Sundays". If we imagine such culture-elements worked up in all directions by Sunday Schools, by systematic revivalist Methodism, and by the distribution of cheap Bibles, we shall be able in some degree to conceive the character of the populace and middle class which burned Priestley's library, and on which the upper-class resistance to the French Revolution could found itself, on the whole, safely.

In so far as these strata came into contact with rationalistic ideas of all, their temper was mostly one of a half-terrified, half-furious ill-will, such as in a previous age had been felt by Protestants towards Catholics, and *vice versa*. Hannah More, a woman of literary culture and capacity, whose recoil from a "worldly" to a pietistic life coincided with her lapse into a state of chronic suffering from intense headaches,[2] herself exhibits this tendency in the unconscious malice of all her references to unbelievers. "Johnson would not shake hands with "an infidel;"[3] she mentally washes hers when she remembers having done it. In her diary for January, 1794, she writes:—" Heard of the death of Mr. Gibbon, "the historian, the calumniator of the despised Nazarene, "the derider of Christianity! Awful dispensation! He "too was my acquaintance. Lord, I bless thee, con- "sidering how much infidel acquaintance I have had, "that my soul never came into their secret! How many "souls have their writings polluted! Lord, preserve

---

[1] Letter of 1792, *Life*, as cited, p. 127. Compare, in her *Moral Sketches*, that entitled "Ill Effects of the late Secession".

[2] In her diary we find such entries as this: "Good health with increased relaxation of mind; thus are the blessings of God turned against himself". *Life*, as cited, p. 141.

[3] *Id.*, p. 79.

"others from their contagion."[1] After writing which (it was on a Sunday) she would doubtless go and tell her scholars that the Gospel commanded them to love their enemies. To tens of thousands of English households such writings as this would come with unchallenged religious authority: the evangelicalism of the Methodists thus finding its way into the sphere of the Church and creating a world of middle-class fanaticism, which might be figured as a feminine variety of the Puritanism of Cromwell's day. Cowper's poetry and Hannah More's prose were types of a whole library of pietism which came into existence in the last generation of the eighteenth century and the first half of the nineteenth.

And yet all through the first period there subsisted, as we have seen, more than enough of the scepticism of the preceding age to give the pietists constant disquiet. The evidence meets us everywhere. Bishop Watson, writing his *Apology for Christianity* in answer to Gibbon in 1776, declaims at length against "a set of men who "disturb all serious company with their profane declama- "tion against Christianity, and .... infect with their "ignorant and irreverent ridicule the ingenuous minds of "the rising generation".[2] Twenty years later, in his *Apology for the Bible*, in answer to Paine, he mentions that he has "conversed with many Deists".[3] In a sermon of 1795, after lamenting that "there never was an "age since the death of Christ, never one since the "commencement of the history of the world, in which "atheism and infidelity have been more generally pro- "fessed,"[4] he goes on to say that "this impious fever of "the mind, this paralysis of human intellect,[5] originated "in a neighbouring nation," and that "its contagion has

[1] *Id.*, p. 140.
[2] *Two Apologies*, etc., edit. 1806, p. 121.
[3] *Id.*, p. 177.
[4] *Id.*, p. 399.
[5] In other passages, he expressly admits that many Deists are, to his knowledge, upright men. *Id.*, pp. 447, 464.

"been industriously introduced, and is rapidly spreading "in our own"; but his previous writings show that the statement could not be meant merely of the Revolution period. It would seem as if, while the writings of the earlier Deists were superseded in educated and "polite" society by those of Hume, Bolingbroke, Voltaire, and D'Holbach, they had been unsuspectedly building up a new stratum of unbelief among the more studious of the working classes, in despite of and alongside of all the Methodism and revivalism of the time. At least it is clear that when Paine's *Age of Reason* came upon the English public in 1794-5, it met with a welcome which could not be accounted for by the mere previous vogue of his *Common Sense* and *Rights of Man*. The success of the new treatise must have been mainly among the working classes. Not that Paine, as so many apologists have told us, could only appeal to the workers; for when all is said that can be truly said against his style and his occasional slips of grammar, it remains the fact that he makes fewer slips of the kind than Bishop Watson himself, to say nothing of earlier men,[1] and that his writing is incomparably superior in energy and fitness to that of nine polemic writers out of ten in his own day or ours. But in reference to his case there occurred a social metamorphosis which is peculiarly interesting from the point of view of this inquiry. Those very aristocrats who a few years before had been scandalising the pious by their Deism and their disrespect to the reigning creed were hastily converted, not to orthodoxy, but to a strong conviction that orthodoxy must be maintained among the vulgar. There thus occurred a curious

---

[1] A generation earlier, Lowth had declared, in his *Introduction to English Grammar* (ed. 1769, pref.), that "Grammar is very much neglected among us", and had implied that Swift's remarks on that head fifty years before were as valid as ever. "A grammatical study of our own language," writes Lowth, "makes no part of the ordinary method of instruction." See pp. 106-108, 121, 128, 130, etc., for samples of bad grammar from Swift, Pope, Dryden, Atterbury, Clarendon, Shakespere, Milton, Bentley, Bolingbroke, and the Bible.

inversion of the process that took place in the seventeenth century, when the upper class became irreligious because sedition was associated with religion. We have seen, of course, that the sceptical movement of that age had plenty of intellectual stimulus; but it hardly needs saying that gentlemen's ears were much more readily opened to Hobbes by reason of the fact that piety had been mainly on the side of the regicides. In each age that way of thinking became unfashionable which had annoyed the fashionable class. In one case it was pietism, in the other the reverse.

It was with the upper-class sceptics in this matter even as it had been with the bulk of the upper-class Whigs, who rather took Burke with them in reaction than were taken by him. Practical Whiggism was all very well when it meant only bloodless fencing between factions alike aristocratic; but when "the naked Caliban, "gigantic," began to shake the frame of things and propose to have his hand in the business of government, the once warring factions were unified by their common class interest. It was a part of the same process that the fashionable sceptics should rally to the cause of law and order; and their state of mind is sufficiently recorded in the story, preserved by Brougham, of the Duke of Queensberry's demand for the suppression of Paine's writings. "They are true," said his Grace, "and that is their "danger, and the reason I desire to see them put down "by the law; were they false, I should not mind them "at all."[1]

The argumentative reply to *The Rights of Man* was what might be expected from a generation of that way of thinking; not that Watson was really an out-and-out unbeliever, as some thought, but that his *Apology* might

---

[1] Brougham, *Men of Letters of the time of George III*, chapter on Voltaire. Works, vol. ii, p. 10, edit. 1872. Brougham makes the remark apply to "the writings of Paine and other assailants of the Constitution"; but the context points to attacks on religion, in which reference alone is the duke's remark credible.

have been written by a lawyer conscious of having a weak case, and convinced that his best course was to throw himself on the gentlemanly sympathy of the jury. Some special credit is indeed due to him for his comparative courtesy in controversy, in an age in which reviving fanaticism called for a malevolent vocabulary. His civility to Gibbon, in reply to whom he wrote his early *Apology for Christianity* (1776), was in marked contrast with the tone of Gibbon's other clerical gainsayers, and elicited from Hurd, the satellite of Warburton, the comment that "it was well enough, if he was in earnest".[1] In a speech in the House of Lords in his episcopal days (1795), Watson gave colour, as opinion then went, for fresh doubt as to his othodoxy by speaking of the French freethinkers as having "mistaken the corruptions of Christianity for "Christianity itself", and by predicting a purer system as a result of their attack,[2] thus making admissions where pious fervour demanded invective. And he himself tells, in regard to his friendship with the Duke of Grafton, that he "never attempted either to encourage or to discourage "his profession of Unitarian principles; for I was happy "to see a person of his rank professing with intelligence "and with sincerity Christian principles;" adding, "If "any one thinks that an Unitarian is not a Christian, I "plainly say, without being myself an Unitarian, that I "think otherwise".[3]

It is not surprising that such mild disclaimers should leave in the minds of his contemporaries a suspicion that the bishop was himself a Socinian. Even his own account of his mental habit makes little pretence to religious fervour:—"The fact is, that I was early in life accus-"tomed to mathematical discussion, and the certainty "attending it; and not meeting with that certainty in "the science of metaphysics, of natural or revealed "religion, I have an habitual tendency to an hesitation

[1] *Anecdotes of the Life of Watson*, 2nd ed., 1818, vol. i, p. 99.
[2] *Id.*, vol. ii, p. 23.
[3] *Id.*, vol. i, pp. 75-76.

"of judgment, rather than to a peremptory decision on many points".[1] He seems indeed to have taken up the business of religious apologetics very much as he took up the study of chemistry. He stood for and obtained the professorship of chemistry in Christ's College, Cambridge, at a time when he "knew nothing at all of chemistry, had "never heard a syllable on the subject, nor seen a single "experiment in it";[2] and though in fourteen months he had qualified himself to lecture, it is no very violent inference that intellectual conscientiousness was not his strong point. After some years of chemistry, he succeeded (1771) in obtaining "the first office for honour in the "university", the Regius Professorship of Divinity; whereupon, he tells us, "I reduced the study of divinity "into as narrow a compass as I could, for I determined "to study nothing but my Bible, being much unconcerned "about the opinions of councils, fathers, churches, bishops, "and other men, as little inspired as myself".[3] Even were he not an avowed Whig, and as such in ill favour at court, it would not be unintelligible that such a theologian should be held in the profession to have been sufficiently provided for by the Bishopric of Llandaff, despite his bitter complaints[4] of the smallness of that reward for services to Christianity outweighing, in a friend's opinion, those rendered by "all the bench of bishops together".[5]

This was specially said in view of his answer to Paine; but posterity will hardly take such a high view of the *Apology for the Bible*. As Dr. Moncure Conway has pointed out, it is a surrender of the old case, and a re-statement in terms of a conception forced on the defendant by Paine's attack. At times it smacks of the Old Bailey to an extent that must have edified the Queensberrys of the day. We can imagine their cast

---

[1] *Id.*, vol. ii, p. 353.
[2] *Id.*, vol. i, p. 46.
[3] *Ib.*, p. 62. Compare p. 396.
[4] Vol. i, p. 439; vol. ii, pp. 116, 118, 278, 329, etc.
[5] Vol. ii, p. 115.

of feature over the Bishop's falsetto repudiation of Paine's plain and true statement that in the Mosaic narrative the Israelites were exhorted to slay all the male and married Medianites, but permitted to keep the girls for concubinage. The windy weakness of the defence at that point was however characteristic of the pass to which an orthodoxy half-conscious of its hollowness had come. Against the decorous trimming of Watson, Paine's argument is to this day deadly in the last degree. But it is no less so against the general apologetics of Paley, whose *Evidences* appeared in the same year (1794) with Paine's First Part, neither writer having seen the other's work. In his Second Part, without reference to Paley, Paine puts out incidentally one argument which by its single impact annihilates the whole Paleyan system of proof.

That system is an elegant forensic *plaidoirie* based upon the monumental work of the Unitarian Lardner on *The Credibility of the Gospels*, the most learned attempt of the century to answer the Deists as regarded the New Testament. For his own part, though he had been a tutor in his college, Paley was capable of putting a bad false quantity in a word occurring in the second line of the Æneid, pronouncing it *profūgus* in his Latin sermon on the taking of his degree of D.D. at Cambridge;[1] but he had manipulated the learning of Lardner with a skill which testified to a high literary gift. Of his argument, however, as of Watson's, it is possible to feel that if the pleader had been retained on the other side he would have made out at least as good a case for that. What is special to his argument is its quasi-psychological rebuttal of doubts as to the Gospel narrative by the plea that the sincerity and trustworthiness of the Gospel-writers and the Apostles is proved by their taking of their obvious risks—an argument which of itself might show what is fully proved by the composition of such a treatise, that

[1] *Life* prefaced to Edinburgh edition of Paley's *Works*, in 1 vol., 1831.

scepticism had on some lines been gaining rather than losing ground since the early days of Deism. Against the very heart of this argument, however, Paine incidentally deals a blow of singular simplicity and effectiveness, which seems not to have been thought of by his predecessors, when he points out that Paul, cognisant of all the procedure in connection with Jesus, entirely disbelieved the claims made for the new cult until he was miraculously converted. That is to say, Paul did not see any adequate evidence, and had to be convinced by miracle; yet ordinary people are asked to believe on remote hearsay of the evidence to which Paul as a contemporary gave no credit. There could not be a more telling application of Hume's saying that faith needed a fresh miracle in every instance.

What marks out and preserves Paine, however, in the history of the controversy over Christianity, is not so much the force of his critical arguments, though they are in general forcible enough, as the significant combination in him of the force of direct criticism with two others, new in that discussion. One was the spirit of modern science, or rather the mood produced by it; the other the very spirit of democracy. The sententious Young had made one of his epigrammatic hits in the line, " The un- " devout astronomer is mad," a sentiment which speedily grew dear to pulpit and parlour. Paine was the first thinker whom we know to have met that platitude, taken in its intended sense, with the rejoinder which turns the tables on the dogmatist, and which might be tersely put in the form of the explicit contradiction that it is the devout (= orthodox) astronomer who is mad. In Paine's book it takes the higher form of an utterance of the emotion roused in him by the astronomic studies which had engrossed him in his obscure youth, when he "had " no disposition for what is called politics ". It is interesting to contrast the growth of his mind with that of Watson's, concerning whom we have his own testimony that after doing a good deal of work as professor in chemistry, he turned completely aside from the study when he became a priest, even burning his unpublished papers. And nothing beyond a verbal trace of his scientific experience can be found in his theological writings. In Paine, the spirit of science was a more organic thing; and perhaps there is no more inward or pregnant statement of the effect of a felt recognition of man's place in the cosmos on his religion than this passage of his *Age of Reason* :—

"After I had made myself master of the use of the
"globes, and of the orrery, and conceived an idea of the
"infinity of space and the eternal divisibility of matter,
"and obtained at least a general knowledge of what is
"called natural philosophy, I began to compare, or, as I
"have before said, to confront the eternal evidence those
"things afford with the Christian system of faith. Though
"it is not a direct article of the Christian system that
"this world we inhabit is the whole of the habitable
"creation, yet it is so worked up therewith, from what is
"called the Mosaic account of the Creation, the story of
"Eve and the apple, and the counterpart of that story,
"the death of the Son of God, that to believe otherwise,
"that is, to believe that God created a plurality of worlds,
"at least as numerous as what we call stars, renders the
"Christian system of faith at once little and ridiculous,
"and scatters it in the mind like feathers in the air. The
"two beliefs cannot be held together in the same mind;
"and he who thinks that he believes both, has thought
"but little of either."[1]

On this follows a grave, insistent pressure of the main known facts of the cosmic system, in plain speech, on the minds of plain men, leading up to the plain question: "From whence there could arise the solitary and strange "conceit that the Almighty, who had millions of worlds "equally dependent on his protection, should quit the

---

[1] It would appear, however, that Paine has here somewhat antedated his rejection of Christianity. He only says, indeed, that after studying astronomy he "began" to compare the creed with the cosmos. In any case, he avowed no unbelief till much later in life.

"care of all the rest, and come to die in our world, because, they say, one man and one woman had eaten an apple! And on the other hand, are we to suppose that every world in the boundless creation had an Eve, an apple, a serpent, and a redeemer? In this case, the person who is irreverently called the Son of God, and sometimes God himself, would have nothing else to do than to travel from world to world, in an endless succession of death, with scarcely a momentary interval of life."

It is not likely that the orthodoxy of that age, variously hypnotised by ritual and platitude and hysteria, could feel at once the full shock of the challenge here given to the endowed creed. "The astronomical discovery," says Mr. Lecky, "that our world is . . . . but an infinitesimal point in creation, in as far as it is realised by the imagination, has a vast and palpable influence upon our theological conceptions."[1] But it is part of the work of theology to prevent the necessary imaginative realisation of the truth. A scientific conception of the universe had been nominally established from Newton's time; and in the case even of the half-hypnotised Newton the conception had been fatal to the Trinitarian fantasy; but the university system secured that astronomic knowledge should be a machinery for the study of mathematics, not a psychological possession modifying the whole intelligence.[2] It was left to the man of the people, sincere with their sincerity, to put the gist of the new lore in the people's hands, with the main lesson it could convey to them; so that henceforth rationalism had a new foothold in their knowledge. But if the endowed priesthood were in part incapable of seeing the argument against them,

[1] *History of Rationalism in Europe*, Introd.
[2] Baxter, who in his diffuse quarto on *The Reasons of the Christian Religion* (1667) raises the question of the vastness of the cosmos and the probability that millions of other orbs than ours are inhabited, educes only the singular argument that in that case the damnation of the bulk of the human race would be a very small matter, and no proof of cruelty on God's part (Work cited, pp. 388-390).

they could not but see its influence on plebeian readers; and we find Hannah More noting in her diary soon after the appearance of Paine's First Part, that she was "conjured by the Bishop to answer Paine's atheistical "book, with a solemnity which made me grieve to "refuse. Lord, do thou send abler defenders of thy "holy cause!" And the entry goes on, in her manner: "Heard of the death of Mr. W——, an awful death! "Profane, worldly, unawakened, in the extremest old age!" The poor lady, with her culture of Johnsonian *belles lettres*, was indeed no match for the revolutionist; and she had her solace in calling him atheistical. To Atheists, and to Theists, there is something pathetically absurd in this ever-repeated helpless snap of pious unreason at a doctrine of which the express purpose was to vindicate the God-idea from the special degradation it had sustained at Christian hands, and to put down Atheism by the same process. Notably enough, even Watson makes no attempt to meet this side of Paine's argument, his answer being made to the Second Part of the book, which appeared a year later. A more heated apologist, writing in 1799, does make an attempt to prove "the consistency of "the Scripture doctrine of Redemption with the modern "opinion of the magnitude of Creation";[1] but his angry argumentation mainly serves to illustrate the difficulty with which the "modern opinion" entered into the psychic states of believers. Twenty years afterwards, Chalmers undertook in his *Astronomical Discourses* to deal with the argument from the modern conception of the cosmos, making no reference to Paine, but avowing that it was often met with in conversation. But, though the preacher's sonorous rhetoric won for his book a passing literary success, it could satisfy only those whose conclusion was foregone, and can have had no modifying effect on the progress of the new naturalist agnosticism. In contrast with the writing of Paine it is rhetoric and

---

[1] *The Gospel Its Own Witness*, by Andrew Fuller, as cited. Part II, ch. 5.

nothing more, being rather a brazening out of the orthodox difficulty than an attempt to surmount it. And to-day Paine's First Part is just so much more unanswerable as our knowledge of the primitive ignorance that gave birth to religion is more complete. Paine, in fine, may be said to have written the preface to modern rationalism, in that he is not merely a logical critic of religious documents and doctrine, but a mind bent on and built up by scientific thinking; his favourite occupations having been the practical inventions on which he brought that thinking to bear. Between his application of the test of scientific cosmology to the whole Christian scheme, and his definition of its details as so much " Christian mythology ", lies the whole scope of scientific hierology.

But that which was the most significant fact in Paine's propaganda for his own day remains permanently significant for ours—the fact, namely, of his intense democracy. Apart from his *Age of Reason* he was already twice famous, first as the American author of *Common Sense* and the series of pamphlets entitled *The Crisis*, perhaps the most decisive ever written; and later as the author in England of *The Rights of Man*, the most popular revolutionary treatise in modern English history. His new work on religion, written just before his arrest in France by the party of Robespierre, was avowedly begun " lest in the general wreck of superstition, of false systems " of government, and false theology, we lose sight of " morality, of humanity, and of the theology that is " true ; " but to the Conservatives of England he was already the very symbol of revolutionary evil, and his opinions were hated as his before they were heard. His panegyric of Jesus and his adoration of Deity, indeed, did but aggravate his offence: his enemies would have been less exasperated if he really were the ribald Atheist they called him. As it was, his Republicanism constituted him an Atheist for a generation which, as Burke claimed for it, feared its God, but "looked up with awe to kings ".

The political circumstances sufficed, as regards the upper and middle classes in general, to give the cause of orthodoxy a new and immeasurable advantage, which lasted for nearly two generations. The reaction against the French Revolution lasted as regards religion when it was worn out as regards politics.

On the other hand, Paine's politics gave Freethought a democratic life it had never had before. Of all the Deists of the eighteenth century, Woolston and Annet alone could be said to catch to any extent the popular ear. There was indeed no working-class reading-public before the latter part of the century; and the leading Deists never thought of trying to create one. But the industrial masses of the later period were not wholly given up to Methodism, especially in the larger towns; and among these, especially in London, Paine created a movement which has never since ceased, and which, perhaps, constitutes the most practical danger to the Church as a revenue-drawing corporation. So long as the mass of the people remain credulous of its creed and claims, no amount of scholarly and scientific exposure can endanger its income; and even if the moral pressure of criticism should keep out of the priesthood all the more intelligent and capable men, there will for many a day be enough of unintelligent wealth, upper-class and middle-class, to give any body of clergy a sufficient social status. But when a vigorous rationalism has got a fixed footing among the workers, whose economic insecurity carries with it the grim compensation of economic independence on the side of opinion, there arises a new possibility of a steady forcing back of ecclesiasticism. The normal rationalism of the Socialist workers on the Continent seems to point the way; and, if in any measure their political battle is ever won, it would seem impossible that the Churches, already so vitally discredited alike in France, Germany, and Italy, should have anything but a dwindling future.

Meantime, of course, we are far from having reached even the present Continental stage in England; and at the end of last century, when the terrified propertied classes found Paine's freethinking going hand in hand with "sedition" so-called, and visibly creating a habit of thought which would keep men politically critical even when special causes of revolutionary discontent were not pressing, they began an effort of repression such as had not been seen in England for over a hundred years. Paine had only escaped their vengeance on the publication of *The Rights of Man* by a sudden flight to France; and in default of prosecuting him for the later work the Government prosecuted in all directions those who sold it. The Society for the Suppression of Vice, with the customary effrontery of such bodies, put all freethinking literature on their list for attack; and one after another publisher or seller of Paine's books was duly imprisoned. In 1797, Thomas Williams, a poor bookseller, was sentenced to a year's hard labour for selling a few copies of *The Age of Reason*, the judge taking credit for much Christian charity is thus "mitigating" the punishment the law allowed. It would appear that one of the two avowed publishers of the book (the other being out of the country) was left alone because he sold replies to the book, and also the libellous *Life* of Paine. In 1812, after Paine's death, his avowed publisher Eaton was sentenced to the pillory and eighteen months' imprisonment. All this while there was no thought of prosecuting the publishers of the works of Gibbon, Hume, and Voltaire, which, as Eaton's counsel argued, might be held to do more harm to religion than the attacks of Paine. The principle of the Vice Society was that freethinking literature likely to reach the poor must be prosecuted, but no other: their action being in fact largely an expression of the political anger of the upper class against the democratic movement. Wilberforce was an active Vice-President of the Society. It may be that his name, now somewhat bare of its humanitarian renown, will survive a little longer in respect of the due measure of ill-fame for his action as a persecutor. It appears that he did not admit such action to be of the nature of persecution. " It was "the constant maxim of my revered friend Mr. Wilber-"force," writes Brougham, "that no man should be "prosecuted for his attacks on religion. He gave this "opinion in Parliament; and he was wont to say that the "ground of it was his belief in the truths of religion."¹ Apparently the pietist supposed that by calling freethought "vice" he was excluding it from the category of "attacks "upon religion". But, though he doubtless acted in part on motives of political malice, there was none the less of malice in his feeling towards the freethinkers. He seems even to have been more cruel than some of his colleagues in this particular case.² All censure apart, it is extremely interesting to observe in such cases as his how men who positively perspired unction as preachers of a doctrine of evangelical love, were turned at a breath, by the denial of their creed, into more malignant persecutors than the educated Pagans whose gods were blasphemed and whose temples were violated by the evangelists' predecessors. For when we consider the average value placed on life in ancient and in modern times, the temper of the upper-class Christians of a hundred years ago towards their gainsayers was incomparably more ferocious than that of the Pagans of the same class; and the language of their judges simply indecent in comparison with that held by some of the Roman magistrates.

Nor was the ultimate slackening of the modern persecution in any way due to a change for the better in the temper of the persecutors. They only gave up when they found that persecution did not avail. Richard Carlile, who was first prosecuted in 1819, spent altogether nine years in jail, solely for publishing freethinking books. At different times after 1819, his wife, his sister, and a number of his shopmen were tried, convicted and imprisoned for different periods on similar charges, the

¹ *Men of Letters of the time of George III*, as cited, p. 10.
² See Mrs. Bradlaugh Bonner's edition of the *Age of Reason*, 1896. Introd., p. xvii.

judges almost always exhibiting an infamous prejudice. It was only when it was found that well-to-do sympathisers persistently subscribed money to keep Carlile's shop going, and that men and women could always be found to face imprisonment for selling books over the counter, that the vindicators of Christianity gave up in grief, wearying of their well-doing. In later decades, fresh experiments have had to be made, with the result of renewed stimulus to the persecuted cause, before new generations of Christians could assimilate the painful secular lesson involved. But in the palmy days, under the good Wilberforce, it took some thirty years of Christian warfare to abate the "perseverance of the "saints".

Yet with all this stress of persecution, which in a commercial community must needs have an enormous indirect force against outward profession, and consequently against propaganda, it is clear that the pietists never felt intellectually sure of their cause. In 1806, Van Mildert published his *Historical View of the Rise and Progress of Infidelity, with a Refutation of its Principles and Reasonings*,[1] a work which compensates for commonplace matter by a consistently rabid manner, in thorough harmony with the religious temper of the time. It is part of the method of such vessels of wrath to treat "infidelity" as refuted past all plausible revival; and it describes Paine's *Age of Reason* and Godwin's *Political Justice* as "works now sinking fast "(it is to be hoped) into oblivion, and consigned to just "execration by every friend of truth and social order".[2] Yet it shrieks that Paine's book had been widely circulated "among the very dregs of the populace, by whom "it was devoured with an avidity which spoke the innate "depravity of their minds"; and it goes on to declare that "we cannot form an adequate conception of the "extent and variety of the means employed in these latter

---

[1] Being the Boyle Lectures for the years 1802-1805, the first set that had been printed since 1783.
[2] Work cited, 2nd ed., vol I, p. 405.

"days for the overthrow of the Gospel, unless we take
"into account the more insidious devices of the enemy, in
"raising up from among the very 'household of faith' foes
"to its doctrines and principles, who, under the semblance
"of giving it their support, were employed in secretly
"undermining its foundations."

These traitors were the rationalising theologians of
"Germany, Holland, and perhaps other parts of Europe";
yet even of these "none perhaps appears in a more dis-
"graceful light than" the Scottish Catholic Geddes,
author of a new translation of the Bible (vol. i, 1792), and
of *Critical Remarks on the Hebrew Scriptures* (vol. i, 1800).
Of this case, nevertheless, the devout historian takes a
hopeful view. "Had the author lived to complete his
"design, it is impossible to say how much Revealed Re-
"ligion might have suffered. But happily his efforts
"(highly as they have been extolled by critics of similar
"principles with his own) have not obtained a very exten-
"sive circulation, and as it has pleased God to remove
"him before his labours were nearly completed, we may
"trust that not all the unmerited condemnation of his
"infidel encomiasts will be able to rescue his work from
"speedy oblivion."[1] Yet with all this Christian confidence, the historian felt "compelled to assign to our own
"country a considerable share in the general impiety of
"the age," only reserving the right to "boast, with honest
"pride and gratitude, that our own countrymen appear to
"have been less generally contaminated than those of
"other countries; that Infidelity has not yet dared to
"rear its crest so insolently among us; and that some
"degree of veneration still prevails for that pure and sound
"branch of Christ's Church, which under God's good pro-
"vidence flourishes in this favoured land." The reverend
gentleman's services to the branch in question were duly
rewarded with a bishopric.

Twenty years later we find Hugh James Rose,

[1] *Id.*, p. 413.

"Christian Advocate in the University of Cambridge," excusing the return, in his Hulsean Lectures, to old objections to Christianity, by the fact that " no persons " have stood forward very recently as the *avowed* " opponents of Christianity, whose characters or whose " works give them any claim to considerations or reply ".[1] But at this very time, Rose was concerned to hold up the German Rationalists to English reprobation; and at the close of a tract published by him in the following year he avowed that " the view which we have been taking of a " part of [the features of the times] is not a very pleasant " or encouraging one for the friends of Christianity ".[2]

In point of fact, a new tribe of writers were arising who, without offering any help to the hardier workers who kept up a freethought propaganda on the lines of Paine, and generally without making any avowal of unfaith, had silently assimilated the rationalism of the last century, English and foreign, and were visibly non-religious in their way of thought. Rose avowed, when publishing his tirade against the German Rationalists, that "some of " the most noxious works are in common use amongst " us"; and while this would apply mainly to churchmen, there was an abundance of lay rationalism independent of German study. Bentham's scepticism was notorious; James Mill's was easily to be inferred; Hallam was visibly no friend to evangelical belief; already John Mill and George Grote had formed their philosophical bent; the London University, though destined to do little to further the ideal of its founders, had been set up to promote education on secular principles; and the *Westminster Review* gave a platform for all manner of guarded heresy. The factor of terrified class interest, combining with that

[1] Advertisement to *Christianity always Progressive*, 1829. In his earlier and more vituperative work (1825) on *The State of the Protestant Religion in Germany*, Rose says (p. 6) that in England " the rationalist party is below contempt ".
[2] *Brief Remarks on the Dispositions towards Christianity generated by prevailing opinions and pursuits*, 1830, p. 85.

of the now enriched and strengthened Church, had indeed for a generation ostracised rationalism, brute force and fear doing what argument had failed to do. The religious Antæus had once more set foot on the revivifying soil—the pecuniary and political interests of the power-wielding majority; and "revealed truth" was once more in the ascendant. Yet still, all the while, the immortal adversary, the "wild, living intellect of man," was gathering strength for a fresh wrestle.

It was in this generation of reaction and transition that Butler's *Analogy* began to win the celebrity which, as we have seen, is since mistakenly credited to it as regards its own age. As was noted later by Professor Baden Powell, the apologetic school of Paley began to be "superseded "by a recurrence to the once comparatively neglected "resources furnished by Bishop Butler; of so much less "formal, technical, and positive a kind, yet offering wider "and more philosophical views of the subject".[1] The *Analogy* had only reached its seventh edition[2] in the year 1775, forty years after its publication, and only its tenth in 1802. But in the present century it has passed through more than thirty editions, many of them very large, continuing to be re-issued when its very editors—at least as represented by Mr. Gladstone—admit that it no longer deals with living arguments. In truth, the first half of the century was the Golden Age of Christian Evidences. Despite the alleged sufficiency of Paley and Watson, there were dozens of minor performers—so many that even a collector with a hobby that way soon tires of rescuing samples of their work from the "penny box". Their very number is the proof of the persistent vitality of the spirit of doubt, at the very height of the reaction: indeed, nearly every polemist in turn deplores the "spread of infidelity among us". What Butler did for this blustering generation was to give it in a quasi-classic form the

[1] *Essays and Reviews*, ninth edit., p. 104.
[2] Published in Aberdeen.

essence of the most judicious argumentation on the religious side, purged of the personalities alike of the past and of the present. Students found in the *Analogy* the one valid argument urged by Watson against Paine; and when Paley gave them uncomfortable sensations as of listening to chicanery at *nisi prius*, they could turn to Butler for a grave and almost masculine handling of some of the deeper issues involved, he measuring the average strength of human certainty all round, while his skilful successor made out a quite too glittering case for the concrete credibility of the twelve apostles.

It would have been strange if in the England of ever-expanding commerce, of an ever-increasing wealthy class, and of an ever-increasing population, such pleading as Butler's did not avail to satisfy a sufficiency of reasonably intelligent youths that an income could be made in the priesthood without much loss of self-respect. It would be strange, indeed, if they had not been able so to convince themselves in the first half of the century, when the habit as well as the fashion of religion was so strong, seeing that they contrive so abundantly to reach the requisite persuasion in the second half, after Darwin and Strauss, the higher criticism and the comparative mythologists, have done their share in explaining religion away. But it remains to trace these later adaptations in some detail.

CHAPTER II.

THE BEGINNINGS OF THE BROAD CHURCH.

IN such a corporation as the English Church, recruited from the whole of the middle class, it is impossible that what of liberal thought there is among the laity at any period should not show itself in some form. We have seen how it did so even in the eighteenth century; and in the nineteenth, when the worst of the reaction against the French Revolution was over, the expression of resumed progress was bound to be as much more marked as the progress itself was more vital. But nothing could prevent the counter-pressure set up by the very conditions of the Establishment; and the conflict between common-sense and economic necessity has been and will remain a constant source of hesitancy and dissimulation, as knowledge deepens.

The first signs of the modern spirit, within the century, were symptoms rather of dislike of tyranny and persecution than of rational doubt, and seem to have always had a political basis. In Bishop Watson, we have seen such traits: the expression of the Whig frame of mind in matters theological; the typical Whig being too much a creature of compromise to be an unbeliever in such a stage of culture, but too much a lover of freedom and moderation to take any satisfaction in violence against infidels. He was indeed the most advanced type of mind that in such an age could safely express itself at all. After Watson we have Sydney Smith, like Watson a believer by habit, and so little given to deep doubt as to be positively malevolent towards doubters; but at the same time averse to sacerdotalism and the fanaticism of dogma. He was the only clergyman in the diocese of

York, in 1825, who stood for Catholic Emancipation;[1] but he was as staunch a churchman as any in point of creed. "My father," says his daughter in her Memoir of him, "however much he might indulge in attacks on what he "thought the shortcomings of the Church, never for a "moment tolerated anything approaching to irreligion, "even in his most private transactions. He received "about this time a work of irreligious tendency from the "house of a considerable publisher in London, who was "in the habit of occasionally presenting him with books. "Many men might have passed this over as of little im- "portance; but he felt that nothing was unimportant "that had reference to such a subject. He immediately "wrote to the publisher, saying that 'he could not but be "'aware that he had sent him a work unfit to be sent to "'a clergyman of the Church of England, or, indeed, of "'any church'; and after counselling him against such "publication, even with a view to mere worldly interests, "he adds, 'I hate the insolence, persecutions, and in- "'tolerance, which so often pass under the name of "'religion, and, as you know, have fought against them; "'but I have an unaffected horror of irreligion and im- "'piety, and every principle of suspicion and fear would "'be excited in me by a man who professed himself an "'infidel.' These feelings were strongly evinced on "various occasions, in some of his early letters to Jeffrey. "He not only deprecates the injury to the *Edinburgh* "*Review* by the admission of irreligious opinions; but "declares his determination, if this were not avoided, of "separating himself from a work of which he had felt "hitherto so justly proud. He writes to Jeffrey: 'I hear "'with sorrow from Elmsley, that a very anti-Christian "'article has crept into the last number of the *Edinburgh* "'*Review*. . . . . You must be thoroughly aware that the "'rumour of infidelity decides not only the reputation, but "'the existence of the *Review*. I am extremely sorry,

---

[1] *Memoir of Sydney Smith*, by his daughter, Lady Holland. Edit. 1869, p. 139.

"'too, on my own account, because those who *wish* it to have been written by me, will say it *was* so.' And again, in another letter: 'I must beg the favour of you to be explicit on one point. Do you mean to take care that the *Review* shall not profess infidel principles? Unless this is the case I must absolutely give up all connection with it.'"[1]

It is perhaps not far wrong to read in these excited protestations, so curious in their contrast with the prevailing humour of the Dean's letter-writing, the fear of the man of common-sense to let common-sense have a hearing in matters of creed. There is nothing to show that Smith had what are commonly called "religious convictions". He was a shrewd and humane humorist, pushed into the Church against his will by his father in his youth, and conscious of a thorough incapacity to be zealous about abstruse dogmas. It was a natural consequence that he should be afraid to scrutinise in any degree the foundations of the doctrines he had to preach. He accordingly fulfilled his bent by leaving dogmatics carefully alone, and preaching tolerance to an intolerant generation, breaking out vehemently against those daring spirits who seemed to him to put all peace and quietness in jeopardy by their doubts and denials. To the unbelievers he transferred much of the blame for the social penalties which followed on even a charge of unbelief. "It matters not," he remarks in one of his reviews, "how trifling and insignificant the accuser, cry out that *the Church is in danger*, and your object is accomplished; lurk in the walk of hypocrisy, to accuse your enemy of the crime of Atheism, and his ruin is quite certain; acquitted or condemned, it is the same thing; it is only sufficient that he be accused, in order that his destruction be accomplished."[2] Smith, with his English dislike of the speculative habits of mind of his Scotch friends, was not the man to make the inquiry whether a

[1] *Id.*, p. 142.
[2] Article on *Trimmer and Lancaster*, in *Works*, edit. 1869, p. 85.

religion which normally worked in this fashion might not profitably be superseded by the "irreligion" he dreaded. What he saw was that it was hard enough in that day to make a fight for a moderate Liberalism in politics without also having to fight the worst forms of religious prejudice. So he felt towards the sceptics somewhat as he felt towards the Tories, whose walk and conversation he has so vividly described. "From the beginning of the "century . . . . to the death of Lord Liverpool was an "awful period for those who had the misfortune to "entertain liberal opinions, and who were too honest to "sell them for the ermine of the judge or the lawn of the "prelate:—a long and hopeless career in your profession, "the chuckling grin of noodles, the sarcastic leer of the "genuine political rogue — prebendaries, deans, and "bishops made over your head—reverend renegadoes "advanced to the highest dignities of the Church for "helping to rivet the fetters of Catholic and Protestant "Dissenters, and no more chance of a Whig administra-"tion than of a thaw in Zembla—these were the penalties "enacted for liberality of opinion at that period; and not "only was there no pay, but there were many stripes. It "is always considered as a piece of impertinence in "England if a man of less than two or three thousand a "year has any opinions at all upon important subjects; "and in addition he was sure at that time to be assailed "with all the Billingsgate of the French Revolution— "Jacobin, Leveller, Atheist, Deist, Socinian, Incendiary, "Regicide, were the gentlest appellations used; and the "man who breathed a syllable against the senseless "bigotry of the two Georges, or hinted at the abomin-"able tyranny and persecution exercised upon Catholic "Ireland, was shunned as unfit for the relations of "social life. Not a murmur against any abuse was "permitted . . . . ."[1] So the sceptics were to be ostracised; and as the good Dean saw that the Tories were

---

[1] Preface to *Works*, 1839.

as much exasperated against Methodism as against unbelief, he fell foul of the whole sect as a "trumpery faction", and exhorted people to be good Christians "without "degrading the human understanding to the trash and "folly of Methodism".[1] From which procedure on the part of a preacher of "charitable forgiving indulgent "Christianity"[2] we can the better realise that of the party which did not pretend to be indulgent. These were, as he says, "some four or five hundred thousand English "gentleman, of decent education and worthy characters, "who conscientiously believe that they are punishing, and "continuing incapacities [legal disabilities], for the good "of the State; while they are in fact (though without "knowing it), only gratifying that insolence, hatred, and "revenge, which all human beings are unfortunately so "ready to feel against those who will not conform to their "own sentiments".[3]

In the propaganda of Sydney Smith, it is evident, we have an expression of temperament rather than of reason; and the same characteristics appear in most of the pioneers of the Broad Church. Men attached by prejudice to the Christian creed, sought to resist the line of action to which confident faith in that creed tended to lead ordinary people. Thus we find in Dr. Arnold, the father of Matthew—Goliath, the father of David, as some friend of Mr. Swinburne's defined him—a positive virulence of aversion to non-Christian opinion, with a constant leaning to liberalism on the ecclesiastical side. Of a journal entitled *Cottage Evenings* he declared: "I delight in its "plain and sensible tone .... but as it is, so far from "co-operating with it, I must feel utterly adverse to it. "To enter into the deeper matters of conduct and prin-"ciple, to talk of our main hopes and fears, and yet not "to speak of Christ, is absolutely, to my mind, to

---

[1] Article on *Hannah More*, in *Works*, p. 168. Compare the article on *Methodism*, p. 97.
[2] P. 85.
[3] Article on *Toleration*, p. 227.

"circulate poison."[1] Not that the journal was anti-Christian: it simply represented "a cold Deism". In this spirit he vehemently insisted on making Biblical knowledge a part of the examination for the B.A. degree in the new London University,[2] and denounced the Gower Street College as "Antichristian, inasmuch as it meddles "with moral subjects—having lectures in History—and "yet does not require its Professors to be Christians". He even carried his Christianity to the length of opposing the relief of Jewish disabilities, on the score that "the "Jews are strangers in England" and "have no claim "to become citizens but by conforming to our moral law, "which is the Gospel".[3] But he was not only willing to have Arians within the fold of the Church, he would have allowed its buildings to be used for their services by dissenting sects, barring only the Catholics, the Quakers, and the aggressive Unitarians. So confusedly does the spirit of toleration begin its work.

As time went on, a certain measure of rationalism of opinion began to mix with this ecclesiastical liberalism; and the recoil from hard-and-fast dogmas began to take the shape of a recasting of doctrine. Watson and Smith had stood very much where Locke did, desiring to make orthodoxy a very simple matter; but men of a more analytic turn of mind must needs go further. It is hard to-day to see any heterodoxy in Whately: "to us of "this generation," as his biographer remarks, "who are "accustomed to see men high in the confidence of "respective church parties assume the boldest license in "approach towards Romanism on the one side, and "Rationalism on the other, it seems almost out of date to "notice the special grounds of disqualification which

---

[1] Letter of June 18, 1831, in Stanley's *Life of Arnold*, one-vol. edition, p. 172.
[2] Letters of April 30, Nov. 18, and Nov. 28, 1837. *Id.*, pp. 260, 309, 314, 316, 317.
[3] Letters of April 27, May 4, and May 16, 1836. *Id.*, pp. 273-277.

"were urged against Whately".[1] His main inspiration unquestionably was that dislike of party malice and persecution which made him privately add the petition "that we may not be persecutors" to the prayer against persecutions.[2] But the author of *Historic Doubts relative to Napoleon Buonaparte* must have read at least Volney and Dupuis, if not some of the German rationalists; and we find Newman, who had at first been influenced by his critical attitude of mind, writing to him in 1834 that "when I first was noticed by your Grace, gratitude to "you and admiration of your powers wrought upon me; "and had not something from within resisted I should "certainly have adopted views on religion and social "duty which seem to my present judgment to be based "in the pride of reason and to tend towards infidelity, "and which in your own case nothing but your Grace's "high religious temper and the unclouded faith of early "piety has been able to withstand".[3] A second letter specifies some of the Archbishop's "anti-superstition "notions" to which Newman had always inwardly demurred, such as "the undervaluing of antiquity, and "resting on one's own reasonings, judgments, definitions, "etc., rather than authority and precedent; . . . the "notion that the State, as such, had nothing to do with "religion; . . . . the abolition of the Jewish Sabbath; "the unscripturalness of the doctrine of imputed "righteousness, ... and the impropriety of forming "geological theories from Scripture". Finally, Whately had acquiesced in "the project of destroying the Irish "Sees"; and then "all was over".

Here, again, it was rather temperament than fundamental belief that marked off Whately from the right

---

[1] *Life and Correspondence of Whately*, by E. Jane Whately, abridged ed., p. 60.
[2] Stanley, *Christian Institutions*, p. 239. Stanley observes that this was a thought "which perhaps before our age it would hardly have occurred to "any ecclesiastic to utter."
[3] *Apologia pro Vita Sua*, edit. 1875, p. 382. The correspondence is also given in Whately's *Life*.

wing of the Church. He was satisfied that his *Historic Doubts*, though written long beforehand, "served as an "answer to Professor Strauss's theories";[1] and his common-sense revolt from certain extremities of creed never reached anything like critical scepticism. But he had the common-sense bias, within the limits of the "un-"clouded faith of early piety", which had hypnotised him like other people, and he tried to be rational where he could; whereas the craving of Newman's sacerdotal spirit was for something rigid and definite to hold by in a whirl of speculation to which, by reason of his subtler sensitiveness, he was by nature far more pliable than the briskly ratiocinative Whately. As he has told us: "From "the age of fifteen, dogma has been the fundamental "principle of my religion; I know no other religion; I "cannot enter into the idea of any other sort of religion; "religion, as a mere sentiment, is to me a dream and a "mockery".[2] He could see well enough that the spirit of criticism which took Whately a certain way could very well take others much further who could make a more penetrating analysis. Hence his recoil from "the pride "of intellect", a recoil crudely enough expressed by some of his followers, who are duly castigated in a letter written by Whately to a friend in 1839:—

"The 'twaddlers' to whom it seems I have introduced "you, however intrinsically despicable, derive great im-"portance from circumstances. Theirs is the last new "fashion. As the fine gentlemen of Queen Elizabeth's "time delighted to exhibit themselves in masks as salvage "men with wreathed boughs round their loins, so it is in "vogue among a certain set of educated men to declaim "against evidence, reason, science, argument, learning, "and all, in short, that they denote by the title of 'pride "'of intellect', and to cry up the purity and the pious "faith of our worthy forefathers, and of unsophisticated "peasants; and as the costume of the above-mentioned

---

[1] *Life*, as cited, p. 159.   [2] *Apologia*, p. 49.

"make-believe salvages was admired because it was known that they *had* handsome clothes in their wardrobes, so these irrationalists are listened to with wonderful favour in their 'babbling o' green fields' because it is known that many of them do themselves possess the intellectual cultivation which they decry."[1]

It is instructive to reflect how little difference of supernaturalist creed there was between the "irrationalists" and their critic, and on the other hand how important is the difference of temperament which could set up such divergence of policy. Whately contrasts with Newman to peculiar advantage in his treatment of their common friend Blanco White, the ex-priest from Spain, who had made a great figure in the English religious world by first renouncing his ancestral Catholicism on grounds of general scepticism, and then embracing the creed of the Church of England, and writing against that of Rome. He had supplied a neat and telling argument against the Papal claim, in telling how, while yet a priest, he had reflected "that the certainty of the Roman Catholic faith had no better ground than a fallacy of that kind which is called reasoning in a circle; for I believed the infallibity of the Church because the Scripture said she was infallible; while I had no better proof that the Scripture said so, than the assertion of the Church that she could not mistake the Scripture".[2] The Catholics could reply, as Whately noted, that "if we rest our religious belief on the Sacred Scriptures, and refer to tradition for the assumption that they are the Sacred Scriptures, our belief must rest ultimately on tradition";[3] and the Archbishop's answer that he rested on his own judgment, which he admitted to be fallible, would hardly have satisfied the devout of his Church. But White's dilemma was for them very satisfactory as it stood, and Oxford

---
[1] *Life*, p. 159.
[2] Cited in *Outlines of the Life of Blanco White*, prefixed to his *Observations on Heresy and Orthodoxy*, edit. 1877, p. xviii.
[3] Letter to Baden Powell, March, 1839, in Whately's *Life*, p. 146.

gave him an honorary degree. When, however, in his latter years the ex-priest gradually veered round to Unitarianism, and published his essay *On Heresy and Orthodoxy* (1835), one of the first fruits of the new Deism, he was treated by Anglicans with a bitterness proportionate to their former favour. He has told that Newman, who had been one of his most intimate friends, cast him off[1]— "a circumstance," says Newman, "which I do not "recollect, and very much doubt".[2] But just before making this statement, Newman has told how he had written fiercely of heresiarchs, declaring that they should meet no mercy; how he would have no dealings with his own brother, and " put his conduct upon a syllogism "; and how he fomented a family schism. In the circumstances we have every reason to accept White's recollection rather than his. Candidly narrating his old fanaticisms, Newman urges: "it is only fair to myself to "say that neither at this nor at any other time of my life, "not even when I was fiercest, could I have even cut off "a Puritan's ears, and I think the sight of a Spanish "*auto-da-fè* would have been the death of me". This is all very well; but he had joined the Church that wrought the *autos-da-fè* and never once repudiated them. In any case, he had not scrupled to persecute and boycott where he had the power. Whately, on the other hand, was much more tried by White's change, White having resided with him from the time of his appointment to his archbishopric. But though White has told how he felt bound to leave his friends, it was in no way brought about by Whately, who treated White, then in a very distracted state of mind and body, with the most affectionate forbearance, and helped to maintain him till the time of his death in Liverpool, six years later.[3] One of Whately's letters to White at this time contains the remarkable avowal that "as far as external persuasions

[1] *Life of Joseph Blanco White*, edited by J. H. Thom, 1845, vol. iii, p. 132.
[2] *Apologia*, p. 48.
[3] Whately's *Life*, pp. 106-107.

" go, the temptations to separate from the Church are at
" least as strong as those towards adherence to it : I mean
" to a man of my disposition ".[1] But this had reference
to the "opposition, insult, calumny, suspicion, contempt,
"hatred," he had to endure "from the violent, the
"thoughtless, the weak, the worldly, the partisans of
" all sides," not to any doubts on the Christian
" fundamentals ".

Educated in our day, without a clerical preparation, Whately would almost infallibly have become a rationalist, probably a practical man of science. Educated in our day, without that grounding in pietism which shaped his whole career, Newman might become either a dreamer or a Comtist. The circumstance which turns two such types alike to clericalism is just the existence of the endowed clerical profession, as it is in England ; and if only the progress of rational culture did not now tend to keep the best brains of all types outside of the Church, we might count on a perpetual balance of its forces between the elements of Broad and High.

Looking back, we see the Broad Church emerging as a grouping of the men who reasoned and criticised to a certain extent, growing uneasy over doctrines and narratives that jarred on the civilised moral and critical sense, but feeling satisfied if they could substitute something just a little more refined for the original incredibility. To some extent they found their type and teacher in Coleridge, whose bias to ratiocination, coupled with his constitutional need for extraneous support, led him to put a quasi-rational form on a number of the Christian dogmas. The result was a number of attractively shadowy theorems. Such was the improvement wrought on the doctrine of Blood Redemption by Maurice—a partially systematic development of the old latitudinarian Whiggism which sought to simplify and rationalise dogma as far as possible. The educated moral sense which in

[1] *Id.*, p. 110.

the seventeenth century had begun to revolt at the theory of salvation by blood sacrifice, was bound to revolt more generally and more forcibly in the nineteenth; and it was almost a matter of course that it should be argued by some one that the doctrine of blood sacrifice was no part of true Christianity; that the New Testament only seemingly lent itself to such a principle; and that the purpose of the Incarnation and the Crucifixion was not to placate an offended Deity but to educate mankind. This modification must needs have been agreeable to many nominal Christians, even before the Eucharist was seen to be historically but a ceremonial development of the primeval practice of ritual cannibalism; but there is one decisive obstacle to its adoption by the Church, and that lies in the Church's constitution, its biblical basis, and its financial footing. Mr. Green has said of that Church—his Church—that it "stands alone among all "the religious bodies of Western Christendom in its "failure through two hundred years to devise a single "new service of prayer or praise".[1] So has it been: so will it be. New services and new articles are equally impossible in a Church in which, despite the greatest legal latitude of doctrine, all innovation means risk of attack, followed by loss or limitation of income, at the hands of the irrational majority. And by the same law every important rational advance made by members of the Church, supposing it to be even set forth in an important book, must remain in the status of a non-pious opinion, held without avowal if at all, since any general and open acceptance of it would theoretically endanger the Church's endowments. The surest stronghold of Theism is the Church which sees its way to repel all attacks on its funds by the charge that the assailants are "robbing God".

Of this law of religious conservation, whereby the machinery of a Church endowment always secures the outward maintenance of primeval orthodoxy, there is no

[1] *Short History*, p. 610.

more interesting illustration than that supplied by the works of one of the most intelligent of the pioneers of the Broad Church, who was already influential when Newman and his colleagues were publishing their *Tracts for the Times*. Even now, after nearly sixty years, a real importance attaches to Milman's *History of Christianity*, which with his earlier *History of the Jews* may be reckoned the first overt result within the English Church of two generations of German rationalism, and of the occult discussion in England of the problems raised by the English and French Deists of the last century concerning the New Testament and Christian history. In many ways the *History of Christianity* carries the critical principle, howbeit cautiously, further than is now ventured on by any professed Churchman. Milman indeed was so prudent in his vocabulary and his formulas that many loosely orthodox people can still read him without seeing how his reasoning tends: in fact, we cannot be sure that he himself saw it, even in the analysis of Newman. There are always Churchmen with intelligence enough to see the unreasonableness of thorough orthodoxy, but without mental courage and keenness enough to go the whole length of criticism. Such become the exponents of half-way positions, in which they do not forfeit income or status, and to which numbers of similarly-minded laymen, with a certain sprinkling of unbelieving conformists, are glad to resort. But Milman's book is, as Newman showed, in effect a rationalistic account of Christianity as a strictly "human" phenomenon, a religion marked-off from others only through making in general a better moral application of theological principles common to other systems.

There could be no better elucidation of all this than Newman's review, which should always be read with the *Apologia*, as showing in detail the movement of Newman's mind on the side of its recoil from the tendencies of the "liberal" school. With an insistent earnestness often verging on bitterness, but never lapsing into clerical virulence, after first guarding Milman from unfair interpretation, Newman proceeds to show, step by step and point by point, how the professedly non-theological method of the historian is one that logically undermines and negates theology; and how, despite his profession of neutrality, he at times reveals the anti-theological animus which really inspires him. On this head Newman's comment is specially piquant. Finding Milman first disclaiming theology and then deprecating polemics, he takes it as a foregone conclusion that the book is going to be intolerant. "As liberals are the bitterest persecutors, so "denouncers of controversy are sure to proceed upon the "most startling, irritating, blistering methods which the "practice of their age furnishes."[1] Considering Newman's own efforts in the way of blistering in the *Tracts* and the *Lyra Apostolica*, the complaint against the moderate Milman is not impressive; but in the subsequent critical dissection the palm for sincerity, for consistency of attitude, is clearly with the Catholicising critic, whatever may have been his vacillations in other matters. Once, indeed, he comes within sight of the point at which the intelligent Catholic must perform his juggle with his conscience, dealing as he does with Milman's cautious demonstration that all the elements of the Christian system are to be found piecemeal in other and older systems. Newman claims "to show that the genuine-"ness of the Catholic creed, ethics and ritual, was "unaffected by this fact, there being an existing Catholic "theory" [to the effect that "from the beginning the "Moral Governor of the world has scattered the seeds of "truth far and wide over its extent"] "on which the "fact could stand without detriment to Catholicism, as "well as a popular and liberalistic theory acccording to "which the fact would throw discredit upon it. But," he goes on, "the professed fact itself needs careful looking "after, for it has been before now, and is continually, "shamefully misstated. *We had intended in this place to have*

---

[1] *Essays, Critical and Historical*, 7th edit., vol. ii, p. 214.

"*added some words upon it, but our limits forbid*".¹ Thus the acute critic leaves it an open question whether he admits the facts under discussion, and he is no less careful about the ultimate argument. " There is another question which " obviously arises out of the fact under consideration, viz., " as to its effect upon the *authority* of Revealed Religion. " It may be objected, that originality is necessary, if not " for truth of doctrine, at least for evidence of divinity; " and though there is nothing very profound in the " remark, it ought to be answered ; *and we mention it, that " we may be seen not to have forgotten it.*" This is the sole mention, the sole pretence of answer. It was doubtless the judicious course.

Despite his final caveat that "the professed fact needs " careful looking after", Newman had explicitly accepted Milman's account, thus summarising it in his own words: " The phenomenon, *admitted on all hands*, is this: that a " great portion of what is generally received as Christian " truth is in its rudiments or its separate parts to be " found in heathen philosophies and religions. For in- " stance, the doctrine of a Trinity is found both in the " East and in the West; so is the ceremony of washing ; " so is the rite of sacrifice. The doctrine of the Divine " Word is Platonic; the doctrine of the Incarnation is " Indian: of a divine kingdom is Judaic; of angels and " demons is Magian ; the connexion of sin with the body " is Gnostic ; celibacy is known to Bonze and Talapoin ; " a sacerdotal order is Egyptian ; the idea of a new birth " is Chinese and Eleusinian ; belief in sacramental virtue " is Pythagorean ; and honours to the dead are [a feature " of] polytheism. *Such is the general nature of the fact " before us.*"²

Milman, of course, was far from drawing the logical conclusion from his premises. Certain parts of the Gospel narrative he was prepared to let go by the board

¹ *Essays, Critical and Historical*, as cited, vol. ii, p. 246.
² *Id.*, p. 231.

as every-day " Orientalism "; but when it came to the
main doctrines, though he had shown them to be equally
common property, he reasoned very much as did
Newman. Noting the universality of the doctrine of a
Mediator, he professed that he should be "content with
" receiving it as the general acquiescence of the human
" mind in the necessity of some mediation between the
" pure spiritual nature of the Deity and the intellectual
"and moral being of man "[1]—Omnipotence on this
theory being under disabilities from which lesser powers
were free. But, asks Newman, "what is to hinder a
" writer less religious-minded than Mr. Milman, pro-
" ceeding to infer concerning the doctrine of mediation
" what he himself does infer concerning the angelic
" host?"[2] And so with the other sacrosanct doctrines.
That of the Logos, Milman pointed out, "had already
" modified Judaism; it had allied itself with the Syrian
" and Mithraic worship of the sun, the visible Mediator,
" the emblem of the Word; it was part of the general
" Nature worship; it was attempting to renew Paganism,
" and was the recognised and leading tenet in the higher
" mysteries ".[3] Newman could see clearly enough what
Milman would not see, that all this led to the absolute
surrender of the Christian system, since its precepts are
traceable to other sources in the same way as its dogmas.
And Newman put the question plainly: " What tenet of
" Christianity will escape proscription, if the principle is
" once admitted that a sufficient account is given of an
" opinion, and a sufficient ground for making light of it,
" as soon as it is historically referred to some human
" origin? What will be our Christianity? What shall
" we have to believe? What will be left to us? Will
" more remain than a *caput mortuum*, with no claim on
" our profession or devotion? Will the Gospel be a
" substance? Will Revelation have done more than

---

[1] *History of Christianity*, vol. i, p. 74.
[2] *Essays*, vol. ii, p. 238.   [3] *History*, vol. ii, p. 428.

"introduce a *quality* into our moral life-world, not "anything that can be contemplated by itself, obeyed "and perpetuated? This we do verily believe to be the "end of the speculations, of which Mr. Milman's volumes "at least serve as an illustration. If we indulge them, "Christianity will melt away in our hands like snow; we "shall be unbelievers before we at all suspect where we "are. With a sigh we shall suddenly detect the real "state of the case. . . . ."[1]

Theoretically, the case is clear enough. But, practically speaking, Newman was needlessly apprehensive. For his own part, seeing the facts thus plainly, he could save himself from rational unbelief by a suicidal effort of the morbid will; and he underestimated the remaining resources of the human intelligence in the matter. Given twenty thousand priests faced by the above dilemma, it is safe to say that nineteen thousand nine hundred will find a solution compatible with the retention of place, power, and peculium. Many will perform the Newmanian operation with a Maurician difference; many will simply say nothing and sigh nothing, in which case the visible Church will not be affected; and many more will find a *Via Media* as did Milman. In the Broad Church there are many corners; and a man is pretty safe so long as he says with Milman: "While, however, Christianity necessarily submitted to "all these modifications, I strongly protest against the "opinion that the *origin* of religion can be attributed, "according to a theory adopted by many foreign writers, "to the gradual and spontaneous development of the "human mind. Christ is as much beyond His own age, "as His own age is beyond the darkest barbarism."[2] That historic falsism will doubtless be found serviceable for many years to come.

Milman for his part found it quite sufficient for his day. Of his *History of the Jews*, Stanley remarked in an obituary article (1869) that "it may be doubted whether any sub-

---

[1] *Essays*, as cited, pp. 241-242.   [2] *History*, vol. i. p. 50.

"sequent tumult or obloquy has been more passionate
"than that which beset the first appearance of the *History
of the Jews* [1];" and the *History of Christianity* cannot have
regained the confidence that was outraged by the representation of the early Hebrews as barbarians, and by a
quasi-rationalistic treatment of Abraham, the "sheykh",
and Lot's wife, and the quails and manna. It is hard
to-day to realise the fury then excited by manipulations
which are now ordinary expedients of the conciliatory
preacher, and ethical views which are endorsed by Mr.
Gladstone: indeed it may be suspected that a good deal
of the storm against the *History of the Jews* came from
Tory artillery directed against the Whig. "Will it be
"believed," asks Milman in the appendix to his second
edition, "that after all the clamour, proceeding in some
"instances from quarters where such ignorance is almost
"incredible, the interpretations [of miracles] in this work,
"with two or three exceptions, are the same with those
"which have been long current in the most popular books:
"in Calmet, in Natural Histories of the Bible, and even
"in the Family Bible of the Society for Promoting Chris-
"tian Knowledge?" No degree of ignorance is incredible
in writers so orthodox as some of those who attacked
Milman; but the political explanation will probably hold
to some extent. When he got his Deanery from Peel,
the hostility would tend to subside; and when he produced his really learned *History of Latin Christianity*,
despite its very plain avowal [2] that Christianity progresses
with the progress of knowledge, by a law of human
nature—a doctrine which, like many of those in the
History of Christianity, leads up to the cancelment of all
Christian pretensions—he had little to fear from outcry;
his guarded rationalism having now an odour of orthodoxy as against the Romanism in which Newman had
ended.

In sum, he remains an edifying study to clerics, who,

---

[1] *Essays on Questions of Church and State*, 1st edit., p. 576.
[2] Vol. i, p. 12. Cp. *History of Christianity*, ed. 1867, vol. i, p. 48.

save as regards his treatment of Hebrew miracles and Hebrew barbarities, are careful not to reproduce his teaching; and he has a certain special claim on the attention of general readers in respect of the perfectly unconscious humour of many of his handlings of myth— as in his remark, which so tickled Carlyle, on "the extra-"ordinary conduct of Judas Iscariot"; and in his description of Rahab as "a woman who kept a public "caravansary". And to the culture-historian, finally, he remains remarkable in respect of the comparative fulness with which, while thoroughly deistic in his theory of things, he developed rationalistic views of Jewish and Christian history in the England of 1830-40, at the very start, as it were, of the revival of criticism after the great reaction. He was not original, having drawn largely from foreign sources, both French and German; his work, as Stanley says, "was the first decisive inroad "of German theology into England";[1] but it was none the less a notable advance on the religious thought of his own Church and country; and the fact remains that all the extension of scholarship in the last fifty years has not led to any more straightforward handling, within his Church, of the main issues on which he touched and on which Newman challenged him. That he was in his day, in Stanley's words, the Church's "foremost man in "the world of mind,"[2] is of course only another proof of how little the world of mind owes to the Church. But that is not a point to be pressed in his case in particular.

[1] *Essays on Church and State*, as cited, p. 576.
[2] *Id.*, p. 572.

CHAPTER III.

THE TRACTARIAN REACTION.

THE extent to which the outwardly orthodox Liberalism of the new generation was inwardly removed from the old faith is first made clear by the sudden rise of the " Oxford " movement", associated first with the names, in particular, of Keble and Newman, but most enduringly with the latter. We should indeed be wrong if we saw the so-called religious liberalism of that time with Newman's eyes, even apart from his animus; for much of what he regarded as a rationalising liberalism within the Church was really the mere political action of a Dissent that was as far from rationalism as he was, indeed further, since it had not his intellectual power of seeing the strength of the rationalist tendency and of the atheistic position. But it remains the historic fact that the Tractarian movement began as a revolt of neo-fanatics in the Church against the politically rational policy of lopping off its dead or decaying limbs, in particular that of the Irish Establishment. It was a fulfilment of the often-quoted speculation of Bishop Jebb, of Limerick, in 1814, that " a little of persecution, *or of somewhat resembling persecu-* " *tion*, may be providentially permitted to train up men " with an attachment to the Church as a hierarchy, dis- " tinct from the State ". A very slight "resemblance" sufficed.

To later historians, the movement will probably be a notable proof of the extent to which the English Universities in the first quarter of the century had contrived to shut out the influence, and even the bare knowledge, of the critical movement that had so long been going on in Germany. We can hardly say now with Stanley and the post-Tractarian Liberals that Newman would never have become a Catholic if he had been able to read German. His criticism of Milman showed that he knew something of the German critics, whose tendencies had been plainly brought before his circle by the discussion between Rose[1] and Pusey,[2] both friends of his; and he would have met the Germans as he met Milman, with a *reductio ad atheismum*, so to speak. Even if he had been brought up from childhood in a rational atmosphere, it is doubtful whether, with his peculiar mixture of psychic weakness and intellectual strength, he would not have swung to Catholicism in some mood of obscure hysteria; though on the other hand he might have swung into a neurotic pessimism. But his movement as a whole, from its beginning with Keble, was made possible only by the hot-bed of new pietism developed in England after the French Revolution, when the contagion which we have seen previously spreading from Wesleyanism through the middle classes was reinforced by the new class politics.

Of what the hot-bed was like at its hottest we may get some idea by going back to a writer "to whom", says Newman, "humanly speaking, I almost owe my soul— "Thomas Scott of Aston Sandford".[3] He might have added that he even owed him a little of his style and autobiographic method, there being in Scott's autobiography,[4] which Newman possessed from his boyhood, a curious foreshadowing of the *Apologia*, both in form and tone. But Scott is visibly what Newman can only doubtfully be surmised to have been in part—a neurotic organism. His meticulous narrative of his pragmatic changes of creed, from a semi-rationalistic Socinianism (accompanied by "gross defilements"), by zig-zags to

---

[1] *The State of the Protestant Religion in Germany* (1825) above cited: and *Letter to the Lord Bishop of London* in reply to Pusey, 1829.
[2] *The Causes of Rationalism in Germany*, 1828.
[3] *Apologia pro Vita Sua*, ch. i.
[4] *The Force of Truth: an Authentick Narrative*, 1779, 8th edition, 1811.

·evangelical Calvinism and Methodism, is merely the record of the search of an ill-balanced temperament for the precise form of supernaturalism which would most completely lap it in emotional comfort; the haven of happiness being at length found in the consciousness of election to grace by God's predestination. The form of reasoning which accounts for the steps taken is really only a register of emotional changes for which reasons were found after the event. As a systematising commentator, Scott was indeed able to show that every Christian system short of high Calvinism was inconsistent with itself; and when challenged on the ethical side of Calvinism he could use the Butlerian parry. "The "doctrine of personal election to eternal life, when "properly stated, lies open to no objection which may "not likewise with equal plausibility be urged against the "conduct of God in placing one nation in a more favour-"able condition than another. .... In fact the grand "difficulty in the whole of the divine conduct equally "embarrasses every system of Christianity, and every "scheme of Deism, except men deny that God is the "Creator and Governor of the World."[1] But inasmuch as Scott's only ostensible reason for giving up his previous positions was just that they involved "grand difficulties", ethical and other, his last position is no more defensible than they, since it professes to be ethical after having negated rational ethics. He could but stolidly repeat, in the Calvinist fashion, the old shibboleth that, though God elects his saints at his own good pleasure, with no regard to their works, and though those elected cannot possibly fall away from grace, nevertheless there is no risk that the conviction of having found grace will lead the saint into license.

Here was a sufficient grounding in irrationalism for the future Catholic, who had only to carry Scott's temper and method a step or two further in order to put himself

[1] Work cited, 8th ed., pp. 78-79.

in the hands of the infallible Church. Calvinism, in historical fact, was but a creation, in terms of doctrine, of a scheme of life which could practically countervail the Catholic by reason of quadrating with it, setting up against the outward infallibility of Pope and Church the pietist's consciousness of being himself infallible in his doctrine. While professing to subject reason to revelation, of course, the Calvinist was really making reason the criterion of revelation, in the very act of deciding that revelation in general was genuine, and in selecting for his system the particular parts which suited him; but he was at bottom in the same case with the Catholic, who in turn must needs decide by his reason that the Church was infallible, and as such the proper court of appeal. In all cases alike, then, the determining force was just the degree of emotional unrest, relatively to knowledge and self-reliance: and probably the kind of temperament which in Scott's day could rest in Anglican Calvinism, would in Newman's day struggle further, apart from any direct lead to Catholicism. Newman, whose logic, faithfully followed, would have led him into scepticism, sank to rest in Catholic pupillage, as did Scott in the conviction of predestinate grace. In a sense, Newman had yielded to a rational pressure which Scott did not feel— the pressure of common-sense criticism on Calvinistic ethics. He remarks that he admired in Scott, " besides " his unworldliness, his resolute opposition to Antino- " mianism, and the minutely practical character of his " writings. They show him to be a true Englishman; " and I deeply felt his influence. . . . ." But Scott's opposition to Antinomianism was merely the exhibition of his crux, for his theory *was* Antinomian; and his practice was just the old quandary, seen in Paul, between immoral theory and moral practice. The rationalism of the eighteenth century, ecclesiastical as well as lay, was really a practical recoil from the practical Antinomianism that has always visibly followed on Antinomian theory, from Paul to Luther and from Luther to our own day. In the

English transitional period, under new life conditions, the old experience had to be gone through afresh; the creed of grace had to yield the old graceless fruits before men fell back once more towards the check of common-sense, which put works above faith and preferred incoherent system to dissolute practice. Scott represents the reappearance of the mystic contagion in the State Church at a time when sheer self-seeking and insincere conformity had discredited the common-sense check. Newman's lot was cast in a time of fresh common-sense reaction against fanaticism and self-seeking alike. Hence his early modification of the creed of " grace ".

But, over and above this concession to the new social rationalism which remained from the revolutionary movement, Newman had also from his generation a strong æsthetic lead to Catholicism, in respect of its literary return to the past. While the abstract pursuit of reason characteristic of the eighteenth century criticism was kept up among us by a succession of economists and moralists from Smith to John Mill, the temperamental reaction from the vast tumult of modern politics and the grime of modern industry towards the picturesque Middle Ages, was no less marked in England than in France. In spirits divided against themselves, such as Coleridge, we see both tendencies in continuous play. In firmer personalities, such as that of Hallam, the mediæval interest expresses itself in an orderly historic record, devoid of the enthusiasms of the Thierrys and Fauriels no less than of those of the Chateaubriands and de Maistres, but turned to the account of the modern mood of reform. In the novels of Sir Walter Scott, however, the backward-looking sentiment expressed itself with a contagious power which could not but touch all men with the literary instinct and the poetic bias towards the far-away; and it is probable that Newman's reaching-out towards antiquity, which he notes as one of the momenta in his career, was due far more than he knew to this " psychological climate ", which can so easily be traced in the poetics as well as the poetry of

Keble. We have Newman's own testimony that he was much impressed by the *Thalaba* of Southey, who joined to a delight in the past a keen sense of the "features of "unqualified deformity" to be seen in everything connected with modern manufacturing industry.

The bearing of the medieval sentiment on Newman's ecclesiastical ideals is vividly revealed in his paper on Keble:—

"Poetry is the refuge of those who have not the "Catholic Church to flee to and repose upon, for the "Church itself is the most sacred and august of poets. . . . "Her very being is poetry; every psalm, every petition, "every collect, every versicle, the cross, the mitre, the "thurible, is the fulfilment of some dream of childhood, "or aspiration of youth. . . . . Now, the author of *The* "*Christian Year* found the Anglican system all but "destitute of this divine element, which is an essential "property of Catholicism;—a ritual dashed upon the "ground, trodden on, and broken piecemeal;—prayers "clipped, pierced, torn, shuffled about at pleasure, until "the meaning of the composition perished, and offices "which had been poetry were no longer even good "prose;—antiphons, hymns, benedictions, invocations, "shovelled away;—Scripture lessons turned into chap-"ters;—heaviness, feebleness, unwieldiness, where the "Catholic rites had had the lightness and airiness of a "spirit;—vestments chucked off, lights quenched, jewels "stolen, the pomp and circumstances of worship anni-"hilated; a dreariness which could be felt, and which "seemed the token of an incipient Socinianism, forcing "itself upon the eye, the ear, the nostrils of the "worshipper; a smell of dust and damp, not of incense; "a sound of ministers preaching Catholic prayers, and "parish clerks droning out Catholic canticles; the royal "arms for the crucifix; huge ugly boxes of wood, sacred "to preachers, frowning on the congregation in the place "of the mysterious altar; and long cathedral aisles un-"used, railed off, like the tombs (as they were,) of what

"had been and was not; and for orthodoxy, a frigid,
"unelastic, inconsistent, dull, helpless dogmatic, which
"could give no just account of itself, yet was intolerant
"of all teaching which contained a doctrine more or a
"doctrine less, and resented every attempt to give it a
"meaning,—such was the religion of which this gifted
"author was—not the judge and denouncer, (a deep
"spirit of reverence hindered it,)—but the renovator,
"as far as it has been renovated."

This instructive passage may serve to bring home to us at once what it was that mainly fretted Newman and others into Catholicism, how much of nervous and æsthetic revolt and how little of comparative science; and what it was that sufficed to give a new lease of life to the Anglican Establishment, how much of tuneful platitude and how little of masculine wisdom. For the fact that the name of Keble was "revered" at Oxford for a whole generation is firstly and lastly a proof of the intellectual poverty of the place, on its ecclesiastical side. The one outstanding claim that the author of *The Christian Year*, with his clerical poetry and his academic poetics, could have on the grave esteem of critical people to-day would be in respect of his repute for "saintliness", that is, for singular beauty of character, if only the facts were found to square with the legend. But on enquiry we find that Keble, like so many another so-called saint, was a pietist whose normal serenity of temper broke down into lurid rage as soon as it was tested by a really serious trial, such as the proposal of the political reformers of the day to cut down the disgraceful Anglican Establishment in Ireland. For such a case he had neither wisdom nor patience, neither a sense of justice nor a sense of propriety. "The time had come," says his latest biographer, "when "it seemed to Keble that 'scoundrels must be called "scoundrels';"[1] and in his contributions to the *Lyra Apostolica* the reformers are characterised as "the ruffian

---

[1] *John Keble: a Biography*, by Walter Lock, 1893, p. 78.

"band, come to reform where ne'er they came to pray," as "robbers of the shrines", as "the vile", and as "hell-powers"; and under the heading "Fire" in the collection Keble is the main contributor, singing of the fires of Elijah and the darts of Jehovah, of the flaming sword and "God's all-judging ire".[1] The utterance is thick with passion, the thought darkened by a reek of class prejudice. And when we look narrowly into the Oxford movement, which, as Newman relates, proceeded on Keble's sermon on National Apostasy, we find a very large element of the merest Toryism of temper and principle, with a very small element of knowledge and sagacity. To the retrospective critic of to-day there is little to show for the old repute of the movement as a product of abnormal depth of character and originality or acuteness of thought. The late Dean Church, who belonged to that generation, wrote lately of the Tractarian movement that "a number of able and earnest men, men who "both intellectually and morally would have been counted "at the moment as part of the promise of the coming "time, were fascinated and absorbed by it. It turned and "governed their lives, lifting them out of custom and "convention to efforts after something higher, something "worthier of what they were." "Round Mr. Newman "gathered . . . . the best men of his college, either "Fellows—R. Wilberforce, Thomas Mozley, Frederic "Rogers, J. F. Christie; or old pupils—Henry Wilber- "force, R. F. Wilson, William Froude, Robert Williams, "S. F. Wood, James Bliss, James Mozley; and in "addition some outsiders—Woodgate, of St. John's, "Isaac Williams and Copeland, of his old college, "Trinity."[2] On this we can now only say that the "coming time" has shown nothing to justify an expectation that these young men would distinguish themselves. Among them they have not produced one book of any permanent importance. Their "earnestness" need not

[1] *Lyra Apostolica*, edit. 1879, Nos. cxiv, cxxxiv, clvi, clxv, etc.
[2] *The Oxford Movement*, pref., p. xi.

R

be questioned; their ability must be estimated as not measurably high above the clerical average, from which Newman stands out in virtue of his literary gift, his distinction, his refined energy, his productiveness, and his charm.

One of the typical spirits of the first days of the movement, one perhaps even more potent that Newman in its beginnings, was Hurrell Froude; and all that we know of him, all that Newman tells us of him, is in keeping with the friendly summing up of Dean Church: "Froude was "a man strong in abstract thought and imagination, who "wanted adequate knowledge. His canons of judgment "were not enlarged, corrected, and strengthened by any "reading or experience commensurate with his original "powers of reasoning or invention. He was quite con- "scious of it, and did his best to fill up the gap in his "intellectual equipment. . . . . But circumstances were "hopelessly against him; he had not time, he had not "health and strength. . . . ." Newman said of him: "He had no turn for theology as such," and Dean Church adds that "he was blind to the grandeur of "Milton's poetry. He saw in it only an intrusion into "the most sacred of sanctities."[1] He was in short a superior fanatic, such as has always been to be found in the great churches; a high Tory in politics; high-minded without depth or breadth; self-confident and intolerant; easily capable of becoming a persecutor and an oppressor. Such men make "movements"; they do not make movement in the sense of any lifting or furthering of civilisation. And it is clear from Newman's own narrative that in his days of movement he too was fanatical and bitter; so much so that Hurrell Froude, when calmed by the near approach of death, became in comparison gentle, and told him: "I must enter another protest against your cursing "and swearing. What good can it do? and I call it un- "charitable to excess. How mistaken we may ourselves

---

[1] Work cited, pp. 45, 46.

"be on many points that are only gradually opening on
"us."[1] Newman has frankly told us of his own ferocities
and intolerances; and his brother has since his death given
us fresh details, all pointing in those earlier years to the
spirit of priestly domination, without the strength which
can make domination genial. Dean Church notes how
evangelicalism in those days "too often found its guaran-
"tee for faithfulness in jealous suspicions and fierce
"bigotries."[2] The same is plainly true of the Tractarian
movement itself. In view of Newman's avowals, and of
the early literature of his party, in prose and verse, it was
sufficiently idle for him to write that "Liberals are the
"bitterest persecutors", and that it was the Liberals who
drove him from Oxford.[3] They did by him as he would
have done by them, as his fellow-dogmatists had sought
to do by Hampden; and, though tolerance is largely a
matter of temperament and of political wisdom, and
Newman later acquired much of its spirit, while many
so-called Liberals did not, it is certain that no Catholic
before or since ever compared with the Liberal Dean
Stanley in point of sheer unsectarianism. It was indeed
well for Newman's fame that he found his place in a
Church which exacted from him self-surrender before
according him titular dignity. To the last, we are told,
he was sharply impatient of the troubles of doubters
within the fold. He attracted rather than led: he inspired, but did not instruct. What he says of Keble
was true of himself in his days of action: "What he
"hated instinctively was heresy, insubordination, resist-
"ance to things established, claims of independence,
"disloyalty, innovation, a critical, censorious spirit"
[*i.e.*, critical and censorious of *his* ideals]. "And such
"was the main principle of the school which in the course
"of years was formed around him."[4]

It is not surprising that such leaders should for a time
have many followers. Their position was merely High

[1] *Apologia*, ed. 1875, p. 23.
[2] Work cited, p. 15.
[3] *Apologia*, pp. 203, 292.
[4] *Apologia*, Note A, p. 290.

Toryism in religion; and in 1830 there was no lack of the high Tory spirit. Movements begun by earnest leaders are processes of selection and collection of types; and the Tractarians easily found theirs. "The *Via Media*," wrote one critic, "is crowded with young enthusiasts, who never "presume to argue, except against the propriety of arguing "at all." Newman preserves interesting traces of the influence of the *Tracts for the Times*. Another critic wrote: "The spread of these doctrines is in fact now "having the effect of rendering all other distinctions "obsolete, and of severing the religious community into "two portions, fundamentally and vehemently opposed "one to the other." Yet another wrote of them: "One "of the largest churches in Brighton is crowded to hear "them; so is the church at Leeds. There are few towns "of note to which they have not extended. They are "preached in small towns in Scotland. They have even "insinuated themselves into the House of Commons." And at length a bishop declared in a charge that the movement "is daily assuming a more serious and alarming "aspect. Under the specious pretence of deference to "antiquity and respect for primitive models, the founda- "tions of the Protestant Church are undermined by men "who dwell within her walls, and those who sit in the "Reformers' seat are traducing the Reformation."[1]

This last note gives us the key to the whole later history of the movement, ostensible and occult. That it led to Rome, not only logically but emotionally, is Newman's own teaching; and a certain number of his immediate adherents and friends followed him thither. Yet it is the historic fact that the vast majority of those who followed the Tractarian lead in petitioning against all encroach- ments on the property and status of the Church, remained where they were; and that whatever intellectual impres- sion may have been made by Newman's reasonings, the Church of England is to-day more fully manned than

[1] *Apologia*, pp. 95-96.

ever, without a single alteration in her formulas. To a certain extent the reaction was even recruited by Whigs. Sydney Smith has told how in 1839, when Liberalism had become "a lucrative business", with "the Tories on the "treadmill and the well-paid Whigs riding in chariots", he found himself, to his "utter and never-ending astonishment", fighting "against the Archbishop of Canterbury "and the Bishop of London, for the existence of the "National Church".[1] The clerical upheaval, in fact, was a matter of corporate interest. The High Church party is doubtless the outcome of the Tractarian movement; but the High Church remains Anglican; only a few devotees passing over to Rome. Wheresoever the carcase is. . . . . Here we come back as always to the old truth; the main forces in the making and unmaking of Churches—which in turn maintain religions—are those of personal and pecuniary interest, not at all those of intellectual conviction. The Tractarian movement was strong as such when it was voicing the class interest and class prejudice of the Anglican priesthood. When its leaders went where their drift of emotion and theology led them, leaving behind the fleshpots, their movement as such was at an end. The mass of the priesthood saw clearly enough that, though they might repel political Liberalism in the name of "the honour of God", they could not do it in name of "the Catholic Church". Any overt declaration of allegiance to Rome *within* tha Anglican Church would mean expulsion; any general attempt at denial of the State's authority by the clergy, in terms of anti-Reformation principles, would certainly lead to Disestablishment. Liberalism was and is quite strong enough for that. So the Church remains as she was; and will so remain until haply the sacerdotal party miscalculate their strength.

And this might very well be the answer of Anglicans to Newman, as regards his pleas that only the Catholic

[1] Preface to *Works*, end.

Church is capable of resisting the spread of Atheism, and that an Infallible Church is a very natural and suitable instrument for the Deity to frame to that end. The latter is a Butlerian argument, and as such is quite valid for a Catholic; but it can equally well be adapted to Anglicanism. As thus: Wherever there is a good endowment, priests will be forthcoming; and where some hold of religion on the public mind is necessary to the maintenance of endowments, the clergy may be trusted to work pretty diligently to spread their creed. This holds good alike of the Establishment and of Dissent in England. The success and practicality of the English methods, then, may be taken as a fairly good certificate of *their* divine origin. On the other hand, the claim for the Catholic Church breaks down *a posteriori*. It does *not* prevent the spread of Atheism. There is more Atheism in France and Italy than in England: in Italy and France, unbelief is normal among educated men; while in England the Church has still a very fair educated following. It is quite true that the Anglican Church is honeycombed by the " Higher Criticism ", and that many of the clergy are Agnostics; while in the Catholic Church here it may still be true that it is as orthodox as when Newman wrote: " Now that I have been in the Church " nineteen years, I cannot hear of a single instance in " England of an infidel priest".[1] But the " in England " is significant. We know there are infidel priests in Italy and France; and that in the past there have been thousands of them. In England, naturally, a sceptical Catholic priest either enters the Church of England, where he has so much more freedom, or becomes a layman, in which case he has more still, without any of the odium that attaches to an ex-priest in Catholic countries.

As regards the Bible (we may imagine a prudent Anglican to go on) is it not Cardinal Newman himself who has said that it " cannot make a stand against the

[1] *Apologia*, p. 271.

"wild living intellect of man"[1]—that is to say, that even the Pope has to lay less stress on the Bible than on the Church's authority and practice? Why then may not the Anglican Church do the same, making its position morally strong by admitting the imperfections of the Sacred Books, while eloquently insisting on their value as interpreted and modified by the general judgment of the National Church?

No: decidedly there is no form of the Butlerian argument that will suffice to countervail an endowment of seven millions per annum. Of course if a man wants, as Newman avowedly did, "a fulcrum whereby to keep the "earth from moving onwards",[2] he will not find it in the Anglican Establishment. But neither will he find it in the Papacy; and the Church of England may claim to be about as efficient a preventive of intellectual progress as could be got anywhere for the money. Atheism will never carry all before it while Theism and Polytheism have such a rich source of income. On that principle the Church may repose with Christian confidence, if not *a priori* then *a posteriori*, on a retrospect of her history for the past sixty years, in which time she has maintained her creed intact in despite of Agnostics and Arians within as well as of Catholics and critics without. We have only to note the sequel of that "Liberal" movement which Newman so hated and feared, in order to see that he underestimated the power of the defence, by reason of his own undue spirituality.

This explanation may be held to without implying that Newman was the paragon of intellectual sincerity which even some non-Catholics hold him to have been. Certainly he stood out well enough as against Kingsley; because even where Kingsley was right in their debate, as when he charged Newman with putting married life lower than celibate, he was himself as inconsistent as he accused Newman of being, since the glorification of

[1] *Id.*, p. 245. [2] *Id.*, p. 244.

virginity is explicit in the Apocalypse, to say nothing of the teaching of Paul; and Kingsley ought on his own showing to have repudiated the canonical text itself. Kingsley was indeed the very type of sentimental incoherence in religion. But Newman on the other hand is hardly the type of scrupulous consistency in mental processes. As Dean Church has put it: " The charm of the "*Apologia* is the perfect candour with which he records " fluctuations which to many are inconceivable and unintel- " ligible, the different and sometimes opposite and irre- " concilable states of mind through which he passed, with " no attempt to make one fit into another ".[1] Perhaps he is seen to most advantage in the comparison of his career with that of the common run of prelates of his adopted church, or in particular with that of the contemporary Cardinal whose name divided with his the homage of English Catholics. The dynamics of religion are to be studied to as much advantage in the Catholic Church as in the Protestant; and when we learn that Cardinal Manning was all along ecclesiastically opposed to Newman because he did not think him "a true Catholic", we know all that is needed to correct Newman's own estimate of the single-mindedness of the Catholic clergy. In the Catholic Church as elsewhere the self-surrendering man is overridden by the ambitious, the sincere man by the schemer; and the measure meted out to the first by the second, in the case under notice, may suffice to disabuse us of any false idea of the matter set up by Newman's transfiguring tale.

As the true criticism of dogma, in Strauss's phrase, is its history, so the true criticism of Newman's *Apologia*, taken as a guide to actual Catholicsm, is, to be found in the Life of Manning. It is part of the tragi-comedy of modern Catholicism that Newman, who gave up power and leadership to enter its fold, was there accused of heresy, treason, and "worldliness". The Bishop of

---

[1] Work cited, p. 281.

Newport delated him at Rome for heresy in respect of his article in the *Rambler* on consulting the laity in the matter of faith; his former friend Ward accused him of "disloyalty to the Vicar of Christ, and worldliness"; Manning echoed the charge of "worldliness" on the score of his being "cold and silent on the Temporal "Power"; and Monsignor Talbot, furious at the suggestion about consulting the laity, declared that "Dr. "Newman is the most dangerous man in England".[1] Thus the very unworldliness of the really religious man was imputed to him as a criminal worldliness by his truly worldly co-believers, whose highest concern was the maintenance of that temporal power which would have been their own if they had realised their ambition. From which we learn that temporal power plays some such part in the Church of Rome, where so few can now enjoy wealth, as wealth does in the Church of England, whose power, apart from that of self defence, is too diffused to be used with any consciousness of mastery by any one man. It is reassuring to remember how Manning broke his aged teeth over the question of the admission of Atheists to Parliament. And if anything be needed to protect us from the risk of Catholic influence being wielded among us in the future as Manning sought to wield it in the past, the wide circulation of the copious and candid biography by Mr. Purcell will probably suffice. It is the hardest blow ever struck at the Catholic reaction in England.

[1] Purcell's *Life of Cardinal Manning*, vol. ii, pp. 317, 318, 323-4.

CHAPTER IV.

UNBELIEF WITHIN THE CHURCH.

THE generalisation of Mark Pattison, already discussed, to the effect that the method or movement of rationalistic orthodoxy came to an end with the rise of the Tractarian movement, cannot in any way be reconciled with the facts of English Church history since his essay was published, whether or not it may seem to hold good of the period between 1830 and 1860. It is true that the method of Milman, which was in the direct line of descent from the apologetics of the previous century, was allowed to lapse, as we have seen, because it was found to be dangerously provocative, and that the methods of Strauss and Baur, for still more obvious reasons, were never adopted within the Church at all. But just when the Church had seemed to have settled down in its divided state of Broad and High, neither party avowing, or perhaps seeing, the final bearing of its principles, there arose a twofold trouble which forced on the former a future of more or less modest rationalism within the limits set up by Church law; and, as a matter of fact, a species of rationalistic religion has never been wanting in the Church since the *Essays and Reviews* and the case of Bishop Colenso.

The publication of the *Essays and Reviews* (1860) forms an epoch in English Church history, in respect not only of their avowal of a more or less far-reaching departure from past orthodoxy, but of the resulting legal definition of the freedom allowed to clerical heresy. It was in many ways fortunate that the volume was prosecuted. Dean Stanley has told how the article of some rationalist in the *Westminster Review*, pointing out the critical effect of the Essays, and calling on the essayists, as honest men, to leave the Church and turn Comtists, awoke the orthodox to the situation; and how the outcry of the latter, in turn, made the book at once famous throughout the world. From a sale of 3,000 it seems to have passed in a few months to 13,000; and within a few years that was probably doubled. This was all perfectly natural; and Stanley's lamentation over the process has the touch of fatuity which belonged to his dream of making intellectual revolutions with rosewater and causing the Church to become rational without its own knowledge. If faith was ever to grapple with reason, this was the time. A posse of seven pietists was got together[1] to answer one by one the seven essayists—currently labelled the "Seven Cham- "pions not of Christendom" and the "Septem contra "Christum"—and the evangelical Bishop Wilberforce, son of the philanthropist, contributed a preface calling for "the distinct, solemn, and if need be severe, decision of "authority that such assertions as these [of the original "essayists] cannot be put forward as possibly true, or "even advanced as admitting of question, by honest men "who are bound by voluntary obligations to teach the "Christian revelation as the truth of God. I put this "necessity first," the voluble Bishop went on, "from the "full conviction that if such matters are admitted by us "to be open questions amongst men under such obliga- "tions, we shall leave to the next generation the fatal "legacy of an universal scepticism, amidst an undis- "tinguishable confusion of all possible landmarks be- "tween truth and falsehood." It was all much truer than could reasonably have been expected. The attempt to exercise "authority" against two of the more aggressive of the heretics broke down utterly; and things have to a large extent gone since as Bishop Wilberforce feared.

The gist of this volume, so influential both directly and indirectly, may be worth stating summarily. It

[1] *Replies to "Essays and Reviews,"* 1862.

opened with an essay—first drawn up as a university sermon—on *The Education of the World*, by Dr. Temple, then headmaster of Rugby, afterwards Bishop of London, and now Archbishop of Canterbury. The doctrine of this is to the effect that historic mankind may be conceived as a "colossal man", who has passed through childhood and youth into manhood; that in each stage he has had his appropriate religious regimen—the Jewish law for childhood, the Example of Christ for youth, and the indwelling Life of the Spirit for manhood. A semblance of universality is given to the theory (already conventional) by crediting the Greeks and Romans with contributions to human development; but the main formula is thus adapted to the simple Christian philosophy of things. It is symmetrically fallacious and neatly false, and was so fitted to lead the semi-enlightened believer by an easy inclined plane from an absolute to a modified Scripturalism; Dr. Temple's reassuring conclusion being that "the Bible "from its very form is exactly adapted to our present "want", that want being a free hand with the Bible's contents. For the rest, the essayist is himself comfortingly Conservative, exhibiting an untroubled faith in the accuracy of the historical and biographical parts of Genesis, including the stories of Lamech and the Tower of Babel. To Dr. Temple, it would seem, Colenso must have been as much of a shock as he was to the average curate. On the other hand, the troublous aspect of this essay was that the age of the Founder was somewhat invidiously made out to be inferior to the present, as youth to manhood; and the law was handled a good deal in the manner of Uzziah.

Next came Professor Rowland Williams' review of Bunsen's Biblical Researches, a study making very short work of the "prophecies", the continued defence of which he hinted to be mere sophistry; and of some parts of the Canon, the Book of Daniel for instance, as indisputably spurious. Dr. Williams' procedure was what Newman would have called "blistering". Compared to the exegesis of English orthodoxy, he declared, "even the Conservatism of Jahn among Romanists, and " Hengstenberg among Protestants, is free and rational". In one of his footnotes too there is a passage on Mansel which is still worth quoting :—

" Mr. Mansel's *Bampton Lectures* must make even those
" who value his argument, regret that to his acknow-
" ledged dialectical ability he has not added the rudiments
" of Biblical criticism. In all his volume not one text
" of Scripture is elucidated, nor a single difficulty in the
" evidences of Christianty removed. Recognised mis-
" translations and misreadings are alleged as arguments,
" and passages from the Old Testament are employed
" without reference to the illustration or inversion which
" they have received in the New. Hence, as the eristic
" arts of logic without knowledge of the subject-matter
" become powerless, the author is a mere gladiator
" hitting in the dark, and his blows fall heaviest on what
" it was his duty to defend. As to his main argument
" (surely a strange parody of Butler), the sentence from
" Sir W. Hamilton, prefixed to the volume, seems to me
" its gem [? germ] and its confutation. Of the
" *reasoning*, which would bias our interpretation of Isaiah
" by telling us Feuerbach was an Atheist, I need not say
" a word."[1]

A writer who hit out like this, imputing an uncritical orthodoxy even to the one philosopher of the Church, whose metaphysics had even seemed a trifle heathenish to some of the faithful, naturally awoke a special indignation, and was promptly marked for prosecution. Professor Baden Powell, the Savilian Professor of Geometry at Oxford, author of the essay *On the Study of the Evidences of Christianity*, would in all probability have met the same treatment had he not died soon after the issue of the book. Despite a preliminary safeguarding clause, in the usual manner, as to "the *essential doctrines* of

[1] *Essays and Reviews*, 9th edit., p. 67.

"Christianity, 'the same yesterday, to-day, and for "'ever,'" the whole drift of the essay is so dead against the acceptance of the miraculous element in the Gospels, so directly hostile to all the received apologetics, even the latest and most ingenious, that it may be reckoned the most drastic treatise in the bundle. It upset even the admired *Historic Doubts* of Whately by the unexpected retort that "these delightful parodies on Scripture, if they prove any-"thing, would simply prove that the Biblical narrative is "no more properly *miraculous* than the marvellous exploits "of Napoleon I, or the paradoxical events of recent "histories:'" and it fearlessly applauded "Mr. Darwin's "masterly volume on *The Origin of Species* by the law of "'natural selection', which now substantiates on un-"deniable grounds the very principle so long denounced "by the first naturalists, *the origination of new species by* "*natural causes;* a work which must soon bring about an "entire revolution of opinion in favour of the grand "principle of the self-evolving powers of nature".[2] Finally, it laid down as to miracles the decisively rationalistic maxim: "Testimony, after all, is but a "second-hand assurance; it is but a blind guide; testi-"mony can avail nothing against reason".[3]

Professor Powell being past prosecution, the orthodox party characteristically selected, as its second victim, Mr. H. B. Wilson, the author of the essay on *The National Church*, a review of the *Séances Historiques de Génève*, by Comte de Gasparin, Bungener, and others of the moderate Swiss rationalistic school. Whether the exasperating element in the treatise was its hostility to Scripturalism, and its hardy allusion to "the dark "patches of human passion and error which form a "partial crust" upon the Bible, or its attack on the very principle of creed acceptance, certain it is that it aroused boundless wrath in comparison with the remaining essays. These were: Mr. C. W. Goodwin's *On the*

[1] Vol. cited, p. 138. [2] P. 139. [3] P. 141.

Mosaic Cosmogony; Mark Pattison's, above mentioned, on the *Tendencies of Religious Thought in England* from 1688 to 1830: and Professor Jowett's *On the Interpretation of Scripture*. The first was a merciless rebuttal of all the devices employed to reconcile the first chapter of Genesis with geology; but its position was far too strong even on the traditional side to allow of its being impeached, since even some early Fathers, in the days before Pagan science had wholly lapsed from Christian hands, had taken the Biblical tale as a kind of allegory. Pattison in turn has not a few rasping passages, such as the remark that "in "the present day . . . a godless orthodoxy threatens, as " in the fifteenth century, to extinguish religious thought "altogether; and nothing is allowed in the Church of " England but the formulæ of past thinkings, which have "long lost all sense of any kind";[1] and the verdict that while the evidential school had succeeded in vindicating the ethical part of Christianity—a saying implicitly unsaid elsewhere in the essay—it had failed to establish "the supernatural and speculative part".[2] But with all this there was so much profession of standing at a more truly theological point of view than that of the apologists, so much aftershine of the Tractarian movement of the essayist's youth, that it was not deemed wise to impeach him; and the long essay of Jowett in its turn was so characteristically circuitous and guarded as to be ill-suited for indictment, though some of its sayings cut deep enough. Perhaps nobody has more comprehensively called in question the pretensions of the Church than he did in the sentence: "The theologian, too, may have "peace in the thought, that he is subject to the con-"ditions of his age rather than one of its moving "powers".[3] But in these as in other matters it is not so much the spirit as the letter that "killeth", and Jowett was judiciously general.

Taken as a whole, however, the book can still be

[1] P. 297. [2] *Id. ib.* [3] P. 422.

recognised as the most startling event that had yet occurred in the history of popular English religious opinion. For half a century, Churchmen had been affecting to regard "infidelity" as intellectually discredited. Rose, who only thirty years before had declared it to lack any considerable living expositor in England, was alive to help to denounce the new outbreak; and here in an instant came a powerful and comprehensive utterance of all manner of unbelief from seven accomplished churchmen, all standing high for character no less than for ability. Darwin's book had been out only two years; and here already it was emphatically endorsed by a Professor of Geometry, theologically trained. The roundabout rationalism of Milman was brushed aside by explicit negations of the common belief; the Bible was handled, not merely "like any other book", but in some respects on a more unsparing method than men had yet agreed to apply to Homer. Only the profession of churchmanship distinguished the essayists from the Deists of the last century; and nearly all that the Deists had contended for was here taken as not merely arguable but established and done with. If Strauss and Baur were not avowedly accepted, their method was implied; and the popular unbelief set up by Paine was here endorsed by a body of university dons. The brief period of triumphant orthodoxy, in short, was at an end. Rationalism was seated in the very citadel of the Church.

The episcopally edited set of answers merely made the case clearer, expressing as they did only the anger and the incompetence of the orthodox party. On the general public they made practically no impression: and to the studious reader to-day they would be pathetic, were it not for their pervading spite; for they freshly and fully illustrate the important psychological fact that the most zealous champions of the "religion of love" in any of its stages are almost sure to be themselves acrimonious and malevolent, incapable of debating without spleen, and immeasurably further from loving their enemies than are their enemies from feeling amicably towards them. Of the seven answers, not one is so much as impressive in its tone. The best of the clerical answers to the Deists of the previous century had been the work of men who recognised the difficulties of the orthodox case, and were serene in virtue of their readiness to modify it. But such types were no longer on the orthodox side; and their successors showed the tempers of men consciously cornered.

Nor was the legal crusade any more successful. The prosecution was got up by the Bishop of Salisbury and a country clergyman against the wish of a "large majority "of the Episcopal Bench". In the Court of Arches,[1] Dr. Lushington, following the previous judgment in the case of Mr. Gorham (who in 1847 had been kept out of a living by his bishop for his views on Baptismal Regeneration, and lost his case in the Court of Arches, but won on appeal to the Judicial Committee of the Privy Council), proceeded to quash twenty-seven out of thirty-two charges against Messrs. Williams and Wilson, and let them off with the penalty of a year's suspension. They however appealed as Mr. Gorham had done to the Judicial Committee of the Privy Council; and though the two archbishops, who were members, were avowedly hostile to the doctrines of the appellants, judgment was ultimately given in their favour on all points, the archbishops "partially" assenting. The orthodox revenged themselves as best they could. Dr. Pusey, who in his own youth had been "for three years suspended by the 'Six Doctors "'of Oxford' from preaching", because of his having contravened the Articles in regard to the Eucharist, now wrote to the *Record* (a journal strongly opposed to his party) calling for united action against the "recent miser- "able, soul-destroying judgment". An Oxford Committee drew up a Declaration affirming belief in everlasting

[1] On June 25, 1862.

punishment and plenary inspiration (the two points felt by the framers to be most vital), and sent it to all the clergy of the Establishment, adjuring them to sign it "for "the love of God."¹ While some eleven thousand clergymen signed, however, as many more refused, among them two-thirds of the clergy of London ; and among the supporters were only eight of the thirty English deans, only nine of the Oxford professors, and only one at Cambridge; and only four out of the twenty-eight bishops countenanced its formal reception at Lambeth.

Thus triumphantly did the event bear out the opinion confidently expressed by Dean Stanley in the *Edinburgh Review* before the hearing of the case, an opinion in itself significant of extraordinary developments within the Church : " The questions raised by the Essayists, with " very few exceptions, are of a kind altogether beside and " beyond the range over which the Formularies extend. " It would almost seem as if, providentially, the con- " fession of most Protestant—indeed, we may say, of most " Christian—Churches, had been drawn up at a time when, " public and ecclesiastical attention being fixed on other " matters, the doors had been left wide open to the " questions which a later and critical age was sure to " raise into high importance. In spite of all the declara- " tions on the subject, no passage has ever yet been " pointed out in any of the five clerical Essayists which " contradicts any of the Formularies of the Church in a " degree at all comparable to the direct collision which " exists between the High Church Party and the Articles, " and between the Low Church Party and the Prayer- " book. . . . . On the questions now debated, Articles " and Prayer-book are alike silent."² Stanley of course censured the book in a qualified way, repeating the conventional complaint against "negative teaching", and deploring the combination of the seven essays in one volume; though in point of fact their publication as

¹ Stanley, *Essays on Questions of Church and State*, ed. 1884, p. 80.
² *Essays*, as cited, p. 62.

seven separate books or pamphlets would have made a far stronger impression of heretical strength. But all the while he rejoiced in the legal decision as much as the other side raged. And from his point of view the gain to the Church was great, for a reason which he does not specially mention. During twenty years there had been a steady falling away, not only in the quality but even in the quantity of spontaneous candidates for Holy Orders. The figures are extremely instructive, especially when we remember that Strauss's *Leben Jesu* had been published in 1835 (English translation, 1846); Blanco White's *Observations on Heresy and Orthodoxy* in the same year; C. C. Hennell's *Inquiry Concerning the Origin of Christianity* in 1838; Theodore Parker's *Discourse of the Transient and Permanent in Christianity* in 1841; his *Discourse of Matters pertaining to Religion* in 1842; F. W. Newman's *Phases of Faith* and W. R. Greg's *Creed of Christendom* in 1851; R. W. Mackay's *Sketch of the Rise and Progress of Christianity* in 1854, and so on. A list drawn up by Bishop Sumner shows that, whereas in 1841 there were 242 clerical candidates at Oxford, and 270 at Cambridge, the respective numbers in 1851 were only 215 and 222 respectively: while in 1861 they had sunk to 159 and 219. To meet this falling-off, the Church had been forced to beat up an inferior class of candidates, trained in its own colleges, so that, whereas in 1841 there were only 38 of these "literates" in all, in 1861 there were 241.[1] Evidently the spread of rational criticism was keeping out of the Church many young men even of the not very high calibre of those who had recruited it in the past. Colenso put it that "the great body of the more "intelligent students of our universities no longer come "forward to devote themselves to the service of the "Church, but are drafted off into other professions".[2] In these circumstances, the irreversible legal decision that

[1] See the figures cited by Colenso, *The Pentateuch*, vol. ii, 1863, pref. pp. x, xi.
[2] Vol. i, pref. p. xxiii.

a clergyman not only need not believe in the accepted creed but need not fear to disown it, was something of a turning-point in the Church's development.

It must have seemed, finally, to many pious spirits, as if "the powers of hell" were marching on the gates of the Church when, on the heels of *Essays and Reviews*, came the first volume (1862) of Bishop Colenso's *Pentateuch and Book of Joshua Critically Examined*. The sensation created by that eclipsed even the excitement over the seven essays. Compared with these, the bishop's first volume was as the opening of a methodical bombardment after a flying assault. No anti-theological work on such a scale had yet appeared in England; and whereas the essays had been to a large extent academic in key and even a little dilettantist, the bishop was openly undertaking to bring home to the mass of his countrymen, in the fullest detail, the historical falsehood of the Pentateuchal narrative, in which they were all held to be interested. Finally, he, a bishop, was doing thus methodically and earnestly what Paine had been supposed to have attempted in vain, two generations before, and what Voltaire had tried to do still earlier. A bishop had "refuted" Paine; and the French "scoffer" had been held discredited even in his own country. Wherever there were Bible-readers well enough read to know these things, Colenso's name became a portent. It is so indeed still; for his work is more or less well known in quarters where later names in Biblical criticism are barely heard of.

It is somewhat difficult to gather from Sir George Cox's admirably comprehensive Life of his friend a quite clear idea of the course of Colenso's religious development; but it is perfectly clear that his was one of the most transparently sincere characters ever seen in any Church. He went out to Natal filled with an enthusiastic zeal for missionary work; and he did work devotedly, with the result of winning native affection in an unheard-of degree. But soon he found himself embroiled with fellow-churchmen, first with a High-Church Dean, and later with the High-Church Bishop of Capetown, his ecclesiastical superior, on points concerning the meaning of the Eucharist and the proper way of putting to natives the Christian doctrine of blood redemption. A follower of Maurice, the perplexed disciple of the kaleidoscopic Coleridge, he held by the new Broad Church view, or tendency of feeling, which reduced the primeval ritual to a kind of dramatic symbol, standing for no special historic fact and no distinct dogma. This notable concession to rational morals, in the name of which unbelievers had attacked the doctrine of the Atonement for two hundred years, brought upon Maurice the vehement hostility of the faithful; but Colenso was too simply conscientious a man to alter his attitude on that account. He was indeed the most straightforward soul in the Church of England in his day; and by far the most disinterested of its bishops. Stanley's panegyric, delivered before a furious meeting of the Society for the Propagation of the Gospel, at a time when Colenso was "absent, friendless, unpopular," and "attacked by every epithet which the English language "has been able to furnish," is likely to live. "The "Bishop of Natal is the one Colonial Bishop who has "translated the Bible into the language of the natives of "of his diocese. He is the one Colonial Bishop who, "when he believed a native to be wronged, journeyed to "London, and never rested until he had procured the "reversal of that wrong. He is the one Colonial Bishop "who, as soon as he had done this, returned immediately "to his diocese and his work. For this act he has never "received any praise, any encouragement, from this the "oldest of our Missionary Societies. For these deeds he "will be remembered when you who censure him are "dead, buried, and forgotten."[1] It is said that the concluding words were spoken with a sudden energy of voice and gesture very unusual in the amiable speaker.

[1] *Recollections of Arthur Penrhyn Stanley*, by Dean Bradley, 1883, p. 110.

The story of the bishop's introduction to rational Biblical criticism by the doubts and moral scruples of some of his Zulu converts is well known.[1] That it needed such a lead to make such a man, after the year 1850, begin to open his eyes to the character of a large part of his sacred books, is an eminent proof of the power of early religious teaching and clerical training to benumb even a good intelligence. As he has told, he had in his youth met with some of the "ordinary objections", but had contented himself with "the specious explanations" "which are given in most commentaries". This becomes the more intelligible when we learn from Kuenen that even among professional specialists like himself, occupied in discriminating the documentary sources of the text, the central and decisive incredibility of the narrative was actually unobserved, though it had been dwelt upon both by Voltaire and by Reimarus. It was only when they read Colenso that they realised once for all that "the "exodus, the wandering, the passage of the Jordan, and "the settlement in Canaan, as they are described in the "Hexateuch, simply *could not have happened*".[2] This fact, so plain to any reader not hypnotised by tradition, was actually "in danger of gradually falling into oblivion"[3] through the hebetude of the documentary experts. When, therefore, hostile churchmen averred, among other things, that Colenso in his First Part merely repeated familiar objections, they were not only irrelevant but disingenuous. The First Part, though the most popular, remained, in Kuenen's opinion, the most important and durable of all. The four following parts, which the critics pronounced more scholarly, did but "build upon foundations already "laid", working out and confirming "what was pretty "generally admitted before he wrote. No new light is "struck, no new direction given to research in these "volumes. But it is far otherwise with Part I. Con-

---

[1] *Pentateuch*, vol. i, pref., p. vii; introd., p. 9.
[2] *Origin and Composition of the Hexateuch*, Wicksteed's trans., p. 43.
[3] *Id.*, p. 45.

"tinental criticism of the Pentateuch had been incon-
"siderately busying itself with a constructive work that
"*used these very materials now so rudely tested by Colenso.*
"For myself," adds Kuenen, "I gladly admit that he
"directed my attention to difficulties which I had hitherto
"failed to observe or adequately to reckon with. And as
"to the opinion of his labours current in Germany, I need
"only say that inasmuch as Ewald, Bunsen, Bleek and
"Knobel were every one of them logically forced—if they
"could but have seen it—to revise their theories in the
"light of the English Bishop's researches, there was small
"reason in the cry that his methods were antiquated and
"his objections stale." So that it was in virtue of his determination to make clear to the laity what the scholars were supposed to know, that Colenso put the scholars right, and made his main contribution to Biblical criticism. The record may serve, perhaps, to modify the conviction so common among our quietists, that honesty is never the best policy in the intellectual life.

Certainly honesty was the prime force in Colenso's character. He had closely studied the subject for a little over a year when he began the publication of his book. The life of professional dissimulation lived by thousands of his fellow clerics was for him impossible. "I assert with
"out fear of contradiction," he writes in the Preface to his second volume,[1] "that there are multitudes of the more
"intelligent clergy who do *not* believe in the reality of
"the Noachian Deluge, as described in the book of
"Genesis. Yet did ever a layman hear his clergyman
"speak out distinctly what he thought, and say plainly
"from the pulpit what he himself believed, and what he
"would have them to believe, on this point? Did ever a
"*Doctor* or *Bishop* of the Church do this—at least in the
"present day? I doubt not that some cases may be
"found. .... But I appeal to the laity, generally,
"with confidence. Have you ever heard your Minister—

[1] P. xxvii.

"able, earnest, excellent as you know him to be—tell out plainly to his people the truth which he knows himself about these things? Or . . . . has he ever told these things to you in private? Have not your Clergy *kept back* from you their thoughts hitherto . . . . about a multitude of matters such as those treated of in Part I of this book—which yet, as my adverse Reviewers say almost with one voice, have been all along perfectly familiar to all respectable students of theology?"

Such plain speaking, of course, increased the fury of the orthodox outcry, and nettled the less orthodox at whom it pointed. The appeal in the case of the *Essays and Reviews* not having been yet settled, no immediate action could be taken in England; but in Capetown there was got up an ecclesiastical trial "the outcome of a "plan deeply laid, not by Bishop Gray alone, but by "Bishop Wilberforce and his colleagues in England,"[1] on the score of heresy contained in Colenso's *Commentary on the Epistle to the Romans*, published there in 1861. The offences charged were false doctrines on the forever debated because forever irrational themes of the Blood Sacrifice, justification, sacraments, eternal punishment, textual inspiration, the authenticity of the Pentateuch, and the authority of bishops and the Book of Common Prayer. For these manifold errors he was formally sentenced by the Bishop of Capetown, once his intimate personal friend, to be deposed from his office of bishop. But the sentence was illegal and invalid; and soon the decision on the appeal of Messrs. Wilson and Williams settled that for him as for them there was no possible ecclesiastical punishment. The book was condemned in Convocation, where Bishop Wilberforce expressed his gratified belief that there were many present who had not read the book;[2] but the sentence counted legally for nothing. So Colenso went back to Natal in 1865, after a stay of three or four years in England,

---

[1] Sir George W. Cox, *Life of Bishop Colenso*, 1888, vol. i, p. 280.
[2] *Life*, vol. i, p. 477.

during which he had published his five volumes on the Hexateuch; and despite efforts to excommunicate, to starve, and to fetter him, including, he tells, some of "the "most deliberate theological lying that I have ever met "with",[1] he went on with his work as before, drawing to his sermons many who formerly went to no church, but above all fighting a long and noble battle, ending only with his life, for the natives, against the iniquitous rapacity of his fellow Christians. He made practically no further progress in his thinking, remaining to the end an unphilosophical Deist, and an undogmatic Christist. "Theologians," he wrote, "may dispute—as perhaps "they must—on the history of the Resurrection; critics "may do their work for the God of Truth in sifting its "details. But nothing can touch the spiritual fact that "He, who died upon the cross, now liveth—that He who "died unto sin once, now liveth eternally to God. "For us, Christians, the name of Christ is exalted, as a "living power, over all the earth; for us His Cross is the "emblem of the victory of love, of patience, of faith- "fulness, through suffering."[2] In fine, he could not carry on, as regards the New Testament and his primary theological assumptions, the kind of critical process he had brought to bear on the Old.

At this point, all the elements in the modern conflict between reason and traditional religion may be seen to be fully defined. The State Church had been legally declared to be a corporation within which, while the Bible is unquestionably the basis of all its religious teaching, any member may criticise the text and teaching of the Bible to any extent; and in actual fact the criticism had been so carried to a length which, for consistent people, meant the quashing of the claim of supernatural authority for the book, either in whole or in part. This must be assumed not only to have given a relief to many within the Church, but to have attracted

[1] *Life*, vol. ii, p. 39.
[2] *Natal Sermons*, vol. ii, p. 120, cited in the *Life*.

to the priesthood a certain number who would otherwise have remained laymen. And the freedom was soon further defined by a legislative alteration in the formula of subscription. Under the old Act of Uniformity[1] those who entered Holy Orders had to declare "unfeigned as-"sent and consent to all and everything contained and "prescribed in and by" the Book of Common Prayer. By an Act passed in 1865, on the pressure of the liberalising party in the Church, there was substituted the following form: "I assent to the Thirty-Nine Articles "of Religion and to the Book of Common Prayer and of "the Ordaining of Bishops, Priests, and Deacons. I "believe the Doctrine of the United Church of England "and Ireland as therein set forth to be agreeable to the "Word of God; and in Public Prayer and Adminis-"tration of the Sacraments I will use the form in the "said book prescribed and none other, except so far as "shall be ordered by lawful authority."[2]

Thus the one thing now clearly laid down is adherence to use and wont in the prayers and sacraments and discipline of the Church, nothing being fixed as to the beliefs to be held concerning them. For the formula "I "assent" is implicitly admitted to mean less than "un-"feigned assent and consent to all and everything" in the Articles; it is indeed impossible to evade the inference that it is meant to invite or permit a feigned assent. We have here one of the clearest of the countless proofs that the Church is doomed by its very nature to palter with truth. It cannot, it dare not, draw up a straightforward confession of faith or unfaith. The multitude of the superstitious imposes on the rest a disguising of their opinions; they can be relieved only by making their declaration of belief equivocal. All the while the ceremonial forms of antiquity are strictly insisted on. There is thus no limit to dissimulation in practice. Views of Christianity which were unimaginable

[1] 13 Car. II. c. iv, § 9. 1662.
[2] Act 28 and 29 Vict., c. 122.

to the framers of the Thirty-Nine Articles may be vended by men who nominally "assent" to these Articles, since they do not straightforwardly and explicitly contradict them. On the principles legally laid down in the case of *Essays and Reviews*, it might even be technically quite safe to preach Atheism, under the form either of a consistent Pantheism, which is logically and practically the same thing, or of Mr. Arnold's formula of "something not "ourselves which makes for righteousness". True, the First Article affirms the Trinity, and ascribes "goodness" to infinitude; but then it describes the deity as "without body, parts, or *passions*," and it thus permits of an absolutely impersonal conception, though other Articles contradict that.

It is impossible that this state of things should fail to raise chronic question among clergy and laity as to the honesty of many of the former. The question, indeed, is not a simple one, either in theory or in practice. Colenso was one of the sincerest of men; and he was confident that he did right to stay in the Church. On the other hand, many of the orthodox Churchmen who so loudly called on him to withdraw, were themselves, on other grounds, technically more disobedient to Church discipline than he; and that is the position of thousands of priests at this moment. In the words of Dean Stanley:—
"The Ritualists as a body are what they have been truly
"called, 'Nonconformists within the Church of England'.
"They introduce practices into its worship which con-
"fessedly have not been in use since the time of Elizabeth.
"They desire to substitute for it, as far as the outward
"forms, gestures, dresses, teaching, suppressions, inter-
"polations will allow, the worship of another Church.
"They speak with the utmost disparagement of the
"Articles. They explain away the meaning of many of
"them to such a point as to reduce them to an absolute
"nullity. They set aside the authority of bishops almost
"as entirely as if they were Presbyterians or Indepen-
"dents. They abhor the union of Church and State, on

"which the whole of the existing constitution of the "Anglican Church is founded."[1]

There remains the argument of legal-minded laymen against both classes of priest alike: that those who join a church and take its pay ought in honesty to conform to its regulations, or else leave. And this argument is not wholly disposed of by Stanley's eloquent protest:—" It is "almost openly avowed (and we are sorry to see this ten- "dency as much amongst free-thinking laymen as amongst "fanatical clergymen) that Truth was made for the Laity "and Falsehood for the clergy—that Truth is tolerable "everywhere except in the mouths of the ministers of the "God of Truth—that Falsehood, driven from every other "quarter of the educated world, may find an honoured "refuge behind the consecrated bulwarks of the Sanc- "tuary. Against this Godless theory of a National "Church we solemnly protest. It is a theory tainted "with a far deeper unbelief than any that has ever "been charged against the Essayists and Reviewers . . . "As regards his own religious belief, the main question "for a clergyman to consider is whether he can sincerely "accept as a whole the constitution and the worship of "the Church of which he is a minister. Those to whom, "as a whole, it is repugnant, will spontaneously drop off "in one direction or another without any pressure from "without. Those to whom, as a whole, it commends it- "self as the best mode of serving God and their brethren, "will in spite of any lesser differences count it treason to "the Church and to its Divine Head to depart either "from its ministry or its communion."[2]

This has clearly the accent of conscientiousness and elevation; but as an argument it is obviously lax and insufficient. The position it repudiates does not set aside falsehood for the clergy. It rather prescribes for them a course of special sincerity—the withdrawal from a false position; and Stanley on his part would virtually put

---

[1] *Essays on Church and State*, edit. 1884, p. 226.
[2] *Essays*, as cited, p. 61.

them there. His reasoning is sophistical. What are we to understand exactly by "as a whole" and "repugnant"? And why set up the criterion of a belief as to "serving God" or even "brethren"? Stanley and his friends held that the majority have wrong notions as to sacrifice and redemption—two of the fundamental doctrines of historic Christianity; and they could not reasonably propose to exclude Socinians. But a Socinian with Colenso's views of the composition of the Bible would be simply a Deist of the last century type. Then if such a one could accept the constitution and worship of the Church "as a whole", why should he not go further and become an Atheist of Arnold's type, taking a literary satisfaction in the manipulation of the sacred books, and an æsthetic satisfaction in the ritual? He could on this footing make out, as Arnold did, that his adaptation of the old machinery was a serving of his "brethren"; but in view of the undisguised concern of so many quite orthodox priests in all ages for their own incomes, above the interests of either lay or clerical brethren, it seems invidious to demand professional altruism from the clerical Atheist alone.

It will be answered that such a position ought to be "repugnant" to an unbeliever; and so of course it should. But then it ought to have been repugnant to Stanley to stand by all manner of superstitious practices, to go through the form of prayer, and to treat as a fetish a collection of ancient books. And to many of the clergy, without doubt, some or all of these proceedings are repugnant. But on these proceedings their income depends, just as the incomes of thousands of men in business depend on proceedings which are more or less acutely repugnant to them; and the priest, like the layman, under the economic pressure too often sees no escape from his present way of life save into some course that is only repugnant with a difference, or into hardship without end. When it comes to this, it is hardly just to pass special blame on the inconsistent priest, save on the score that he makes special pretence to righteousness, posing as an ethical authority and a judge of human actions in general. And when, as sometimes happens, he makes as little pretence as possible, or not more than is made by men of the world, his is not quite such a censurable case as in the abstract it might be made to appear. Like the majority of other men, he is in the grip of a profoundly faulty social system; and his derelictions are to be classed with the innumerable deflections of other men from their ideals under stress of circumstances.

And there is yet another argument that the impartial sociologist must put on behalf of the half-believers and unbelievers in the Church. The question rises, To whom do the Church's endowments really belong? Rational politics gives only one answer: they belong to the nation. The claim of mere prescription, as urged by Protestants against Catholics, cannot avail against the title of the nation to do again what it did before. The claim of the Catholics, again, cannot avail against the verdict of modern ethics and modern politics, that the old endowments were in the first instance politically made, and that the Catholic Church, in its turn, obtained the inheritances of Paganism. We must come back to the ownership of the State. But then it is quite certain that the State to-day, were the matter open, would not re-endow the Church on the old footing, though the Church's vested interest may suffice to hold its own; and in any case it is morally clear that the majority have not the right to give public property for the propagation of one set of religious opinions against all others. This was admitted long ago by Liberals like Arnold, though they drew their theoretic line to exclude Jews and Rationalists. A Rationalist to-day could unanswerably argue that he has a right to a share in any national endowment of mere quasi-philosophical or ethical opinion; that his opinion is at least as well thought out as any; and that if ancient and irrational law attaches the endowment to certain abracadabral formulas and practices, the blame for his insincere conformity lies on those who maintain the unjust appropriation. The Ritualists practically reason and act on such lines.

It is thus clear that the problem is not to be set aside by a mere moral impeachment of any set or type of priests. There is no ethically accurate line of differentiation. Like all other sociological problems, this must be viewed in a larger light than that of the old instinctive primitive ethic, if we are to see it either scientifically or practically, either accurately or to useful purpose. The Church is no more to be discredited by an impeachment of individual Churchmen than private property is to be discredited by an impeachment of individual rich persons. But there *is* a sociological impeachment of the Church, and that had need be framed all the more stringently because the other is withdrawn.

In the light of the very considerations under view, then, the Church is an instrument of a twofold demoralisation, a " two-handed engine " of retrogression. Primarily, it is an endowed machinery for the preservation of worn-out beliefs and disproved dogmas, for the imposition of the dead hand of an ignorant past on the living present. To say nothing of its being deducible from the Christian gospels themselves, this truth is implied in the reasoning of all the men who have brought to the questions of religion any fresh thinking power whatever, be they Deists, Atheists, or Unitarians, of the school of Paine, or the school of Maurice, or the school of Arnold. It is impossible to overrate the historic hindrance thus put upon the greatest human interests by organised religion: no rhetoric can do the truth justice. Under the social and political system which permits the perpetual financial endowment of the Christian system, no religious or intellectual progress could have been made in antiquity at all. The Pagan systems, in so far as they were similarly endowed, would have subsisted as systems for ever, were it not for the various forms of political violence which subverted them. There is no grosser historic falsity than the pretence that Christianity triumphed by sheer superior attractiveness over those systems which confronted it. Throughout all Europe it obtained forcible possession of their endowments; in the case of the most primitive northern heathendom with which it came in contact, the power of king or chief or conqueror was employed to alter the course of existing revenues. Christian clericalism thus subsists among us, to the general detriment of our intellectual life, very much as many morbid organisms are maintained to the general detriment of our physical stamina, in virtue of the political civilisation which restricts all violence, public or individual, without providing scientific and humane preventives to do the work done of old by immoral violence and by destructive stress of environment.

That the systematic endowment of a body of traditional doctrine is a stumbling-block to true thought needs no proving. It is an organised violation of the first principles of intellectual progress. This holds true, of course, not merely of State Churches but of all. The State Church is an economic norm, on which Dissident Churches form themselves; and these strive for endowment only the more zealously because of their greater need. Thus the Catholic Church everywhere builds up wealth to perpetuate itself; and the separate Protestant Churches continually exhort their adherents to give and to bequeath. Wealth so amassed must be employed in the ways specified : it cannot be diverted. Even where the clergy are well disposed towards rational culture, they are coerced by their colleagues and their surroundings. And they themselves, however sympathetically we view their case, are doubly morbid elements in the social life, in so far as they are sceptical of the creed they are forced to preach. When we say that the dissembling priest is not a specially unveracious person, as men go, we must remember that the other unveracities of life are like his an outcome, for the most part, of economic pressure, varying in degree. When a social system is seen to multiply commercial fraud, we must count that a vice in the system; but we do not the less dislike the fraud. The dissembling priest gets very easy measure as compared with the swindler in commerce; but by any rational test he must in his degree be ranked as a social evil. Even such a one as Dean Stanley, with his gift for peace and peace-making as between the warring tribes of the clergy, wrought not a little for intellectual confusion and the jerrymandering of principles; and if he with his intellectual and educative bias had such an influence, the masses of more deeply doubting conformists in the Churches, for whom dissimulation is a rule of life, cannot fail to taint intellectual morals in all directions. If there is no country where intellectual chicanery is commoner than in England, it is largely due to the wealth of the Churches, which undermines honesty in thousands at the very opening of their career, and in connection with the very deepest interests. It is a fact as obvious as it is unpleasant that not a single step is made in the rationalising of the Church's teaching save by way of all manner of prevarication. On the issues handled by Colenso, there is now general agreement among studious Churchmen: the old positions are utterly discredited save among the unscholarly. "I cannot name," says a leading Broad Churchman, "a single student or professor of any "eminence in Great Britain who does not accept, with "more or less modification, the main conclusions of the "German school of critics. In Germany itself, the land "of laborious and devoted study, there are scores of "learned professors; and among their entire number there "is said to be only one—and he a man of no name—who "clings to the old '*mumpsimus*'. Truth is great, and "will prevail."[1] But the truth thus vouched is not great, and it does not prevail in any worthy manner. It is manipulated as equivocally as error ever was. From the conclusions referred to, it follows that the old idea of inspiration is a chimæra; that the Biblical literature

---

[1] Archdeacon Farrar in *The Bible and the Child*, 1897, pp. 24-25.

T

is not only human but in large part deliberately fictitious : that there is hardly a page in which forgery and fraudulent adaptation do not enter. Yet instead of frank and complete revision of doctrine we have only a new literature of Jesuitry and equivocation, no less hollow than the old. One of the leading scholars of the Church, for instance, admits plainly enough that "It is impossible
"to doubt that the main conclusions of critics with
"reference to the authorship of the books of the Old
"Testament rest upon reasoning, the cogency of which
"cannot be denied without denying the ordinary prin-
"ciples by which history is judged and evidence
"estimated. Nor can it be doubted that the same con-
"clusions, upon any neutral field of investigation, would
"have been accepted without hesitation by all conversant
"with the subject : they are only opposed in the present
"instance by some theologians, because they are
"supposed to conflict with the requirements of the
"Christian faith. But the history of astronomy, geology,
"and, more recently, of biology, supplies a warning
"that the conclusions which satisfy the common un-
"biassed and unsophisticated reason of mankind prevail
"in the end. The price at which alone the traditional
"view can be maintained is too high."

Yet, after this apparently unambiguous surrender of the old delusion as to the nature of the Hebrew literature, we have the delusion thus set up again :—" It is not the case
"that critical conclusions, such as those expressed in the
"present volume, are in conflict either with the Christian
"creeds or with the articles of the Christian faith. Those
"conclusions affect not the *fact* of revelation, but only its
"*form*. They help to determine the stages through which
"it has passed, the different phases which it assumed,
"and the process by which the record of it was built up.
"They do not touch either the authority or the inspira-
"tion of the Scripture of the Old Testament. They
"imply no change in respect to the Divine attributes re-
"vealed in the Old Testament ; no change in the lessons

"of human duty to be derived from it; no change as to
"the general position (apart from the interpretation of
"particular passages) that the Old Testament points for-
"ward prophetically to Christ. That both the religion
"of Israel itself, and the record of its history embodied in
"the Old Testament, are the work of men whose hearts
"have been touched and minds illumined in different
"degrees by the Spirit of God is manifest; but the re-
"cognition of this truth does not decide the question of
"the author by whom, or the date at which particular
"parts of the Old Testament were committed to writing;
"nor does it determine the precise literary character of a
"given narrative or book. No part of the Bible, nor
"even the Bible as a whole, is a logically articulated sys-
"tem of theology; the Bible is a 'library', showing how
"men variously gifted by the Spirit of God cast the truth
"which they received into many different literary forms
"as genius permitted, or occasion demanded."[1]

If any apologist has paid a heavier price for the maintenance of a traditional view than is paid here, he has by
this time passed out of memory. Two steps of reasoning
may suffice to show any man that on the apologist's own
principles the "Spirit of God" is only a shibboleth for
moral earnestness, and that in that sense the phrase
might be more fitly used of Rousseau, or of Mill, or of
Feuerbach, than of the bulk of the compilers of the Old
Testament. But the form of the phrase is as it is because
of the writer's position and antecedents: he must compound for rationalism in the analysis of documents by a
double dose of obscurantism in philosophy; and he
gravely quotes for us the deliverance of the documentist
Riehm: "Everyone who so reads the Pentateuch as to
"allow its contents to work upon his spirit, must receive
"the impression that a consciousness of God such as is
"here expressed *cannot be derived from flesh and blood*".
Thus is a measure of conformity to reason paid for by a new

[1] *An Introduction to the Literature of the Old Testament*, by Canon Driver edit. 1891, pref. pp. xiv., xv.

flout to it; and in place of the old phantasy of inspiration we have one much more lawless and much more grotesque, in which a confessed series of primitive sacerdotal forgers figure as supernaturally endowed in comparison with scrupulous civilised men.

The same sequence is seen in the quasi-critical handling of the New Testament by clerical scholars. Even when we get something better than neck-or-nothing attempts to antedate the Fourth Gospel, in complete disregard of the fact that, the earlier the date is put, the worse is the quandary for those who want to believe in the Synoptics, there is a visible and perpetual evasion of the scientific conclusions in the matter. While there has been obvious progress in the analysis of the Old Testament by clerical scholars, that of the New is not so far advanced in their hands as it was in those of Hennell, nearly sixty years ago. Every concession to criticism is heaped over with evangelical rhetoric, reaffirming the supernaturalist view in the process of destroying its bases. Among specialists in the textual criticism of the Old Testament we rarely find a modicum of critical insight into either the central problems of religion or the special historical problem of Christianity. Professor Robertson Smith was a case in point. Of this lopsidedness and inconsistency, much is doubtless due to the irrational conservatism of habit in general; but much is also due to the bribe held out by the Church, as an institution, for all treason to the spirit of truth, all surrender to tradition and routine.

Such are the reactionary forces with which rationalism has to struggle in England. Obviously they will tend to affect rationalism from within as well as from without, modifying and stinting men's utterance of their thought, as well as resisting what is uttered. It only remains, then, to examine broadly the methods and results of the rationalist movement of the past generation, before we seek to strike a balance and estimate the probabilities for the future.

CHAPTER V.

LAY RATIONALISM.

WHEN we turn from the state of affairs within the Church thirty years ago to the state of affairs outside, it would seem as if the conflict between faith and criticism had really reached the beginning of the end. Within the Church there remained no distinctly orthodox man of anything like eminent intellectual power. Apart from Mansel, Dr. Thomson was almost its only writer on philosophical subjects. Whately, who by this time might rank as orthodox in comparison with the new rationalisers, died in 1863. Whewell died in 1866. Bishop Thirlwall, strong as a historian, half-articulate as a thinker, could hardly be called orthodox; the other good scholars in the Church could hardly be called thinkers. Nor did the laity make up for the ecclesiastical defect. Even the "God-intoxicated" Carlyle was a sad heretic; and the eloquent Ruskin counted for nothing in philosophy or apologetics, being besides the friend and admirer of Colenso. True, Browning and Tennyson were in some degree Christian, as poets might be expected to be; but they were hardly stablishers of the faith. As against these, the list of names that could now be cited on the side of what was still called "infidelity" was overwhelming. There were Grote, Mill, Spencer, Darwin, Bain, Buckle, Draper, Lewes, F. W. Newman, Greg, and Harriet Martineau; the least of them an important writer; half of them destined to rank among the important names of their century. If none was greater in his department than Hume or Gibbon, they constituted together such a body of distinguished unbelievers as had never before existed at one time in England, and among them they covered far more ground than had ever been covered by their predecessors, Mr. Spencer applying natural science to the whole cosmic problem; Darwin applying it to the whole of biology; and Buckle, the most outspoken of them all in his anti-clericalism, although a Deist, applying it to the whole field of human history. And if as great a number of new names of equal importance with the greatest of these have not appeared since, it will not be disputed that the tendency of thought has since run on the same lines, or that the balance of forces remains unaltered. From 1860 onwards there were added to the list the names of Professors Huxley, Tyndall, and Clifford, Mr. Lecky, Matthew Arnold, Mr. Morley, Mr. Leslie Stephen, Viscount Amberley, Mr. Frederic Harrison, and his fellow Positivists, the author of *Supernatural Religion*, Mr. A. W. Benn, Mr. Grant Allen, Professor Karl Pearson, and others; to say nothing of the clearly anti-theological tendencies of the new school of mythologists and anthropologists, among whom only Professor Max Müller and Mr. Andrew Lang have shown themselves concerned to plead for "some religion or other", as against the scientific impartiality of Dr. Tylor and Sir John Lubbock, and even of Sir George Cox.

On the side of systematic or unsystematic orthodoxy it is impossible to cite any names of admitted importance, with the solitary exception of Mr. Gladstone, who in his latter years has given to religion the powers that he considered to have grown ineffective for politics, striving not only to rout modern unbelief with the weapons of Butler (while admitting their irrelevance to the main part of the modern criticism of his creed) but to discredit by letters to traditionalists the textual criticism of the specialists of his own Church, after having somewhat disastrously grappled with Professor Huxley on Genesis and the affairs of Gadara. Mr. Gladstone stands practically alone among the eminent publicists of his day, as a defender of Biblical religion; for it will hardly be pretended that the argumentation of his political antagonist,

Mr. Balfour, is a defence of Christianity by a Christian; or that the emotional volumes of the late Mr. Henry Drummond amounted to an argumentative vindication of his creed; or that the treatise of Mr. B. Kidd on *Social Evolution*, which attracted attention a few years ago, can pass as a serious plea for any body of dogmas whatever. And one recalls nothing else, save such scholarly skirmishing as the vain attempt of the late Bishop Lightfoot to answer *Supernatural Religion*, and the gracefully ineffectual and already forgotten essays entitled *Lux Mundi*. It has been remarked by a freethinking writer, *àpropos* of the pathetic recantation of the late Dr. Romanes, that whereas a generation or more ago the "sensations" of the serious reading public were set up for the most part by the issue of some new heretical work, such as those of Strauss, Buckle, Colenso, Darwin and Renan, and the *Essays and Reviews*, "what now excites our reading world, or the "gossipping part of it, is a serious and moderately intel-"ligent attempt to defend that religion the questioning of "which a generation ago was a portentous thing".[1] And this appears to be broadly true, though the writer is perhaps not without bias in his diagnosis.

At the same time, there is no sign of anything like a revival of religion among the working-classes. Not only are there constant complaints on the part of the clergy that they "will not go to church", but there has been a fairly popular freethinking propaganda among them. In 1872, Mr. Arnold remarked how in former times, though religion had not much practical hold of the masses, "they "did not question its truth, and they held it in con-"siderable awe". Exact knowledge of the past was never Mr. Arnold's strong point, and here his words may be doubted; but we may accept his testimony when he adds: " But now they seem to have hardly any awe of it "at all; and they freely question its truth. And many " of the most successful energetic and ingenious of the

---

[1] *University Magazine*, April, 1897. p. 1.

"artisan class, who are steady and rise, are now found
"either themselves rejecting the Bible altogether, or
"following teachers who tell them the Bible is an
"exploded superstition."[1] This had reference to the
"Secularist" propaganda in particular. Systematically
begun a generation ago by Mr. G. J. Holyoake, Mr.
Bradlaugh, and others, it had a vigorous life while Mr.
Bradlaugh lived; and though at present it appears to be
less flourishing, the cause, so far as the present writer can
discover, is not at all any fresh growth of faith among the
people, but rather their more and more complete emancipation from religious interests. Twenty or thirty years
ago, Secularist lectures were almost the only forms of
non-religious intellectual excitement that were widely
accessible on Sundays in most English towns; and it was
perhaps their vogue that set up the rival movements which
have gone so far to eclipse them. To say nothing of the
multitudes of workmen's clubs, of which so many run
courses of Sunday lectures on political and other topics,
or of the propagandist activities of the Socialist movement, there are now in nearly all the large towns
"Sunday Societies" which provide gratis lectures of
good quality on secular subjects; and in the nature of the
case these are frequented by the more rationalistic
citizens, who in an over-worked age, in England as on the
Continent, are likely on their rest-day to seek relaxation
and entertainment rather than critical argumentation,
whether or not they have broadly made up their minds on
the general religious question.

 This last phase of the case, however, brings us face to
face with a problem that would suggest itself even on the
strictly literary aspect—the problem, namely, as to how
far ecclesiastical and religious influences are still indirectly powerful, even where they do not command
respect and adherence. The Sunday Societies are
financed by voluntary subscriptions, which presumably do

---

[1] *Literature and Dogma*, 5th edit. Pref. p. vii.

not in general come from devout Christians. If these subscribers, or those of them who do not believe in Christianity, chose to give their money for rationalist propaganda, for the communication to the unstudious public of right ideas about the origin and history of religion, they could make a very powerful and educative propaganda indeed. If they dislike the Secularist propaganda, they could set up one of their own. But they do nothing of the kind; and why? They would doubtless give various reasons, such as the simple shibboleth that rationalism is " in the air ", and the older shibboleth that religion is "still useful"; but these shibboleths would not give the real reason for their course. That reason we must look for in economic conditions.

When we go back on the course of the rationalism of the second half of the century, that "cultured" rationalism which took up the old task recommenced by Paine, and carried on after him by men in touch with the working-classes, we note a certain gradual falling-away in explicitness of doctrine. Those of the earliest works coming under this heading, the *Inquiry Concerning the Origin of Christianity*, by C. C. Hennell (1838);[1] the *Phases of Faith* of Professor F. W. Newman (1850), and *The Creed of Christendom*, by Mr. W. R. Greg (1851), were in their different ways perfectly explicit. The *Phases of Faith* retains, and will long retain, much of the interest of the *Apologia* of the Professor's more famous brother, since it is a spiritual autobiography written with no less frankness and trenchancy and earnestness, if with less of literary charm. Indeed it would seem to have given the lead to the *Apologia*, which came out fifteen years later, and which in many ways resembles it, through all their absolute contrariety of purport, more than it does the evangelical autobiography of Scott, of Aston Sandford, which probably gave a lead to both, since Francis, like John, mentions Scott as one of the writer he read in his

---

[1] Second edition, 1841. This work, which went nearly but not quite as far as his own, was translated into German by Strauss in 1840.

youth.[1] However that may be, the *Phases* is a wonderful record of a thoughtful youth's painful progress from orthodoxy to rationalistic Deism, and, at the same, of the rigid narrowness of spirit of the religionists around him, among these being included his brother, and another clergyman of no less exemplary disinterestedness. And though its final Deism is in its simpler way just as arbitrary as the more complicated assumptions of the Christian system, its critical argumentations against the latter must have persuaded a far larger proportion of its readers than that led to Romanism by the *Apologia*, for they are both sincere and cogent. Of its kind, no more genuine book has been written.

It chanced to evoke, among many other criticisms, that of Mr. Henry Rogers, a contemporary man of letters who had held several literary professorships, and who set himself, in an anonymous work of didactic and dialogistic fiction entitled *The Eclipse of Faith*, to defend orthodox religion against its assailants in general. This work, which passed through ten editions in ten years, may be taken as the measure of the educated lay orthodoxy of the period, and as in a less degree a clue to the tone of some of its lay heresy. It is written in a would-be humorous tone of stedfast religious malice, with an unchanging *rictus* of self-complacent spite, which soon becomes rather more unpleasant than the downright passion of the ordinary clerical apologist; and its diffuse argument resolves itself into the two propositions that unbelievers take contradictory views of the Bible, and that Deists like Newman have no better ground for their Deism than Christians have for their Christism—the old argument of Butler.[2] To this Professor Newman, in his second edition, made a rather freshly effective reply.

---

[1] There is, of course, a great difference in the tone. Francis speaks of Scott as " a rather dull, very unoriginal, half-educated, but honest, worthy, " sensible, strong-minded man ". The words of his brother, already cited (above, p. 235), were perhaps meant as a partial counterblast to these.

[2] An issue of whose works Professor Rogers had edited.

"With energetic and dogmatic earnestness he [the critic] "enforces upon me, that God, as revealed to him and me "in Nature, has no consistent or trustworthy moral "character. Well: *if so*, how can any Bible have any "authority? Can anything be more imbecile than to "talk of an authoritative Revelation from a God who may "be a devil? *If, for aught I know, God is a liar, why am* "*I to believe his word, if I be ever so sure that it is his* "*word?*" The fervid Professor at the same time suggested that his critic, who had thus set up the principle of an immoral God, was not improbably a concealed Atheist—a suggestion which gave the author due matter for retort in his *Defence of 'The Eclipse of Faith'*.[1] But on the logical issue, Professor Rogers, who had employed the weapon of Butler with the usual shortsighted confidence of his fellow-Christians, could offer only this hopeless defence:—"I believe firmly that the prevailing "characteristics of the universe indicate unlimited power "and wisdom; and in general, goodness; the last, how-"ever, so chequered as to admit of being blessedly "confirmed by an external revelation, assuring the "faltering reason of man, amidst the conflicting "phenomena around us, that the goodness of the Deity "*is* unlimited and perfect".[2] So that once more the Bible of the Butlerian is on all fours with the Koran, which also says that "God is good", and is entitled to acceptance accordingly.

Thus within a hundred years of the supposed collapse of the Deism of last century, Deists were attacking orthodoxy more vigorously than ever, and with the fuller critical knowledge amassed in the interval. Professor Newman is at the philosophic position of Tindal, feeling like him that he had "within" the assurance and knowledge of the "goodness" of Omnipotence. And nearly all the other beginners of the modern rationalistic movement up to this date are Deists—even Mr. Spencer

[1] This is turn went through three editions in ten years.
[2] *A Defence of " The Eclipse of Faith "*, 2nd ed., 1854, p. 37.

at the outset taking that position, as did Buckle. Blanco White had been as confidently deistic as Milman; so was Theodore Parker. Harriet Martineau alone among the well-known writers of that time reached an atheistic philosophy,[1] for her avowal of which[2] she was assailed with due bitterness by her deistic brother, the Rev. James Martineau.[3] As early as 1842, Mr. G. J. Holyoake had been sentenced to six months' imprisonment for incidentally avowing something like Atheism[4] in a discussion after a lecture given by him as an Owenite Social Missionary; but this represented no propaganda; and Mr. Bradlaugh was not heard of till many years later. Robert Owen had himself struck very directly at orthodox ethics in his teaching, but had not gone beyond a species of Lucretian Deism.

Despite their limitation of their doctrine, however, all of the deistic writers mentioned, and Harriet Martineau no less than they, had been very direct in their dissent from orthodoxy. Professor Newman had done something almost entirely new in the controversy, in expressly challenging the conventional doctrine of the perfectness of the character of Christ—a doctrine often assented to in large measure by professed unbelievers. Mr. Greg, who on the contrary stood somewhat inconsistently to that doctrine, was none the less explicit in arguing down the supernaturalism of the Gospels, and in pointing out the

---

[1] Not of the clearest, certainly. She explained that she was "an atheist "in the vulgar sense, that of rejecting the popular theology—but not in "the philosophical sense, of denying a First Cause".—*Autobiography*, vol. ii, p. 351.

[2] In the *Letters on the Laws of Man's Nature and Development*, by H. G. Atkinson and herself, 1851.

[3] In the *Prospective Review*, No. xxvi, 1851, she had been converted by her friend H. G. Atkinson, a writer of somewhat erratic ability, but in no way deserving of the insolent contempt bestowed upon him by Mr. Martineau, who in this matter illustrated the strong tendency to bigotry so often associated with modern Unitarianism.

[4] Mr. Holyoake's pamphlet, *The Last Trial for Atheism* (5th edit., Trübner and Co. 1878) gives an interesting picture of the utter brutality of the orthodoxy of the time.

impossibility of society's acting on certain of the Jesuine precepts as to conduct. Doubtless Christian society had never attempted to act on those precepts, and there was not the faintest likelihood that it ever would; but the open disavowal was remarkable for the time. Equally above-board was Charles C. Hennell's deistic *Inquiry Concerning the Origin of Christianity*, which may rank as the first systematic and effective application of rationalistic criticism to the Gospels in England in the present century, following as it did close on the heels of Strauss. Himself a Deist or " Christian Theist ", Hennell struck a new note of catholicity by declaring that in his observation "neither Deism, Pantheism, nor even Atheism, " indicate modes of thought incompatible with up- " rightness and benevolence; and that the real or affected " horror which it is still a prevailing custom to exhibit " towards these names, would be better reserved for those " of the selfish, the cruel, the bigot, and other tormentors " of mankind ".[1] The tone of Parker's *Discourse*, again, was markedly aggressive. Then came the clerical *Essays and Reviews*, and Colenso on the Pentatench, carrying criticism far on certain lines, in the name of academic culture. But it cannot be said that there has been an ostensible and continuous development on the same lines since, though as a matter of fact opinion has unquestionably moved in the main towards rationalism. Something has checked the rate of open discussion among the middle-class laity since the apparent triumph of rationalism over repression in the Church. The publication of Buckle's *Introduction to the History of Civilisation in England* (1857-1861) marks an energy of anti-clericalism in the educated laity that can hardly be matched since. During the past twenty years the note has been systematically sounded only among the Secularists, who have carried on in their journals and on the platform an all-round popular criticism embodying

[1] Preface to new edition, 1841.

the results of specialist research, besides pressing the historical criticism far on Buckle's lines. But, as we have seen, the Secularists in turn seem to have felt an economic pressure; and their propaganda apparently languishes at a time when religious terrorism, despite the nominal maintenance of the blasphemy laws, has almost ceased openly to exist. The general phenomenon, then, calls for explanation.

Before putting any theory, however, it may be well to pass under review the manner and matter of the leading rationalistic writers among the laity since 1863, in order that the main data for a conclusion may be before us. It is, indeed, necessary to make such a survey in order to complete our general notion of the action and reaction of forces in our culture-history. And first we may take a writer who stands in a curiously midway position between the past and the present of cultured opinion.

Of all the great serious writers of our period, excepting perhaps Mr. Ruskin, Mr. Arnold is at once the most promising and the most disappointing, by reason alternatively of his vivacious amenity and his intellectual wilfulness. The latter quality he shared with Carlyle, who was so destitute of the former; but the air and promise of "sweet reasonableness" make the ultimate arbitrariness seem only the more perverse. He must clearly be classed with the rationalists, inasmuch as he repudiated as completely as any of them the whole body of supernaturalist beliefs; and yet his whole influence was finally directed to a fantastic maintenance of all supernaturalist institutions. Broadly speaking, he is to be described as a case of a survival of deeply rooted æsthetic habits in an intellectual climate entirely foreign to that in which they were indigenous. From his evangelical-liberal father he had that grounding in pietism which stunted the whole intellectual life of that and the previous generation; and while his literary interest in ideas enabled him to acquire many of those later current, his native defect in reasoning power, and the absence of all thinking-discipline from his early training, left him a singular compound of incoherent conservation and critical audacity. And what critical progress he did make would seem to have been set up by different sets of special surroundings. Saved by some temperamental difference from complete sympathy with his father, and turned away from clerical life by his employment as political secretary to Lord Lansdowne, he seems first to have reached toward some forms of poetic pantheism, such as that expressed in the *Empedocles on Etna*, written when he was about thirty. He was slow to "find himself" as a publicist. In 1863 he sharply attacked Colenso, on the singular score that he had not published his treatise on the Pentateuch in Latin; and though the critic later professed to stand by his previous position, he himself completely disregarded it in 1873, when in his own *Literature and Dogma*, happily written in his own excellent English, he did for the God-idea and for miracles in general what Colenso had done for the ethics and history of the "Mosaic." books. In the first *Essays in Criticism*, collectively published in 1865, when he was forty-three, his vantage-ground consists a good deal in his having sat at the feet of critical France, and so learned to recognise the limitations of his countrymen, albeit without reaching any scientific view of the case; and on questions of philosophy he writes as a supercilious and partly dissembling Liberal. At least, if he then held the views which he set forth a few years later in *Literature and Dogma*, some of his proceedings in the essay on *Spinoza and the Bible* are sufficiently disingenuous. The Dutch scholar Van Vloten had written of Spinoza—in a Latin which Arnold is careful to disparage—that " By keeping " the name of God, when he did away with his person " and character, he has done himself an injustice. . . . . " It is in his having done away with final causes, and " with God along with them, that Spinoza's true merit " consists." On which Arnold remarks that "to use " Spinoza's denial of final causes in order to identity him "with the Coryphæi of atheism, is to make a false use of "Spinoza's denial of final causes"—the kind of pontifical formula with which he waved aside any reasoning he did not like and could not refute. Now, if not at the time of writing, certainly when he wrote *Literature and Dogma*, Arnold was himself an Atheist; and it is a comprehensive illustration at once of his way of dismissing opponents with a graceful insolence, and of his own and of the English public's want of real lucidity, that he could save himself from the charge by a phrase about "the "Coryphæi of atheism" when he himself was as aggressive an Atheist as his day had seen, outside of the Secularist Society. In academic slang, "Coryphæus" serves always as an impertinence; and if we called Jesus the Coryphæus of the Twelve we should be counted ribald. Arnold, having no party to lead, felt safe in casting the appellation at unspecified Atheists. But not a single one of his leading contemporaries more explicitly derided the God-idea in all its current forms. "A magnified non-natural Man," was his account of its philosophic phase: "three Lord Shaftes- "burys" was his account of the Christian Trinity. Atheism could no further go; and his suggestion of an "Eternal Something-not-ourselves" which makes for "righteousness" was merely a tub thrown to the whale of superstition, a form of words to cover the void left in the liturgy by the depersonalising of deity. Had Arnold been asked whether he believed that the whole energy of the Cosmos made for righteousness, or whether he believed that there were two Somethings, of which one made for Unrighteousness, he would have answered that he had "no turn for abstruse reasoning" and that "the "athletes of logic" always went astray. It was one of his pet irrationalisms to argue that the absurdities of the current creed were the result of an excessive "gift for "abstruse reasoning" among the theological, a form of attack which they found easier to parry than his thrusts at their miracles and their Trinity. If he had said, as

George Eliot did earlier, that " there is nothing like acute
" *deductive* reasoning for keeping a man in the dark ", he
would have indicated a logical and psychological truth ;
but when he credited the Trinitarians with being
" athletes of logic " he merely contradicted the truth
contained in his own saying that the current " materalis-
" ing and mechanical theology " is " really the result of
" the poverty and inanition of our minds ". The thesis
that philosophic absurdities and self-contradiction come
of a special talent for metaphysics is perhaps the most
gratuitous compliment ever paid to theology.

All this was his way of assimilating the doctrine of the
Positivists, as his appeal for an English Academy was his
way of assimilating French culture. But as his political
science never went beyond dividing his countrymen into
" Barbarians, Philistines, and Populace," so his plan of
action never went beyond emptying the Bible of its
supernaturalism and using what was left as a guide to
" three-fourths of life "—all this in the name of practical
ethics and a straightforward appeal to the conscience of
the nation. He had become so habituated, apparently
under his father's guidance, to reading transcendental
meanings and modern applications into the primitive
moralities of the Old and New Testaments, that he had
positively lost all perception of what the Sacred Books were
for those who wrote and those who originally received
them. Nothing can be more fantastically remote from the
historic facts than his notion of ancient Israel as a kind
of moral solidarity, a people with a collective genius for
righteousness, who created a specially high type of Deity
as a kind of poetic incarnation of their moral sense. This
conception, indeed, he would qualify on challenge till it
had lost all coherence ; but as soon as the stress of argument was over it would reappear as before. Thus he
avows, what other men had pointed out, that " Religion
" in the Old Testament is a matter of national and social
" conduct mainly. First, it consists in devotion to Israel's
" God, the Eternal who loveth righteousness, and of sepa-

"ration from other nations whose concern for righteous-
"ness was less fervent,—of abhorrence of their idolatries
"which were sure to bewilder and diminish this fervent
"concern. Secondly, it consists in doing justice, hating
"all wrong, robbery, and oppression, abstaining from inso-
"lence, lying, and slandering. . . . . But it is evident
"that . . . . as time went on . . . . for the mass of the
"Hebrews their God came to be a mere magnified and
"non-natural man, like the God of our popular religion
"now. . . . . One may observe rites and ceremonies,
"hate idolatry, abstain from murder and theft and false
"witness, and yet have one's inward thoughts bad,
"callous, and disordered. . . . . Then even the ad-
"mitted duties themselves come to be ill-discharged or
"set at nought, because the emotion which was the
"only security for their good discharge is wanting. . . . .
"Therefore the Israelites, when they lost their primary
"intuition and the deep feeling which went with it, were
"perpetually idolatrous, perpetually slack or niggardly in
"the service of Jehovah, *perpetually violators of judgment
"and justice*".[1]

That is to say, the Israelites, with their Bible growing in their hands, grew worse than the Greeks, worse than the Romans, worse than the modern civilised peoples.

To say nothing of the strange ignorance of Jewish and all other primitive history displayed in the conception of a primary transcendental intuition and purity of ethic, lapsing into anthropomorphism and misconduct, let it be noted here how the doctrine squares with the previous assumption that the time of *Abraham*[2] was "probably the moment" when "the idea of The Eternal as righteousness "became fixed and ruling for the Hebrew people, and "marked it permanently off from all others who had not "made the same step".[3] That was "the intuition in

[1] *Literature and Dogma*, 5th edit., pp. 85, 86.
[2] This view was held in common by Mr. Arnold and Professor Max Müller.
[3] *Literature and Dogma*, p. 32.

"which their greatness began ".[1] Despite this, the bulk of the texts on which the accomplished Bibliophile relies for his evidence of the element of emotion in Hebrew ethics are from the Psalms, which even for him were Davidic, and for scholars are much posterior to David. So that the time when Israel was going most quickly down hill in conduct was just the time when its most emotionally religious literature—including the work of the prophets—was either already grown sacred for it or was being freshly thrown out; until, "with Malachi's testi-"mony on its lips to the truth of *Israel's ruling idea,* "'Righteousness tendeth to life,' *died prophecy*".[2] All the while, the emotionalism of the Psalms "is the "*Essence of Christianity, it is what the Jews needed*, it is the "line in which their religion was ripe for development. "And (*sic*) it *appears* in the Old Testament. Still, in the "Old Testament it by no means comes out fully."[3]

This indescribable line of argument Mr. Arnold in all seriousness supposed to be a vindication of the indispensableness of the Bible as a guide to conduct, and of the unparalleled genius of "Israel" for morals and religion. Having gone so far, he proceeded to establish the credit of the New Testament on the ruins of that of the Old, by demonstrating that Jesus Christ supplied in perfection the element so abundantly and yet so scantily present in the older books, and "touched morality with "emotion" once for all. The result of this undertaking is a presentment of Jesus which, by any student who undertakes to relate it to Jewish actualities, will be found absolutely unintelligible. Reading the New Testament as uncritically as he did the Old, Mr. Arnold assumes the historic genuineness of all the utterances which the Gospels put in Jesus' mouth, *excepting* those which put Jesus in an awkward and unattractive light. He does indeed, in his Preface, accept as genuine the invectives against the Pharisees, admitting them to be "defensible

[1] *Id.*, p. 192. [2] *Id.*, p. 76. [3] P. 87.

"*although* violations of Jesus Christ's established rule of "working, never commendable as exemplifications of it". He evidently felt that it would have been much more sstisfactory if Jesus had called the Scribes and Pharisees "Barbarians, Philistines, and Populace," or perhaps Coryphæi, instead of children of the devil and a brood of vipers. But for the rest his Jesus is simply a benign personage who went about telling people to love each other, and The Eternal, and Righteousness, and be sweetly reasonable; but who had a trying time because "a type of soul more and more hard, impervious, and "impracticable, was formed in the Jewish people" by its religion, and because the general level of intelligence was so low that his selected disciples, when he spoke to them of the leaven of the Pharisees, were mystified by what seemed an irrelevant allusion to yeast; and who finally was crucified for reasons best known to those who did it.

It is needless to follow Mr. Arnold through his adaptation of Paul's Christianity, which was effected as easily as the adaptations above noted, the adaptor being hampered by no regard to historical facts, and having a method by which, as Butler put it in a phrase Mr. Arnold himself applies to the current theology, "anything could be made to come out of anything". His Paul is as much a literary chimæra as his Abraham, his Israel, and his Jesus. He seems to have grown, through sheer indulgence of his literary and æsthetic bent, incapable of realising how anybody in Biblical times, or any of his own religious authorities since, really felt about any religious doctrine. And if anything could be more intellectually grotesque than his sophisticated Bibliolatry, his belief that civilised people could be guided only by an ancient lore of which one-half made its own framers progressively worse till their downfall, and the other had led men into what on his own showing was a mass of delusion—if anything could be more bewildering than this, it was his apparently serious faith that the nation could be persuaded to go on with its religious institutions more zealously than ever after realising that every one of the beliefs which had led to their establishment was false. A belief that he could persuade his countrymen to this is the reason he gives for coming forward. The theologians, with their "insane licence of affirmation about God", and their "insane licence of affirmation about a future "state", were driving the populace into the party of Mr. Bradlaugh; and he felt that that could be prevented by explaining to them that the word God did not mean any reality, that miracles did not happen, that Jesus did not rise from the dead, that prayer is an anachronism, and that there is no future state, but that the Bible may be made to yield excellent advice if read in a reverently atheistic spirit.

It was all of a piece, no doubt, with his way of deciding that the Hebrew religion of blood and thunder began in a refined ethical abstraction, and that Abraham was a historic character; his way of insisting that the Fourth Gospel is genuine history, and that those who think otherwise lack "real critical insight".[1] He was in some directions entirely wanting in the sense of reality: there seems to be no other way of explaining him, though the proposition is a good deal in his own manner. The surprising thing is, however, that with all this he is so clear in his recognition of the hollowness of the God-idea; of the certainty that miracles "will drop "out, like fairies or witchcraft, from among the matters "which serious people believe;"[2] of the absurdity of the two bishops with their yearning to "do something for the "honour of Our Lord's Godhead". We can only conclude that he gradually absorbed these rational ideas from his intellectual surroundings; but that in matters of literary estimate he felt himself supreme, and that the proper handling of the Bible was always to him a matter of literary estimate. The result is that he signally misses, in this connection, that potency of "culture" which he

[1] *Id.*, p. 174.   [2] P. 259.

laid down as necessary for a right view of religion. "In "every study," he admitted, "one has to commence "with the facts of that study. .... Now, English "religion does not know the facts of its study, and has to "go to Germany for them."[1] But he does not seem even to have sought to master the facts of his study to begin with, so that his further remarks on German lack of delicate perception — true enough in themselves — are beside the case. "To read to good purpose," he declares again, "we must read a great deal, and be content not "to use a great deal of what we read." He may have proportionally fulfilled the second stipulation, but hardly the first.

But there is another partial explanation of his course which cannot here be entirely evaded, because it tends to arise in the case of a number of his contemporaries. That is, the element of concern for respectability, or for social weight, or at least for social comfort—a concern which would be set at rest by the amount of conformity involved in standing for the Church after giving up all her beliefs. There can be no question that this concern is felt and acted upon by thousands of the upper and thousands more of the middle classes who, without religious belief, go to Church. Has it not then an nfluence on freethinking men of letters, even on those who have more or less plainly avowed their rationalism? We have noted the absolute outspokenness of Mr. F. W. Newman's *Phases of Faith*, and the straightforwardness of Mr. Greg's *Creed of Christendom*. These and other early critics of the popular creed were so far hedged against obloquy that their Deism gave them the support of many Unitarians; but they were none the less furiously attacked by Christists; and this may well have been the cause of the small output of similar criticism by Mr. Greg in later life. Arnold, for his part, always went to church: a fact which, taken singly, deepens the mystery

---

[1] Pref. p. xxiii.

hanging over that English proclivity, when we consider how irreverent was his feeling towards most of the preaching. But it may be partially explained as a phase of the extensive concession made to the Church among us on social and economic grounds. Even in France, educated freethinkers of the middle and upper classes resort to the Church for the marriage ceremony, and— what counts for a very great deal—take it as a matter of course that their wives should be believers. When we note in England the force of the same tendency, and add to it the factor of financial interest—the interest of multitudes of men in keeping the goodwill of the orthodox who would be quick to injure them in business and public and professional life were they known to be unbelievers— we cannot but surmise that the partial and inconsistent conformities of Mr. Arnold and other heretics are to some extent due to similar causes. It would indeed be unwarrantable to question the sincerity of Mr. Arnold's Bibliolatry, any more than that of Professor Newman's Deism; but in this direction we may perhaps find some light on its origin. There is in most innovators a natural willingness to be on a friendly footing with the majority on some questions, and they are not unlikely to magnify what notions they may have in common with that majority. The exaggerated patriotism of Strauss is a case in point.

Whatever the truth may have been as regards Mr. Arnold, there are many signs that, even after the episode of the *Essays and Reviews* had revealed the impotence of orthodoxy to suppress heresy within the Church, the heretics outside felt cause to garble the extent of their unbelief. Mr. Spencer, as before noted, was really a Deist when he wrote *Social Statics* and his treatise on *Education*; but, apart from that, he and Mr. Huxley in those days had a way of talking of "true religion" which implied that they were more anxious to be supposed essentially devout and God-fearing men than to be known as disbelieving the main points of the current faith.

Even the famous "reconciliation" of Religion and Science in the *First Principles*, cold as is the comfort it offers to the religious side in the transaction, expresses an anxiety for armistice such as is not seen in the philosopher's later dealings with Socialism, for instance. Even as late as 1870, we find Professor Huxley, in connection with the election of the School Boards, publishing an extraordinary panegyric of the Bible as a school book. His argument was so consummately unscientific that it must have been sharply criticised in the scientific camp; and Mr. Arnold has preserved[1] the record of how, when he was actually on the London School Board, Professor Huxley confided to his fellow-members that if religion were not actually established in the country on the Biblical basis, he would never dream of making the Bible a popular handbook. Meantime he had been elected on the other declaration. It was his own claim in later life, nevertheless, that he had sacrificed his ambition for scientific fame to—among other things— "untiring opposition to that ecclesiastical spirit, that "clericalism, which in England, as everywhere else, and "to whatever denomination it may belong, is the deadly "enemy of science ".[2] So that, despite his precautions, he had doubtless felt the hostile force of orthodoxy in other ways than those of argument.

Other rationalistic writers indicate a similar experience. Mr. Lecky's *History of the Rise and Influence of the Spirit of Rationalism in Europe* (1865) was reviewed at the time by George Eliot as one of those serviceable works which, though not original or subtle or closely reasoned or finely written, "have enough of organising purpose in them to "make their facts illustrative, and to leave a distinct "result in the mind even when most of the facts are "forgotten; and . . . enough of vagueness and vacil- "lation in their theory to win them ready acceptance "from a mixed audience. The vagueness and vacillation

---

[1] *Literature and Dogma*, p. 14.
[2] *Autobiography*, in *Collected Essays*, vol. i, pp. 16-17.

"are not devices of timidity; they are the honest result of the writer's own mental character, which adapts him to be the instructor and favourite of the 'general reader.'" She further noted "an apparent confusedness of thought and an exuberance of approximative phrases", a "fatiguing use of vague or shifting phrases', such as 'modern civilisation', 'spirit of the 'age,' 'tone of thought,' 'intellectual type of the age,' 'bias of the imagination,' 'habits of religious thought,' unbalanced by any precise definition"; so that "the spirit of rationalism is sometimes treated of as if it lay outside the specific mental activities of which it is a generalised expression", the historian frequently writing as if he had never yet distinguished between the complexity of the conditions that produce prevalent states of mind, and the inability of particular minds to give distinct reasons for the preferences or persuasions produced by those states. In brief, he does not discriminate, or does not help his reader to discriminate between objective complexity and subjective confusion." All this, barring the decision that "timidity" plays no part in the process, is exactly and pointedly true; and it exhibits in the critic a power of analysis not possessed by the writer criticised, a power, indeed, not always to be inferred from her accounts of her own attitude in these matters. It seems not impossible that she in turn, partially ostracised as she was for her sane and straightforward but informal union with George Henry Lewes, was driven by her constitutional need of sympathy into some of the reactionary positions we find her taking up in her correspondence; into the didactic views she puts in the mouths of some of her characters in *Romola*, and into the gospel of neo-Judaism which she weaves into *Daniel Deronda*, and preaches in the essay entitled *The Modern Hep! Hep! Hep!*

However that may be, we are almost bound to surmise that social pressures have had something to do with the peculiarity chequered exposition of Mr. Lecky, alike in the *History of Rationalism* and in the *History of European Morals from Augustus to Charlemagne.* Certainly he has all the constitutional confusedness which George Eliot noted. The Introduction to the *Rationalism* might very well serve students as an exercise for correction in logic, so packed is it with overt fallacies and contradictions. It anticipates one of Mr. Balfour's recent propositions in the special form Mr. Balfour has given it, as thus: " The great majority even of those who " reason much about their opinions have arrived at their " conclusions by a process quite distinct from reasoning. " They may be perfectly unconscious of the fact, but the " ascendancy of old associations is upon them; and in " the overwhelming majority of cases, men of the most " various creeds conclude their investigations by simply " acquiescing in the opinions they have been taught." Such phraseology is all very well in colloquy, by way of insisting that most men reason very loosely and uncritically. But when a historian of rationalism thus preludes his work he lets us know that he does not realise what reasoning is. There is really no fundamental difference between reasoning and the process he describes: the latter being simply lax and incomplete reasoning. Hume made a similar blunder; but he corrected himself in a note.[1] And, indeed, Mr. Lecky immediately goes on to say that the people he speaks of " speedily *convince* themselves that the *arguments* in " behalf of their hereditary opinions are *irresistibly* " *cogent*, and the arguments against them exceedingly " absurd ". Then we have such a see-saw of irrelated statement as this :—" The number of persons who have a " *rational basis* for their belief is probably infinitesimal. " . . . . But it would be manifestly absurd to conclude " from this that reason has no part or function in the " formation of opinions. . . . . All that we can rightly " infer is, that the process of reasoning is much more

[1] *Inquiry concerning Human Understanding,* Sect. v., Part i.

"difficult than is commonly supposed." Just so. Mr. Lecky has fully proved his point.

Then we have the confusion over again. "The "opinions of a given period are mainly determined by "the intellectual condition of society," as if the opinions were not part of the intellectual condition. And worse remains:—"Those who have appreciated the extremely "small influence of definite arguments in determining "the opinions either of an individual or of a nation . . . . "will feel an intense distrust *of their unaided reason*, and "will naturally look for some guide to direct their "judgment. . . . . The general and increasing tendency ". . . . is to seek such a guide in the collective wisdom "of mankind as it is displayed in the developments of "history. *In other words*, the way in which our leading "thinkers, consciously or unconsciously, form their "opinions, is by endeavouring to ascertain *what are the* "*laws that govern the successive modifications of belief*. . . . "This mode of reasoning *may be said to resolve itself into* "*three problems*." A man may be allowed once in a way to use the terms "unaided reason" in the sense of "ill-informed mind"; but he cannot be allowed to make the statement that men in the past proceeded mainly on unaided reason, when he has just been telling us that in most cases they do not reason at all. And when he affirms that to trace the manner of their *errors*, and so ascertain the laws thereof, is to "seek a guide in the "collective *wisdom* of mankind", he must just be adjudged to have landed his doctrine in chaos. As for a "mode of reasoning" which "resolves itself into three "problems", it must be allowed to compete vigorously with the Athanasian Creed.

At the close of his work, after many sops to the many-headed, Mr. Lecky professes to see a cloud hanging over Rationalism in the shape of a "materialism" which he has never once defined, and against which he has never argued, handling it exactly in the fashion in which his clerical kindred do "infidelity"; and in a passage marked by what George Eliot described as "ill-pitched elevation of "tone" he panegyrises the times in which, despite their cruelties and their delusions, men could be found to sacrifice, with "cheerful alacrity", "all their material "and intellectual interests to what they believed to be "right". His own literary career and performance bear out the remark; for it is at bottom the ingrained habit of setting "material and intellectual interests" above strict fidelity to truth that determines the confused and contradictory cast of such books as his. What is implicit in the books became explicit when, a year or two ago, he stood as candidate for the representation of the university of Dublin in Parliament. "I am a Christian," was the candidate's answer to a question touching his religious views; and he could at need have pointed to many passages in his works which could convey the same impression. In short, no fire could be lit against Mr. Lecky which he could not be trusted to drown with floods of rhetoric. But it consists with all this, of course, that so far as his rationalism goes it has been popularised as completely as rhetoric could avail, and that he has done more, probably, than any of his contemporaries, to civilise the thinking of commonplace people, were it only by his industrious collection and reproduction of information on culture-history.

No less striking is the case of a rationalistic writer of much higher literary quality, Mr. John Morley, whose essay *On Compromise*, and three monographs on Voltaire, Rousseau, and Diderot, would constitute him one of the most considerable English publicists of his day, apart from his work as a politician and political biographer. The volume on Voltaire, the first and least adequate of the three referred to, gives in Mr. Morley's case the best evidence of the indirect influence of the orthodox environment over heterodox critics. In the preliminary chapter there is a notable comparison between the tactic of Voltaire and that of some of the rationalists of our own age.

"The strange and sinister method of assault upon
" religion which we of a later day watch with wondering
" eyes, and which consists in wearing the shield and
" device of a faith, and industriously shouting the cry of
" a church, the more effectually to reduce the faith to a
" vague futility, and its outward ordering to a piece of
" ingeniously reticulated pretence; this method of attack
" might make even the champions of prevailing beliefs
" long for the shrewd thrusts, the flashing scorn, the
" relentless fire, the downright grapples with which the
" hated Voltaire pushed on his work of 'crushing the
" ' Infamous'. If he was bitter, he was still direct. . . . .
" If he was unflinching against theology, he always paid
" religion respect enough to treat it as the most im-
" portant of all subjects. The contest was real, and not
" our present pantomime stage-play, in which muffled
" phantoms of debate are made to gesticulate inex-
" pressible things in portentously significant silence.
" The battle was demoralized by its virulence. True;
" but is this worse than to have it demoralized by
" cowardice of heart and understanding, when each con-
" troversial man-at-arms is eager to have it thought that
" he wears the colours of the other side; when the
" theologian would fain pass for rationalist, and the free-
" thinker for a person with his own orthodoxies if you
" only knew them; and when philosophic candour and
" intelligence are supposed to have hit their final climax
" in the doctrine that everything is both true and false at
" the same time?"[1]

This pungent passage, which, written in 1872, may have been partly aimed at Mr. Arnold and Mr. Huxley, and perhaps even at Mr. Spencer, is followed by further allusions to "unscrutinizing acquiescence in half-thoughts and faint " guesses, and pale unshapen embryos of social sympathy"; and by this pregnant if dithyrambic generalization :—
" The great tides of circumstance swell so tardily, that

---

[1] *Voltaire*, 4th edit., pp. 6-7.

"whole generations that might have produced their share of skilful and intrepid mariners, wait in vain for the full flood on which the race is borne to new shores." Of that account of things we can realise the truth to-day, when, at nearly a generation's distance from the utterance of the words before us, Mr. Morley ranks as one of the leaders of a Liberalism that is in the main ostensibly orthodox, not to say evangelical, he preserving the proprieties by saying nothing as to his thoughts on "the most important of all subjects", though Mr. Gladstone keeps up his polemic for "the Gospel" while he has power to wield a pen. In the *Voltaire*, Mr. Morley created a sensation by spelling "God" with a small "g", thus summarising the philosophy of Positivism, to which he adhered. For that indiscretion he has adequately apologised on the hustings.[1] And that the apology was not a mere submission to electioneering exigencies may be gathered from some of the later chapters of the *Voltaire* itself, where he oscillates in a bewildering fashion between apologies for Voltaire's lack of spirituality, and spasms of reaffirmation that Voltaire's method was the right one for his task. In one passage we are informed that Voltaire " rejoices in the artifice of imposing the signifi-"cance of the letter, where his adversaries strove for "interpretation of the spirit."[2] On the next leaf comes the admission that "*the spiritual instructors and champions "themselves* thrust into the front place legends, miracles, "and the whole of the peculiarly vulgar part of the theo-"logical apparatus, which it would have been as absurd "to controvert metaphysically, as it would be to try to "elevate a Gold-coast negro from his fetish worship by "the transcendental parts of Plato ".[3]

This flat contradiction is repeated by Mr. Morley a round dozen of times. As thus:—" His [Voltaire's]

---

[1] Some interesting details as to Mr. Morley's action over the Parliamentary oaths question have been preserved in the Life of Mr Bradlaugh, vol. ii, pp. 276-277.
[2] P. 179.   [3] P. 181.

" appreciation of religion was wanting in a hundred vital
" things, just as some may say that Luther's was ; but it
" contained the one idea which the *deepest spirit of the time*
" prompted men to desire, the decisive repudiation of the
" religions of the past."[1] " Voltaire failed, partly from
" want of historic knowledge, partly from insufficient
" depth of nature, to see what these ground ideas were,
" against which, he was fighting."[2] " Voltaire's task
" was . . . . spiritual, to shake the foundations of that
" religious system which professed to be founded on the
" revelation of Christ. Was he not right ? "[3] " He is
" perfectly content with the exposure of a fallacy in words
" without seeking to expose the root fallacy of idea."[4]
" It nearly always happens that the defenders of a
" decaying system, when they find themselves surrounded
" by the wholly uncongenial atmosphere of a wholly
" rationalistic method, fall back, not on the noblest, but
" on the ignoblest parts of their system."[5] " Christianity
" to him [Voltaire] meant a set of very concrete ideas of
" all sorts. . . . . Everybody must admit how imperfect
" is all such treatment of popular error."[6] " A *bald deism*
" [such as Voltaire's] . . . . is mainly a name for a
" particular mood of fine spiritual exaltation ; the ex-
" pression of a state of indefinite aspiration and *supreme*
" *feeling for lofty things*. . . . . It was not by a cold, a
" cheerless, *a radically depraving conception such as this,*
" that the Church became the refuge of humanity in the
" dark times of old."[7] " While he [Voltaire] dealt
" mainly with the lower religious ideas, or with the
" higher ideas in their lowest forms, they [pietists such as
" Bossuet and Pascal] put these into the second place,
" and move with *an inspiring exultation* amid the loftiest
" and most general conceptions that fine imagination and
" a soaring reason could discover among the spiritual
" treasures of their religion."[8] " He [Voltaire, in his
" poem on the earthquake of Lisbon] approaches more

[1] P. 207. [3] P. 174. [5] P. 181. [7] P. 201.
[2] P. 195. [4] P. 179. [6] P. 184. [8] P. 197.

"nearly than a quarter of a century before he would have thought possible, to the *deep gloom* of the Pascal against whose terrible pictures he had then so warmly protested."[1] And so on. As any attentive student can easily satisfy himself, the see-saw belongs to Mr. Morley's mental and moral structure. He does not attempt a judicial balancing of pros and cons, of merits and defects. He visibly veers from this side to that, seeing the problem now in one light, now in another; and the whole tissue of contradiction is given out as criticism, the critic being unfortunately gifted with an eloquence which heats up with the same facility for either side of a dispute. The result is a book which leaves on a close reader a distressed impression of vehement vacillation, of rhetoric doing duty for logic, of a vital defect in self-knowledge and stability of thought. Mr. Morley set out with the simple and tenable thesis that Voltaire's polemic was fitted to the work he had to do; but in the process of exposition his heart fails him, and he makes a series of sudden attacks on his subject for not doing what, on his own showing, there would have been no use in doing. There is perhaps no well-written and well-documented book in modern times which so completely misses moral unity of impression. And even in Mr. Leslie Stephen's *History of English Thought in the Eighteenth Century*, as we have seen above, and as could easily be shown in much fuller detail, there is an abundance of anxious hostility to the rationalists dealt with; a hostility often totally unjustifiable by evidence or argument, and intelligible only as either a survival of early prejudice in a critic trained for the Church, or an apprehensive propitiation of the orthodox reader.

In face of such a series of performances on the side of rationalism, it cannot well be dissembled that our rationalists of the second half of the century have been to a large extent only imperfectly rationalistic in their

[1] P. 204.

cast of mind and way of working. Mr. Lecky and Mr. Morley are not more than Mr. Arnold born analysts or reasoners: so far from it, they leave us speculating as to how they ever got outside of the religious camp. They must have owed much to their intellectual surroundings: Mr. Lecky to Buckle, whom he admires but does not very strenuously emulate; Mr. Morley to Comte and the Comtists, from whom he caught his vicious habit (to which we have seen him reverting after assailing it) of denouncing rationalists for straightforward attacks on religion, on the score that a system which was true relatively to the culture of its adherents ought not to be blamed for its faults. All the while, the sincerity of the attitude of the critical freethinker relatively to *his* culture is to count for nothing: it is only the fanatics of faith who are to be sympathised with. But this Comtist influence is itself a phase of that pressure of religious institutions on the rationalism alongside of them which we have already been forced to recognise.

It is needless to ask how far the Comtist attitude derives from the personal equation of Comte, whose later attitude to Christianity was certainly affected by his relation to Clotilde de Vaux. The very fact that his later doctrine was so conciliatory towards the historic Church, and insisted so much on setting up a ritual and an apparatus in place of that, was part of the cause of its acceptance among a certain number of the English rationalists of a generation ago. Like those others whom we have just been considering, these were for the most part not severely rationalistic in their bent, but rather intelligent and sympathetic humanists who had realised in a general way the incredibility of the current creed, and whose administrative ideal was a kind of rationalised version of that of Newman. The point on which they were most confident was that mere critical reason would never avail for mankind as against an ecclesiastical system; and that one "spiritual power" could be superseded only by another. The result is markedly

x

disenchanting. Whatever the Comtist movement may have done for general enlightenment, it has entirely failed to carry out its avowed purpose. One set of its first English adherents turned aside from its polity: the others have altogether failed to make that polity a power. Harriet Martineau, Lewes, and John Mill did most to win a hearing for its philosophy; but all alike swerved from its ecclesiastical development; the enthusiasts of that have remained more or less fixedly in the background; and Mr. Frederic Harrison, who has not done that, has not succeeded in making it clear to the public intelligence what his position exactly is. All that can be said with confidence is that his polemic against Mr. Arnold, the Christianising unbeliever, and against Mr. Spencer, the rationalising Agnostic, has been much more in evidence than any propoganda by him against the popular creed.

A sense of this lack of backing on the Comtist side may have had something to do with Mr. Morley's gradual retreat on the entrenchments of silence. In any case, the retreat has been made; and where we recognise the pressure of economic and other social interest on the quasi-rationalisers within the Church, we must avow a similar pressure as regards the laymen who have sounded the trumpet and then turned aside. Mr. Morley's lack of logic and coherence is doubtless constitutional, like Mr. Lecky's. In such cases, as in that of Renan, and even in that of Mr. Huxley, we are bound to concede that there is in human nature a faculty of self-contradiction, in itself almost mysterious, which is very well worth a scientific study that has never yet been given to it. But, given the faculty, its special exercise implies a special pressure; and when we recognise that in the matter of rationalist propaganda Mr. Morley, for instance, has been much more rotatory and intermittent than in politics, there is nothing for it but to avow that here, as in other cases, pressure of social and intellectual surroundings, and indirect pressure of personal interest, tend to damp down that heat of first conviction of which we have noted some of the literary evidence. What sometimes appears to be a contraction of understanding, or shrinkage of the spirit with growing age, as in Mill's final leanings to a bankrupt Theism, seems often to be in reality the mere gradual perception, by minds grown prudent with maturity, of the dead weight of organised hostility to the free play of reason—a perception followed by a certain economy of zeal and effort. Mill's whole career: his non-committal prudence during early life, save for his one audacity in the matter of Neo-Malthusianism; his careful adherence to abstract argumentation on religious problems; his slight study of the literature of the subject, and his surprising lapse into an old-world empiricism in his posthumously published essays—all this constitutes a difficult section of the problem of the effect of men's social environment on their philosophy. Whatever be the true explanation, the phenomenon is obvious enough, and a large allowance must be made for it in any attempt to forecast the course of opinion in the coming generations.

CHAPTER VI.

THE BALANCE OF FORCES. CONCLUSION.

In a survey of more than three centuries of our culture history, we have seen one principle in force through the widest variations of political action and critical thought—the principle, namely, that religion depends for systematic survival in any form upon financial endowment, which determines the forms of teaching and worship in despite of all movements of rational opinion, and opposes to such movements a dead weight of organised traditionalism. For our own day there is little need to amass evidence: it is as regards the past only that we need take any great pains to show that priests in general may always be trusted to shape their doctrine in the manner that will secure them an income. And when the tendency is thus seen to be normal in all ages, whether of "faith" or of "science", the statement of it ceases to seem a mere indictment against priests or priesthoods, being evidently rather a generalisation of sociological law. To even the card-sharpers of the intellectual life (for there are such) we can afford to apply the tolerant conception of causation and social selection by which we raise those of the physical life from the status of wilful enemies of society to that of moral invalids. Some of us may continue to harbour a special dislike of the priest, as some do of the soldier, some of the lawyer, and some of the cabman; but to the eye of science all such aversions alike are but cases of nervous idiosyncrasy.

The scientific interest lies, of course, in a calculation of the relative strength of the forces at work—a calculation still very hard to make with any confidence, though the data are now fairly abundant. A hundred years ago, or at least a hundred-and-ten years ago, the Freethinkers of the Continent seemed to have good reason to count on the rapid decay and disappearance of revelationism; but though an immense disintegration has certainly taken place, the movement of things has not kept pace with their forecast. It is easy now to see that they miscalculated the intellectual movement because of their optimistic empiricism in politics. Having failed either to master the laws of the body politic or to forecast the coming industrial developments, they were very much in the air in their guesses as to the course of public religion, which as we have seen turns on political and social conditions. In France as in England the political reaction against the Revolution primed the reaction in religious feeling, so that from the rise of Chateaubriand to the fall of Guizot, Christianity was more in fashion in France than it had been for a century. But the course of things there in the past fifty years has on the whole come nearer to a realisation of the hopes of Voltaire than the progress made in any other country; and the circumstances should accordingly be closely considered.

In England, when the Toryism of the Established Church would have alienated the mass of the people from its creed, the Dissenting Churches, which throve by the same dogmas, were there to reconcile faith with Liberalism and a measure of democracy. In France, the suppression of Protestantism by Louis XIV, at a time when the tide of faith had already begun to ebb, had one good result as against the harm it wrought to French industry, that when the grapple came between democracy and the old régime there was a pretty clean cleavage between clericalism and Liberalism. The reaction begun by Chateaubriand and carried on by Guizot succeeded as it did because the interests of the aristocracy and the middle class, now in the ascendant, coincided with those of the Church. But this very fact ensured the discredit of the Church with the mass of the people. The political tie between the clergy and the ruling classes frustrated all the hopes and efforts of Lamennais and Lacordaire; and with the establishment of the Second Empire began the breach between Church and people which has gone on surely widening till this day, when not only the Paris Municipality but the Chamber is substantially hostile to the clergy. Under the Budget of Cults the Church cannot grow; and any development of Protestantism is now out of the question. Thus, dispite all the diplomacies of Rome, religion in France remains the handmaid of political reaction; and whereas fifty or sixty years ago some of the faithful dreamed of a revival of the lost art of religious massacre,[1] they have to-day no power of persecution whatever, save in the matter of stirring up their flocks in the provinces to annoy the Freethinkers who choose to conduct funerals and marriages without religious rites.[2] These rites, in fact, constitute the chief remaining hold of the clergy on French life.

In Germany the course of things has been curiously different. While the religious reaction was triumphing in France, the vast university machinery of Germany, the freest thing there, was preparing a development of learned and methodical rationalism that outwent all former doings; so that in the generation of Strauss and Baur orthodoxy in the schools was at its nadir. But that severance between expert and popular culture which in Germany is the drawback to the strength of the universities, brought about a remarkable popular reaction. The Catholic Church, sundered from the bulk of the educated and the ruling classes alike, and officered by the Jesuits, silently gathered strength among the populace, and so prepared the victory finally won by Catholicism over the anti-clerical Falk laws of 1873. At this moment, despite the course then taken of expelling the Jesuits, Southern Germany seems to be as energetically Catholic as ever; and while the official statistics show in all

[1] Cp. the extracts from *L'Univers* given by M. Larroque, *Examen Critique des Doctrines de la Réligion Chrétienne*, 2e édit., 1860, tom. ii, pp. 70, 71.
[2] See Mr. P. G. Hamerton's *French and English*, p. 170.

Germany some 32,000,000 of Protestants against some 18,000,000 of Catholics, the latter are out of all comparison the more effective religious power, because their numerical strength is real, whereas the thirty millions of Protestants are so for the most part only in name. Save for the merely fashionable revival, set up here and there by the personal example of the Emperor, the Protestant churches are empty, their nominal male adherents being as a rule unbelievers. In this state of things, with no popular rationalistic propaganda, and with blasphemy laws which punish brutally all popular criticism of even the crudest Catholic superstition, the ancient Church is stronger in Germany than in either France or Italy—a sufficient comment on certain theories as to the innate Protestantism of the Teutonic races. The one effective opponent of Ultramontanism is now the Socialist movement, which in Germany, as in France and Italy, is definitely rationalistic. Thus there is a fair likelihood that the Emperor, pressed upon more and more forcibly every year by the Socialist organisation, will at length throw himself into the arms of the one equally organised and equally militant party in his realm; of which course it would be gratuitous folly to attempt here to predict the result. What may reasonably be said is that, in a country already so injuriously affected in culture as is Germany by militarism, a triumph of religious reaction is quite conceivable, especially if war breaks out to paralyse the intellectual forces still at work.

In England, though there too Catholicism has made much progress without State countenance, Protestantism has of course a much better prospect than in Germany, in respect of the great wealth of the Establishment and the long-standing organisation of the Dissenting Churches, who collectively extract an immense income from the faithful still. Speculation as to the future must accordingly run on the lines of three specific questions: (1) Can the simple spread of rational opinion, whether or not by way of an organised and well-supported propaganda, so far weaken the hold of the priesthoods on the middle class in particular as to make church-going unpopular to the extent of destroying the incomes of the Dissenting clergy, and politically imperilling those of the Established clergy? (2) Is the Romanising tendency among the High Church clergy likely to carry them so far as to provoke a determined attempt to disendow the Church? (3) Is it conceivable that the majority of the clergy themselves can be educated intellectually and morally to the point of abandoning of their own accord all the mummeries of supernaturalism, and of turning the machinery of the churches to some rational intellectual and social account?

The last question, which some would fain answer hopefully, may be most readily disposed of, but not in a hopeful tone. In our social system the financial factor is far too strong to permit of the pleasant upward development speculated on, even were the general intelligence in itself so readily progressive as hopeful people assume. We must take into account the two broad facts (*a*) that the community breeds multitudes of intellectually inferior types, and is likely to go on doing so for an indefinite length of time; and (*b*) that where such types enter into competition with the higher types within the Church they have a vital advantage, in that they have the better claim to draw the revenues, at least in the eyes of their own numerous intellectual kindred. We have seen, of course, that the law permits an abundant latitude of heresy to the State priesthood; and it is doubtless true that to a certain extent latitudinarian clergymen can profit by this freedom to attract semi-rational adherents who would be repelled by the old orthodoxy. The laity differentiate gradually, even as do the clergy. But it is found that this kind of attraction is not permanent, depending as it does largely on the eloquence of the individual latitudinarian preacher. Let that be lacking, and people are found to forsake the assembling of themselves together. Oratory, high or low, will attract in the church as on the platform: but oratory is not not a common gift; and, taking the

Church as a whole, it is safe to say that nothing but a fairly common belief in some supernatural authority or efficacy in "divine ordinances" will in general draw audiences enough to ensure the further adherence of those who go for reasons of pecuniary interest.

Thus, if there be no legal limit, there is a practical one. When all is said, the Church depends on adherents, not only for gifts, but for the enforcement of its claim to its revenues; and to keep adherents it must maintain its services, its prayers, its sacraments, its ceremonies—in short, all the apparatus of primeval superstition. There is no choice. The revenues of empty churches in Wales and the City of London may be guarded by menaces against "robbing God"; but if all or most of the churches were similarly empty, it would mean that there was no longer a population that could be bluffed. So, since pantheistic or historical sermons cannot as a rule draw audiences, there must be maintained, in competition with the Church of Rome, the machinery which does so attract; and accordingly, barring some variations of postures and symbols, the ceremonial goes on substantially as it did in the Dark Ages, and probably very much as it did in the temples of Isis and Osiris and the Syrian Goddess before Christianity was heard of. And the types of citizen attracted are probably much the same in all ages: people with a sentiment for ceremony and adoration, for pomp of procedure and solemnity and stateliness of colour and sound: people with little sense for truth and little depth of reflection whereby to raise and chasten their æsthetic leanings; people weary with affairs and craving a grave solace; people who satisfy the slight uneasiness of light natures concerning their own frivolity by stated devotions; people who conform for gain; women feeding their emotions; men following after women. Mr. Arnold has drawn a picture that is worth recalling of the more distinctively religious type among these. Remarking, in his eclectic manner, that the real objection to the Catholic and Protestant doctrine as a base for conduct is, "not "that it is a degrading superstition, but that it is *not* "*sure;* that it assumes what cannot be *verified*", he goes on :—" For a long time this objection occurred to " scarcely anybody. And there are still, and for a long " time yet will be, many to whom it does not occur. In " particular, on those 'devout women' who in the history " of religion have at all times played a part in many re- " spects so beautiful but in some respects so mischievous— " on them, and on a certain number of men like them, it " has and can as yet have, so far as we can see, no effect " at all. Who that watches the energumens during the " celebration of the Communion in some Ritualistic " church, their gestures and behaviour, the floor of the " church strewn with what seem to be the dying and the " dead, progress to the altar almost barred by forms sud- " denly dropping as if they were shot in battle,—who that " watches this delighted adoption of vehement rites, till " yesterday unknown, adopted and practised now with all " that absence of tact, measure, and correct perception in " things of form and manner, all that slowness to see " when they are making themselves ridiculous, which " belongs to the people of our English race,—who, I say, " that marks this can doubt, that for a not small portion " of the religious community, a difficulty to the intelli- " gence will for a long time yet be no difficulty at all ? " With their mental condition and habits, given a story " to which their religious emotions can attach themselves, " and the famous *Credo quia ineptum* will hold good with " them still. To think they know what passed in the " Council of the Trinity is not hard with them; they " could easily think they even knew what were the hang- " ings of the Trinity's council-chamber."[1]

That this is sound, barring the characteristic assumption that there is something specially English in the matter, is not to be disputed. If Mr. Arnold had lived to peruse a certain tale by Guy de Maupassant, entitled *La Maison*

---

[1] *Literature and Dogma*, pp. 321-322

Tellier; or if he had but remembered what he must have read in Plutarch in his youth concerning the mourning of the Athenian women for Adonis, and in his Bible concerning the "women weeping for Tammuz" in the temple of Jerusalem itself, he might have realised, what his own words suggest, that these extravagances of religious hysteria are in no way special to tactless England, but are physiological phenomena common to all ages and all races. What has specially to be noted here is that in our own civilisation, with its gross extremes of idle wealth and toiling penury, its sexual irrationalism, its crude joys and coarse excitements, its ill-distributed æsthetic and literary culture, its grinding reign of industrial competition, the feminine types in question are in particular sure to abound for many a day, and the Churches are thus sure of at least a feminine support for some generations. On that side, though even there there are beginnings of change, religion is perhaps as strong to-day as ever. It is the intellectual, the studious, the hard-headed, and the practical types who now fail the Church—these and the mass of workers who in old days were partly bullied to worship and partly drawn thither as to a place for intercourse, but who now, especially in the large towns, have a hundred other interests and attractions.

And in the Dissenting Churches matters are not essentially different. To a large extent, no doubt, these still receive the support of people who lack only knowledge to make them rationalistic: hard-worked and serious tradespeople without leisure for reading, as well as evangelically-minded women of the middle and working classes. Among these, mere bareness of æsthetic sentiment and the hereditary recoil from Popish-looking ceremony combine to foster preaching as against ritual; but the same main forces are still at work. A measure of rationalism has reached the clergy; so that the last years of the late Mr. Spurgeon were embittered by what he called the infidelity of many of the preachers of his sect. The Dissenting preacher in fact is in many instances, like the Church incumbent, aware of much of the case against his creed; but like the average State priest he must not say so, lest he should alienate the zealous ignorant, who alone are likely to be faithful attendants and subscribers. So he must cater for audiences in his own way, making up by music for lack of ritual, preaching shallow or clap-trap sermons, and scheming "Pleasant "Sunday Afternoons" wherewith to lure young people into the fold. Given so many thousands of men actually in the business, and so many thousands of youths in training to replace them, it must needs be kept going somehow, irrespective of all the results of science, historical research, higher criticism, and ethical discussion. When we consider the economics of the situation once more, it is seen to be vain to denounce the hosts concerned as hypocrites or cowards. The making of a living is at least as hard a problem among us to-day as ever it was; and when fifty thousand men can make a living by carrying on the churches as they stand, it is a matter of course not only that the places should be all taken, but that the holders, who had mostly been set to the business in youth, should stay there even when they realise that the creed taught them had been a delusion. The income is as a rule too easily earned, be it large or small, to be thrown up on the mere chance of earning as much in the scramble of business or journalism: the chances of hardship are too great to permit of men of ordinary character facing them, either for their families or for themselves, at the age at which, in so many cases, clergymen come to a full sense of the intellectual falseness of their position. In a certain degree, of course, these men are demoralised; but, as we have said, it is only fair to rank them with the multitudes of professional and business men who act dubiously under economic coercion, and to put the blame down mainly to the vast tyranny of the struggle for life under a crudely competitive social system. It is probable, too, that in eighty cases out of a hundred the coerced cleric more or less sincerely feels that he is able to do some practical good in virtue of his position and influence, and even to modify usefully the fanaticism of the uneducated believers around him. His case is as a rule pathetic rather than scandalous.

Blame may no doubt be properly passed in the case of highly placed men who openly palter with truth and rectitude of doctrine, avowing their heterodoxy in one breath, and in the next undertaking to make out that they do well to keep up the ancient practices without the ancient faith; standing on the authority of sacrosanct books which they have shown to be mere monuments of ethical and literary barbarism. And this brings us to our first question, namely, whether it is possible by rationalist propaganda to discredit the priesthoods in the eyes of their present followers to such an extent as to put the churches in a clear minority, thus leading up to disestablishment and disendowment? Certainly an earnest and well-supported propaganda might do much, both by enlightening public opinion and by pressing against the clergy the moral and intellectual falseness of their position. The more conscientious among them could ill stand a systematic crusade that refused to accord moral credit to professed moral teachers who live by exploiting what they know to be delusion. It has to be asked, however, first, whether such a propaganda is likely to arise; and next, whether it could do much more than drive the churches back on worse support and worse servants than they had before, unless along with the propaganda there goes on some work of social reform which shall make the struggle of life easier for all.

As regards the possibilities of an organised propaganda, we have already seen the difficulties in the way. There is no denying that people are less ready to give largely for the spread of pure knowledge and criticism than for the spread of fanaticism and supernaturalism. Not only have the givers of the latter class the advantage created by their own unscrupulous readiness to boycott all who differ from them, and of the fact that the credulous type is still in the majority, and can so command the co-operation of the great tribe of mere self-seekers: they have further the strong motive of their belief that by their action they are placating Omnipotence. Avowed or unavowed, that belief is certainly the efficient cause of half the donations to clerical enterprises. Churches built by brewers, gifts of Communion plate by company-promoters, and pious bequests by millionaires in general, can never escape such suspicion. Of the remainder of the revenues of the churches, a great deal undoubtedly comes from the "devout women" who so superabound in England by reason of the constant emigration of the superfluous males, and whose incomes, large or small, the priesthoods can in a large measure command. With these sources of pecuniary aid, rationalism can only to a small extent compete. Much more would certainly be done in the way of rationalist endowment if the monstrous embargo still laid by the Blasphemy Laws on all bequests for rationalistic purposes were withdrawn. A great part of the wealth of the Churches is naturally drawn from bequests; but laws framed two hundred years ago have still the effect of confiscating all funds bequeathed for the support of anti-Christian teaching. Thus rationalists are absolutely prohibited by Christian laws from setting up any such institutions as depend on regular revenues; and the advocates of Christianity all the while, with a tactic which speaks volumes for their morality, point to the lack of such institutions as a proof of the fewness or the poverty or the avarice of unbelievers. It may be presumed that this particular iniquity will not be suffered much longer to subsist; and that in the coming century a good deal will consequently be done in the way of organised provision for rationalistic education and propaganda. To suppose otherwise would be to assume not merely that the higher civilisation is already on the decline, but that normal motives which operate abundantly in other regards will in this count for nothing. That rationalism is on the increase is not denied even by the latest champions of the other side, such as Mr. Balfour.

A large allowance must still be made, however, not only for the continued economic pressure on rationalists, but for the laggard way in which rationalistic teaching itself develops. We have seen how vacillating, how backward-looking, is much of the literature which represents the rationalism of the past forty years. It is not too much to say that a good deal of it may even go to furnish a manual of fresh declamation for unbelieving preachers. Such a preacher could draw, for instance, much useful pulpit matter from Mr. Morley's *Voltaire*, from Mr. Lecky's works on *Rationalism* and *European Morals*, and even from Mr. Spencer's *First Principles*, as well as from Mr. Huxley's testimonial to the Bible, Mr. Arnold's eulogies of the same compilation, Mr. Stephen's essay on "What is Materialism?" and so on. The Church has now more or less openly accepted Darwin; to whom, though knowing him to be an Agnostic, it gave a religious funeral; and from whom it professes to draw new conceptions of the wisdom of "the Creator". Deism still flourishes, even among studious people. Mrs. Humphrey Ward, who may be so classed, has struggled devotedly to stem the tide of atheistic Secularism while popularising the historical conclusions of M. Renan; and she can claim for her deistic creed the authority not only of that amiably incoherent publicist but of the rigorous author of *Supernatural Religion*, to say nothing of the late Professor Green. People work out one side of the problem with more or less loyal logic, and leave the other under the reign of tradition and intuition. And those who still hold by anthropomorphic explanations of the Cosmos are found to battle nearly as bitterly for their view of things as do the theologians. Harriet Martineau has told how on the publication by her and Mr. Atkinson of their *Letters on the Laws of Man's Nature and Development*, they were on the whole more abused by the more "advanced" religionists than by the others. "I certainly had no idea "how little faith Christians have in their own faith till I "saw how ill their courage and temper can stand any "attack upon it. And the metaphysical deists who call "themselves freethinkers are, if possible, more alarmed "and angry still. There were some of all orders of "believers who treated us perfectly well; and perhaps "the settled orthodox had more sympathy with us than "any other class of Christians. . . . . Certainly the "heretical, from reforming churchmen to metaphysical "deists, behaved the worst."[1] Miss Martineau's verdict may be partly coloured by wounded recollection of the specially virulent attack made on the book by her own brother; but the statement remains broadly true, and broadly applicable to later cases. It is affirmed by Freethinkers, for instance, that Mrs. Ward has been more systematically and unscrupulously libellous towards the Secularists than any of their more reputable Christian antagonists. Professor Huxley, too, is quoted as making ill-justified attacks on those who fought the battle while he was making overtures to the other side. Even George Eliot, whom we have seen pulling to pieces so coolly the facile rhetoric of Mr. Lecky, is seen in her correspondence yielding to her own and her friends' reactionary impulses, to the point of finding more in common between her weakening self and the zealots of faith than between her and the hardier combatants on what was once her side.

On the other hand the Comtist school, which though small has not been uninfluential in the last thirty years, even with Mill and Mr. Huxley turning its religious flank, always sets its face against straightforward and self-confident rationalism. It even scouts the "Un-"knowable" compromise of Mr. Spencer, clinging desperately instead to something like a hagiology, something like a worship, something like sacraments, and accusing all other courses of failure to satisfy human nature.

---

[1] *Autobiography*, vol. ii, p. 354.

Perhaps the practical failure of a generation of that policy—the collocation of "three persons and no God"[1]—may do something to set the next generation of positivists (in the fuller sense of the term) acting on other lines. They must see that very little headway has been made on the old; and other types of reformer have had similar experience. Mr. Huxley, who so flatly opposed the sacerdotalism of Comte, as a species of "Catholicism " minus Christianity", and who yet so effectually played into the hands of Christian sacerdotalism by his advocacy of the Bible as a school-book, lived to deplore that " the " green bay tree of bibliolatry flourishes as it did sixty " years ago",[2] and to spend much of his remaining time in attacking Biblical narratives. And Professor Pearson, one of the latest of what may be termed the professorial school of rationalists, or freethinkers of the chair—whose specialty it is that they feel officially bound to disparage at haphazard all who have been bearing the heat and burden of the day on foot—has apparently undergone a similar psychological change. Mr. Pearson to some extent took up the polemic work of Professor Clifford in succeeding to his chair, but began his propagandist work by parading a concern lest Freethought should continue to "batter down old faiths". "That," he affirmed, "has " been long ago effectively accomplished, and I, for one, " am ready to put a railing round the ruins, that they " may be preserved from desecration and serve as a land-" mark."[3] These brave words, however, are sufficiently unsaid in the same volume, Mr. Pearson being one more sample of the self-contradicting rationalist; and he has more recently avowed uneasiness at what he calls Reaction, with a capital R, on the score that obscurantist treatises are still actually written in these days, and that a mathematical specialist such as Lord Kelvin openly

---

[1] Professor Jowett's account of what he saw on a visit to a Comtist meeting-place.
[2] *Collected Essays*, vol. v, p. 23.
[3] *The Ethic of Freethought*, 1887, preface.

Y

proclaims his adhesion to Paley. Considering that Professor De Morgan was a spiritualist, that Professor Crookes has been one for many years, and that Professor Stokes has long been a patron of the Christian Evidence Society, the occurrence of any reaction does not seem to have been very clearly made out; and it appears more probable that it was Professor Pearson's triumphant undergraduate assumptions that were wrong. In any case, there is no better way of assisting reaction than announcing that the battle has been gained when half the world has not realised that it has begun. All things considered, it seems not unreasonable to suspect that if even Mr. Spencer could have realised how slow his age would be to accept his famous " reconciliation " of religion with science on the no-man's-land of the doctrine of the Unknowable, and how much clerical artillery would be discharged at his scheme of things, despite its acceptableness to some of the unbelievers at the altar, he would have taken the more scientific course of simply saying that Theism must be superseded by the teaching that an infinite universe wholly defies finite comprehension; recognising that such substitution of a philosophic for a mythopoeic view of things is no more fitly to be termed a reconciliation of the two than drainage is a reconciliation of miasma with health. However that may be, it seems at least probable that when culture-history is better understood, though private interest will doubtless continue to silence many tongues which in freer conditions would naturally speak, we shall at least hear less of the venerable principle that sound ideas are "in the air" and will do their work without anybody's articulate help. For that simple form of optimism, if we would rationalise our sociology as well as our cosmology, we must substitute the teaching that only those ideas ever are in the air which are put there and kept there, either by disinterested truth-seekers or by ordinary self-interest: and that when many of the latter corpuscles (so to speak) are of the religious species, they can very well neutralise a good deal of activity on the part of the germs of truth.

Through the simple spread of knowledge, too, we may expect to see derision brought on the other well-established platitude that there is a risk of general moral backsliding on the downfall of the Christian creed. That assumption, echoed with other antique arguments in Mr. Balfour's work on the *Foundations of Belief*, might very well serve to disprove itself, amounting as it does to an admission that Christian morality rests solely on fear and on hope of reward, and that the non-Christians who believe in the efficacy of the Christian motives are desirous of maintaining ignorance and superstition among the majority. It takes no great study now to dispose of the pleasing theorem that moral-minded unbelievers are scrupulous only because of the moral atmosphere of Christianity in which they have been reared. As it happens, the proposition involves for Christians the awkward consequence that the traditional perfection of the first adherents of their own faith must have been due to the pure moral atmosphere of Paganism and Judaism in which *they* were reared. But that dilemma disappears with the rejection of the premises, which for instructed men must be once for all superseded by the directly contrary proposition, that modern Christians owe their greater scrupulosity, as compared with their predecessors, to the atmosphere of moral sanity set up around them by modern rationalism. That can be proved in every possible connection. Not that modern Christians, as such, have never wrought for moral advance; but that when they have done so, it has been nearly always in virtue of critical stirrings of mind akin to those of the rationalist. Teachings such as those of Saint Francis and of Tolstoi may colourably be set down to Christism, though few who think much will doubt that such temperaments would have evolved themselves in similar fashion under any religion. But as to the alterations in the general moral code which broadly mark off modern from older ethical habit, they are one and all demonstrably due to rationalistic impulse. The civilising of the penal code derives from the deistic Beccaria; the revolt against slavery became effective only at the French Revolution, when, as later, it had to be forced on against the authority of the Christian Bible; the claims of women have been pressed by a series of rationalistic writers, against the whole Christian and clerical tradition; the new social ethic, which revises all "rights" on the principle of reciprocity of service, is emphatically anti-theological. In theology itself, the main changes are palpably concessions made to unbelieving criticism. The modern pulpit attitude towards Old Testament precept and example is wholly the result of the free-thinking protest: the factitious modern version of the doctrine of redemption, associated with such names as those of Maurice and Stanley, is the acknowledgment within the Church of the force of the attack, begun by the Deists, on the doctrine of salvation by blood sacrifice, a crudity of primeval barbarism which has been enshrined in the Christian faith from its origin, and which is still the creed of the majority of Christians. Progress in real morality, in short, depends on the removal of Christian hindrance. The most vital of all conceivable reforms of life, the scientifically scrupulous breeding of the human race, it is not only opposed to the whole tradition of clerical ethics, it is alien to the spirit of Christian thought from first to last. And when we compare in detail the general claims made for Christian influence with the historic facts, the whole life of the ages of faith with the whole life of the ages of doubt, the moral codes of the pious with the moral codes of the rationalists, the discussion is seen to be at an end. It is quite true that in Lutheran Germany, as we have seen, the withdrawal of the Catholic discipline was followed by a general dissolution of morals; but that was because the motive power in the change was mainly ignorant cupidity, not the pressure of a higher and saner moral standard.

If the whole Christian system is to be overthrown, it must be precisely in virtue of the accumulation of knowledge and the improvement of the moral standard following thereupon.

Assuming, however, that all this will come home to the intelligence of all rationalists in the future, it still falls to be asked as above whether the result of fresh activity on their part will not be rather a driving of the Church back upon the support of worse servants and a worse audience than a capturing of its revenue for higher purposes, unless there are effected at the same time social reforms which shall at once mitigate the struggle for life among the educated and semi-educated classes, and tend to raise the culture-level all round. And on this head it is difficult to dispute that, if the Church and society remain in other respects unchanged, a systematic discrediting of the Christian system, including the theistic principle, will bring about a steady fall in either the character or the culture-standard of the clergy, or both. As has happened in the past, the dearth of capable and fairly educated men will be met by drafts of men less capable and worse educated; or else the clergy in possession will simply lower their standards of honesty further and further. All that has been said above on the force of the general economic pressure points in this direction. And as rationalists cannot well be content with a mere degrading and discrediting of the priestly class, but must in virtue of their bias aim rather at a general social betterment, it seems to follow that they must more and more aim at a policy of social reconstruction as well as one of doctrinal education. Here then we seem to have a new complication. In the general ferment of social theory and practice, some rationalists, and these in general as conscientious as any, are found holding by the individualist ideal of government, in company with many Christians; while some Christians, certainly not less conscientious than the majority, are found holding by the Socialist ideal, which on the Continent is mainly identified with rationalism, and in England tends to become so. Whichever ideal be right, struggle is inevitable; and it is thus difficult for rationalists as such to agree on a social policy. Seeing, however, that the Christian Churches will in the terms of the case be no less divided against each other, it does not appear that the progress of rationalism need be checked by the fact of its dividing into opposed political schools. Rather, the use of rationalistic premisses all round will promote the rationalising habit; and the steady predominance of social interests will undermine the religious bias. Rationalistic individualism can never make for Church endowment without stultifying its political premises, even when it co-operates politically with classes largely clerical in their sympathies. All round, then, the prospects of the Churches are clouded. Indeed the mere emergence of the social problem in the modern sense is full of promise of disaster to the religious ideal, which lives by evasion of the social problem.

Is there then a likelihood that the wealth of the Church will in the coming age be put in jeopardy by new political developments? This query brings us back to that already put, as to whether the Romeward tendencies of the preponderating High Church party are likely to provoke fresh political jealousy. Twenty years ago, when the High Church seemed disposed to go to any lengths, that may have seemed not an unlikely ending to the problem of Church and State; for it may be taken as certain that, whatever relative gains may be made by the Church of Rome in England, the majority of the nation will never in this era consent to give the property of the Church to the Roman hierarchy. But in these twenty years the advance of the Catholic Church in numbers has been greatly checked; its priesthood, here as in Catholic countries, have begun to feel the pressure of the modern spirit of doubt, taking form as indifference among the working-class and the laity in general; and the Anglican High Church party itself, despite a chronic display of energy and influence, has shown itself more or less aware of its legal limitations, and has besides been insensibly modified by the surrounding life. While rationalism goes on spreading among the middle and working classes, yet without systematically attacking the Church, the sacerdotal party cannot if it would maintain the old standards of fanaticism. Whether it be that the Broad Church influence reacts by closeness of neighbourhood, or that the progressive culture outside percolates irresistibly into the universities, the High Church in its turn seems to broaden somewhat, and to abate a trifle of the height of its pretensions.

Writing just after the prosecution of the *Essays and Reviews*, and with that episode in his mind, Mark Pattison drew a picture of the High Church which allowed it the minimum possible of sweetness and light. "An ordina-"tion examination," he reminds his readers, "is confined "to the very rudiments of professional information . . . "It tests ability hardly at all, and general attainments "not at all. These are supposed to have been tested "previously during the university career. A little inquiry, "however, at our universities reveals the fact that the "Church is almost entirely recruited from the Passmen— "this is a name for the students who do not study; that "the pass examinations are at the minimum of re-"quisition, if anything at all is to be required; and that "even this minimum is surmounted with great difficulty, "and after many failures, by a large portion of the future "clergy."[1] This, be it observed, was at a time of clerical revival, as clerically understood; that is to say, the Church was visibly growing more zealously sacerdotal. Mr. Pattison even concedes, in one passage, that the average of "mental refinement" among the clergy so recruited was higher than in the other professions.[2] But on the next leaf we have this: "Energy, without de-

[1] Article on *Learning in the Church of England* (1863) in Pattison's *Essays*, 1889, vol. ii, pp. 272-273.
[2] *Id*. p. 273.

"velopment of either mind or character, appears to
"define the type of clergyman which the church revival
"tends to form. There is a weakness of individual
"character which relies upon the lead of the chiefs of the
"party, and a feebleness of intelligence which supplies
"the place of judgment by tenacious adhesion to dogma.
". . . In our growth of Churchmanship we are fast
"losing even the lowest form of the tradition of learning
"—the form of respect for the well-read gentleman,
"which has been as a feeble ray from the distant sun of
"knowledge, never leaving the church of this country
"wholly dark. . . . The tone of the High Church
"triumph, as it swells louder and louder on the breeze,
"becomes more vulgar, more violent, more partisan.
"Not merely learning in any sense of the word, but
"knowledge is deserting it. . . . The best traditions of
"Anglicanism—its moderation, its learned repose, its
"tolerant comprehension—are thrust aside, and in their
"place we meet the passionate temper of its worst days,
"the spirit of Laud and Sheldon, and of the vengeances
"of the Restoration. To traduce critical inquiry as
"scepticism or rationalism, to hound on the mob to hunt
"down the small handful of clergymen who have dared,
"however unskilfully, to put their hand to theology, is
"the absorbing passion of a party which once sat at the
"feet of Dr. Newman. The literature of the party sinks
"lower with each increase of its strength."[1]

It was one who had himself sat at the feet of Newman that thus laid on the lash; and as if the foregoing were not sufficient, there was added this: "The High Church
"clergy are, as individuals, generous beyond their means,
"sympathetic with affliction, unselfishly ready to bestow
"their time and their money upon doing good among the
"poor. But let any public question, involving those
"very interests, be brought before them at all in an
"abstract shape, and they are as little capable of giving it

[1] *Id.* pp. 275-277.

"an impartial and cordial examination as an assemblage of
"Belgian or Spanish priests. .... When we look at the
"power of the Anglican school to grapple with moral diffi-
"culties, to adjust the social machine, to aid the soul to rise
"above the weary cares of life, or the distracting tones of
"controversy, to aid to contemplate the 'depth of divine
"'wisdom and philosophy'—what impotence, combined
"with what pretension, do we find there! .... Having
"nothing to say itself, its chief effort is to run down the
"attempts of others to handle the mighty theme. Little
"angry books, in which the bad temper is more con-
"spicuous than the bad writing, dealing in denunciation of
"certain imagined 'enemies of the faith'; an enormous
"mendacity and disingenuousness, which is not ashamed
"to enlist in its cause all the prejudices of the ignorant—
"such is the staple of High Church literature. .... Its
"arrogance and its incapacity are commensurate."[1]

How far, one asks, does this criticism hold good to-day? To the eye of an outsider, one answers, it is a good deal less widely applicable. Since 1863 the legal latitude given to heresy has had the effect of diluting the old High Church virus with a good deal of antidote in the way of modified and readjusted doctrine, as well as a measure of the spirit of tolerance. The volume of essays entitled *Lux Mundi* was at least the proof of such a change, if it proved nothing else. And though we still hear a good deal of "the High Church triumph"; though we have even seen the High Church party winning a victory at the School Board polls in London, in its undertaking to bring home to the youthful Christian population the saving truth that Jesus was the son not of Joseph but of Jehovah, the party is no longer at its old level of fervour or even of ignorance. It could not be. Within the Church of Rome itself, the effect of surrounding criticism is evidenced by a string of secessions of agnostic priests, not so numerous indeed as the conversions of

[1] *Id.*, p. 294.

Anglicans to Rome, but numerous enough to tell of the play of forces at work. So that, though in the Anglican Church the intellectual level certainly remains far from high, and the success with which neophytes at the universities are still kept in semi-ignorance of the results of modern anthropology and hierology is wonderful, nothing can hinder that some of these results should come to the knowledge even of young students.

Lord Halifax the other day assured the English Church Union that the clerical Golden Age had been nearly realised; and he attributed it all to the Oxford Movement. But Lord Halifax typifies the earnest unintelligence of a past generation rather than even the semi-culture of to-day; and whether the Church were sunk in incompetence or riddled with agnosticism he would be equally unconscious of it, so long as the ritual machinery was in full swing. The satisfaction of such authorities, then, cannot be supposed to countervail the evidence that Broad Church communications modify High Church convictions; and it is consequently the less conceivable that even a lowering of the High Church *personnel* under pressure of rationalistic attack would lead to such wholesale Romanising of the Anglican priesthood as to stir up on that score alone a vigorous movement of disendowment. The Oxford Movement, blessed by Lord Halifax, originally pointed as we have seen to Rome; but not one Anglican priest in a thousand followed Newman thither; and what the more high-minded or strong-minded zealots would not do, will probably not be done by a lower species, a species, that is, bent still more zealously on worldly well-being, even though they are ready to accept all the dogmas of the Middle Ages. Within the Church of Rome itself, pecuniary interests are zealously fought for by priestly corporations against interfering superiors. It is not very likely, then, that the miscellaneous High Church clergy will carry their Roman affinities to the point of imperilling their Protestant stipends. The decision of the Pope against the validity of Anglican orders will be taken as the overweening snub it is; and the consequent secession to Rome of a few enthusiasts will count for nothing as against the solid hold of the main body on its preferments.

The Church, in fine, is more likely to be put out of touch with the general public by the visible predominance of the latter spirit within the priesthood than by any display of the former. Already the derisive hostility of laymen to the machinery of Missions has gone so far that one may hazard a prediction of serious trouble accruing to the Churches on this score before another generation passes. The blank futility of mission expenditure, on the missioners' own showing and from the believer's point of view, is now generally recognised among the working class; and the temerity with which the clergy still carry on the game is almost surprising. At a recent meeting of the Church Missionary Society they went through the form of "earnestly" praying to their Deity to do as regards the Indian Famine what seemed to him to be fit; and they actually went on to profess a belief that their operations will ere long convert the entire population of India "to Christ". To plain people, who have read the grieved avowals of the more sincere supervisors of mission work in India that the higher education of natives under missionary auspices simply produces unbelievers, this method of obtaining funds is not readily to be distinguished from lay swindling; and as the stress of the struggle for life heightens, and the criticism of society progresses on Socialist lines, the huge revenues still obtainable for "missionary enterprise" are likely to dwindle disastrously, with the result of shaking clerical credit in other ways. They are largely obtained from women and from capitalists; but women are becoming yearly more accessible to social science; and capitalists are becoming yearly more open to social criticism.

After following the inquiry on all its main lines, then, we seem to be led back to the general principle that, as the form and fashion of organised religion has always been intimately related to its financial footing, its future will substantially turn on the future adjustment of the social system. If that is to go from bad to worse, if the problem of the equalisation of wealth is to remain unsolved, if the national life is forever to be nothing better than a blind procreation of a foredoomed proletariat for the maintenance of a parade of empire and the sustenance of a hollow upper world of much luxury, much more of feverish turmoil, a sufficiency of subservient science, and a modicum of illusory culture, then indeed the Churches may go on drawing sufficient crowds of primitive and decadent organisms, rich and poor, until, as Mr. Lang forecasts, we "worry back to barbarism", or until haply England, for final lack of coal and direr lack of political science, topples down into poverty, depopulation, and civic chaos. But even then, unless the march of things is to be recommenced only by peoples now semi-barbarous, there would surely arise the question whether civilisation must always move under the flag of convicted superstition; whether mankind cannot after all live by truth and reason in matters of corporate conduct and culture as in the processes of tillage and manufacture, building and navigation. And if, as most of us would fain believe, the social problem *is* to be solved on this side of ruin, it is not conceivable that the society of the future will allow to subsist socially aught save the architectural vestiges of the system of sophisticated sorcery, traceable down to the crudest hallucinations of primal savagery, which has been maintained, as we have seen, from age to age, in virtue of the economic compulsions of unsocialised life. Men will have learned, indeed, that the intellectual life cannot be civilised and purified for all until the social life is rationalised; but they will equally have learned that the social life cannot be rationalised while the intellectual life remains barbarous and absurd. Primeval instincts of terror and adoration will doubtless recur in a lessening proportion of cases for ages to come, to be dealt with, let us trust, in a spirit of absolute scientific tolerance. But it is not instinct, not any living and general need of creeds and cults, that has thus far maintained in power and credit a medley of primitive beliefs, in the teeth of all the testimonies of science and research and reason. It is economic forces, the inertia of wealthy institutions, the priestcraft which is but handicraft, the sinister interest of men driven to force a livelihood out of the strife of egoisms, the prejudice of corporations living for themselves rather than for the common weal. And if society is truly to be reformed, all these drawbacks must go.

THE END.

INDEX.

A.

Abraham, 290, 293.
ADDISON, 133.
Agnosticism, 82.
ALLEN, Grant, 278.
AMBERLEY, Viscount, 278.
Anabaptists, 6, 7.
Anglicanism and Catholicism, 246, 312, 330.
ANNET, Peter, 176, 207.
Anti-Clericalism, early, 14-24, 56, 77.
Antinomianism, 237.
Antwerp, fall of, 65.
ARISTOTLE, 96.
ARNOLD, Dr., 219-220.
—— Matthew, 269, 278, 279, 286-295, 301, 306.
ARTHUR, Prince, 31.
ASCHAM, cited, 62-63.
ASKEW, Anne, 46, 60.
Astronomy and Creed, 203-206.
Atheism, 63, 80-106, 205, 246, 288.
—— speculative, 103.
ATKINSON, H. G., 284, 319.
AUGUSTINE, 24.

B.

BACON, 35.
BAIN, 277.
BALFOUR, A. J., 279, 298, 323.
BAUR, 250, 256.
BAXTER, 112, 204 n.
BAYLE, 75 n., 97.
BEARD, Dr., cited, 12, 41, 44, 46.
BECCARIA, xiv, 324.
Bel and the Dragon, 148, 152.
BELLAY, Bishop, 30.
BENN, A. W., 278.
BENTHAM, 212.
BENTLEY, 82-84, 88-91, 100, 101, 144-164, 186.
Bequests, propagandist, 134-135.
BERKELEY, 75, 81, 139-143, 182, 189.
Bibliolatry, 59, 181, 194-195, 289-295.
BILNEY, Thomas, 45.
Blasphemy Laws, 318.
"Blasters," the, 140 n.
Blood Redemption, doctrine of, 225, 261, 324.

BLOUNT, Charles, 98, 115-117.
BOLEYN, Anne, 34, 35 n., 38, 40, 41, 51, 182.
BOLINGBROKE, 174, 180, 197.
BOTT on Butler, 165.
BOUCHIER, Joan, 47.
BOYLE, Robert, 104, 133-135, 158-161.
—— lectures, the, 88, 92, 100.
—— Charles, 162-163.
BRADLAUGH, 280, 284.
Brethren, Society of Christian, 21.
BREWSTER, cited, 123 n.
Broad Church, 215-233.
BROUGHAM, 198, 209.
BROWNE, Robert, 56.
—— Sir Thomas, 160.
BRUNO, 64, 74.
BUCKLE, 77, 160, 185, 277, 285, 286, 305.
BURKE, 10, 23, 131, 174, 180, 194.
BURNET, Bishop, cited, 27, 33, 39, 40.
—— Dr. Thomas, 88, 112-115.
BUTLER, Bishop, 72, 75, 78, 165-181, 182, 186, 215-216.

C.

CAIRNS, Principal, 72, 174, 179.
Calvinism, 236-7.
CAMPIAN, 53.
Canon, the Christian, 154.
CARLILE, Richard, 209-210.
CARLYLE, 277, 286.
CARTWRIGHT, T., 59, 185.
Catholicism, 4-5, 10-13, 14-32, 38-43, 51-53, 60, 65, 67, 85, 223-4, 237-240, 246, 249, 309-311, 325, 329, 330.
Celibacy, 25.
CHALMERS, Dr., 205-6.
CHARLES II, 76-77.
CHARLES V, 23, 37.
CHRIST, character of, 231, 284, 291-2.
Christian ethics, 30-31, 182-183, 248, 323.
Christianity and War, 183.
—— and Paganism, 229, 323.
CHUBB, 173.
CHURCH, Dean, 241, 242, 243.

(335)

INDEX.

Civilisation, prospects of, 332.
CLARKE, Dr. S., 89, 102, 117.
Clergy, economic pressure on, 269, 312-317, 325.
CLIFFORD, Prof., 278, 321.
COBBETT, 4-6, 11, 43.
COLENSO, 250, 259, 260-265, 273, 284, 287.
COLERIDGE, 5, 238, 261.
COLET, 20.
COLLINS, Anthony, 84, 89, 126-127, 138, 139, 144-164, 173, 176, 189.
Commerce, Protestantism and, 60, 64-65.
—— and theology, 131.
Communion, doctrines of, 48-49.
COMTE and Comtism, 305-6, 320-321.
Consubstantiation, 48.
CONWAY, Moncure D., 200.
COPERNICUS, 67.
Cosmology and creed, 203-206.
COWPER, 181.
Cox, Sir G. W., 278.
CRANMER, 8, 45, 49, 50, 54-55.
CROMWELL, Thomas, 41, 44.
CROOKES, Prof., 322.
CUDWORTH, 87, 94-99, 111, 112.

D.

DALRYMPLE, Sir J., 139 n.
DARWIN, 254, 256, 277.
Defence, hired, of religion, 130.
Deism, movement of, 71-143, 165-190, 193, 196-7, 256, 283-4.
—— dilemmas of, 96, 111, 132, 167, 236.
—— survival of, 319.
DE MORGAN, Prof., 322.
DE QUINCEY, 155 n.
DESCARTES, 101, 102, 189.
Devil, belief in, 158.
D'HOLBACH, 197.
Dissent, 246, 311-312, 315-316.
Dissimulation, clerical, 263-4, 268, 272-276, 313-317.
Divini, ancient, 157.
Divorce, Christian, 33, 51.
DODWELL, 175.
DORNER, Prof., 188.
DRAPER, Prof., 277.
DRIVER, Canon, 274-6.
DRUMMOND, H., 279.
DRYDEN, 94.
DUPUIS, 221.
DYCE, Rev. A., 162.

E.

EATON, D. I., 208.

Education, clerical, 57-58, 327.
EDWARD VI, 34.
ELIOT, GEORGE, 289, 296-7, 320.
ELIZABETH, 34, 38 n., 55-56.
Endowments, right to, 270.
—— history of, 272.
English character, 51, 60.
Essays and Reviews, 250-259.
ESSEX, Earl of, 63.
Ethics, Christian, 30, 35, 51, 60, 110, 182-8, 248, 323-5.
—— Hebrew, 201, 289-293.
Evidences, Christian, 213.

F.

FARRAR, A. S., 72, 144.
—— Dean, 273.
Fatum, the classic, 156.
FOTHERBY, Bishop, 85.
FOWLER, Prof., 119, 126.
France, reaction in, 238, 309.
—— Freethought in, 293, 309-310.
Franciscans, history of, 23, 26.
FRASER, Prof., 125.
French Revolution and thought, 181, 193, 195, 215, 309, 324.
Friars, begging, 17, 27.
—— quarrels of, 23.
FRITH, 45.
FROUDE, H., 242.
—— J. A., 14, 22, 28, 32, 35 n., 36, 37, 60, 61, 64, 66.
FULLER, A., cited, 195, 205.

G.

GARDINER, Bishop, 50
—— Prof., 61.
GARTH, 103.
GASQUET, Father, 4, 41, 42.
GEDDES, A., 211.
Genesis, 113, 150.
Germany, Reformation in, 6-9, 10-13, 24, 41.
—— Rationalism in, 188, 193, 212, 227, 233, 235, 273, 310.
GIBBON, 174, 175, 181, 188, 193, 195, 196, 199.
GILDON, Charles, 117.
GLADSTONE, 77, 81, 165, 170, 213, 278, 302.
GLANVILL, 80.
GODWIN, 210.
GOODWIN, C. W., 254.
GORHAM case, 257.
Gravity, Newton on, 100.
GRAY, 174.
—— Bishop, 264.
GREEN, J. R., 12, 18-20, 21, 54, 57, 64, 66, 81, 226.

INDEX.   337

GREG, W. R., 259, 277, 281, 284.
GREW, Dr. N., 97.
GREY, Lady Jane, 52.
GROTE, G., 212, 277.
GROTIUS, 64, 108.
Guelphs and Ghibellines, 23.

H.
HALIFAX, Dr., 166.
——— Lord, 330.
HALLAM, 6, 12, 38 n., 39, 42-43, 48, 212, 238.
HALLEY, 103.
HAMILTON, Sir W., 6.
HAMMOND, Matthew, 63
HAMPDEN, Dr., 243.
HARE, Bishop, 177.
HARRIS, Dr. J., 97.
HARRISON, F., 278, 306.
HASSENCAMP, 6.
HEINE, 5.
Hell, doctrine of, 161.
HENNELL, C. C., 259, 281, 285.
HENRI IV, 9, 107.
HENRY II, 15.
——— IV, 17, 20, 22.
——— V, 20, 24.
——— VI, 19.
——— VII, 21, 31, 35-36, 65.
——— VIII, 6-8, 20, 21, 30-46, 51, 73.
HERBERT, Lord, 85, 107-110, 112, 116.
Heresy, early English, 16.
——— under Protestantism, 41, 45, 46, 177-78.
——— laws against, 127-129, 178.
——— permissible, 258, 265, 312-13.
HERRING, Archbishop, 115.
HERVEY, 181.
High Church, 245, 326-330.
HOBBES, 15, 77, 78, 81-84, 86, 89, 92, 112, 122, 160, 189.
HOBBISM, 83, 92.
Holland and England, 53, 61, 65, 158.
HOLYOAKE, G. J., 280, 284.
HOMER, theology in, 146-152.
——— composition of, 157.
HOOKER, 49.
HOWARD, Catherine, 34, 51, 182.
HUME, 173, 174, 181, 188, 189, 193.
Humour, Christian, 23.
HUNT, Dr. J., 71, 112 n.
HURD, 197.
HUXLEY, 278, 295, 296, 301, 306, 319, 320, 321.

I.
ILIVE, Jacob, 176.

Illiterate clergy, 57-59.
Immortality, conditional, 161.
Incarnation, doctrine of, 229.
Industrialism and thought, 131, 176, 332.
Inquiry, value of, 57-58.
Inspiration, dogma of, 274-6.
Intolerance, Christian, 183, 209, 210, 216-220, 224, 241, 256, 310.
Inventions in 17th century, 176.
Ireland, Catholicism in, 60.
——— heresy in, 129.
Irrationalism, 222-3, 244.
Islam and Christianity, 169.
Israel, Arnold on, 289, 292.
Italy, Protestantism in, 17, 23.
——— influence of, on England, 62-63, 75 n.
——— Freethought in, 311.

J.
JAMES I., 159.
JANNIN, 107.
JEBB, Professor, 144, 162-163.
——— Bishop, 234.
JEWEL, Bishop, 159.
Jewish disabilities, 220.
JOHNSON, Dr., 174, 181, 195.
JOWETT, 255.

K.
KANT, 189.
KATHARINE of Arragon, 29, 34, 39.
KEBLE, 234, 239, 241, 243.
KELVIN, Lord, 321-322.
KEN, Bishop, cited, 49.
KIDD, B., 279.
KINGSLEY, 247-8.
KIPPIS, Dr., 165.
KÖSTLIN, 11.
KUENEN, 262-3.

L.
LACORDAIRE and LAMENNAIS, 320.
Laissez-faire, 42.
LAMBERT, 41.
LANG, A., 278, 332.
LAPLACE, 101.
LARDNER, 201.
LARROQUE, cited, 310 n.
LAW, William, 194.
LE BAS, Prof., 16.
LECHLER, 71.
LECKY, 204, 278, 296-300, 319.
LE CLERC, 97.
Lectisternia, 148-152.
LEIBNITZ, 101, 103.
LELAND, 72-74.
LESLIE, 117, 179.

LEWES, 125, 277, 297.
LIGHTFOOT, Bishop, 279.
LIMBORCH, 118, 125.
LINGARD, 39 *n*., 43.
"Literates," 259.
LOCKE, 77, 98, 118-129, 133, 135, 139, 142, 161, 181, 188, 220.
Logos, doctrine of, 229, 230.
LOLLARDISM, 15, 17-21, 45.
London University, 212, 220.
LOWTH, cited, 197 *n*.
LUBBOCK, Sir J., 278.
LUTHER, 6-8, 10-13, 37.
Lux Mundi, 279, 329.

M.

MACAULAY, 77.
MACKAY, R. W., 259.
MACLAINE, 180.
MACKINTOSH, Sir J., 170.
MALLOCK, W. H., cited, 23.
MANNING, 248-9.
MANSEL, 255, 277.
MARBURG, 7.
MARLOWE, 64, 74.
MARTINEAU, Harriet, 277, 284, 319-320.
——— James, 284, 320.
Marprelate tracts, 57.
MARY, 50.
MASSINGBERD, cited, 17, 26, 41, 49.
Materialism, 299.
MAURICE, 225, 261.
Medievalism, 238-240.
MELANCHTHON, 7-8.
Methodism, 131, 181, 196, 219.
MIDDLETON, 173, 179.
MILL, J. S., 81, 167, 212, 277, 306, 307.
——— James, 212.
MILMAN, 227-233, 250.
MILTON, 99, 242.
Miracles, pagan, 146.
——— Christian, 254, 293.
Missions, Christian, 331.
MOLYNEUX, 129.
MONASTERIES, 39-44.
MONK, Bishop, 155 *n*.
MONTAIGNE, 74, 75.
MONTESQUIEU, 181.
MORE, Sir Thomas, 28, 45, 60, 61, 185.
——— Hannah, 180, 181, 187, 194-196, 205.
——— Henry, 87, 101, 102 *n*., 112.
MORGAN, 173, 189.
MORLEY, J., 300-306, 319.
MOSHEIM, 95, 98.
MOYER, Lady, bequest by, 135.

MUELLER, Max, 278, 290 *n*.
MUSÆUS, 6.

N.

NEWMAN, J. H., 221, 225, 227-231, 234-249, 328.
——— Francis, 259, 277, 281-3, 284, 294.
NEWTON, Sir Isaac, 99-103, 118-129, 133, 142, 189, 204.

O.

OLDCASTLE, 18, 20.
OSIANDER, 9.
OWEN, Robert, 284.
Oxford movement, 234-249, 330.

P.

PAINE, 197-210.
PALEY, 201.
Parliament and Henry VIII, 39, 45.
——— and Mary, 51.
PARKER, Theodore, 259, 285.
PARR, Catherine, 34, 41, 45, 51.
PASCAL, 75-76, 102, 123, 304.
PATTISON, Mark, 71, 73, 145-146, 152, 155, 164, 179, 186, 250, 255, 327-329.
PAUL, 201-202, 237, 292.
PEACOCK, Bishop, 20.
PEARSON, Prof. K., 278, 321-322.
Pentateuch, 262-4.
Persecution, Protestant, 41, 45-46, 47, 55, 60.
——— spirit of, 185, 209.
Phalaris discussion, 145, 162-164.
PHILIP of Hesse, 7-8.
Physics and philosophy, 1-2.
Politics and religion, 197-198, 208, 218.
POPE, 180.
POPE CLEMENT VII, 37-38, 39.
——— LEO X, 10.
Population, increase of, 130.
POTTER, Archbishop, 151-152.
POWELL, Prof. Baden, 253.
Presbyterianism, 59.
PRIESTLEY, 181.
Priests and sacrifice, 146-152.
——— burden of, 155.
Protestantism, 1-68.
——— arrest of, 67-68.
——— pecuniary, 15-17, 50-52.
——— and progress, 57-68.
——— in France, 310.
——— in modern Germany, 311.
Puritanism and culture, 55 *sq*., 66, 181, 194-5.
PUSEY, 235, 257.

INDEX. 339

Q.
QUEENSBERRY, Duke of, 198.

R.
RALEIGH, 64.
Rationalism, vacillating, 296-307.
—— propaganda of, 279-286, 317-325.
Reason, meaning of, 298.
Reformation, 1-68.
REIMARUS, 262.
Religion and war, 184.
—— and culture, 271.
RENAN, 177 *n*., 306, 319.
RICHARD II, 17, 20, 27.
RICHMOND, Duke of, 34.
Ritualism, 267, 312-314.
ROGERS, H., 282-283.
ROMANES, G. J., 105, 123, 279.
ROSE, H. J., 211-212, 235.
Royal Society, 76, 158-160.
RUSKIN, 277, 286.

S.
Sacrifice, Pagan, 146-152.
ST. EVREMONT, 172.
SAYOUS, E., 72.
Scepticism, beginnings of, 75-76, 107.
Scotland, Reformation in, 44, 52.
SCOTT, T., 235-8, 281-2.
SEBONDE, Raimond de, 74.
SEYMOUR, Jane, 34.
Secularist movement, 280, 285-6.
SHAFTESBURY, 3rd Earl, 94, 180, 189.
SHAKSPERE, 74.
SHERLOCK, Dean, 113, 143.
SIMON, Father, 118.
Slavery, Christianity and, 324.
SMITH, Adam, 131, 174, 175, 176.
—— Sydr 215-220, 245.
Socialism ... d Christianity, 207, 311, 325.
Socinianism, 106, 113, 122.
SOCINUS, L., 75.
SOMERSET, 50.
SOUTH, 113.
SOUTHEY, 239.
Spain, Protestantism in, 17.
SPENCER, 277, 295-6, 319, 322.
SPINOZA, 141, 287.
SPRAT, 76.
SPURGEON, 315.
STACKHOUSE, Dr., 136-137.
STALLO, 104.
STANLEY, Dean, 231, 233, 235, 243, 250, 251, 258, 261, 267, 273.
STEELE, 139-140.

STEPHEN, Sir James, 165.
STEPHEN, Leslie, 72, 144, 153, 155 *n*., 157-160, 164, 166, 278, 304, 319.
STILLINGFLEET, 119-122, 135.
STRAUSS, 105, 248, 250, 256, 259, 295.
STRAW, Jack, 27.
Subscription, clerical, 266.
SWIFT, 139.
SWINBURNE, 219.
SWINDERLEY, Wm., 48.
SYDENHAM, 159.
SYDNEY, Sir Philip, 64.
SYKES, Arthur Ashley, 137-138, 166, 171.
Sunday Societies, 280.

T.
TACITUS, 6.
TALBOT, Monsignor, 249.
TAYLER, J. J., 72.
TEMPLE, Archbishop, 252.
TETZEL, 10-12.
Theism, formula of, 105.
THOMSON, Archbishop, 277.
TILENUS, 108.
TINDAL, 111, 136.
TOLAND, 101, 120, 129, 189.
TOLSTOI, 323.
Toryism in religion, 241, 244.
Tractarianism, 232-249.
Transubstantiation, 48.
Trinitarianism, 115, 121, 128, 288.
Trinity, doctrine of, pre-Christian, 229.
Tritheism, 95, 113.

U.
Unitarianism, early, 63, 106, 119.
—— modern, 181, 224, 320.
Universities and Henry VIII, 39.

V.
Vacuum, Newton on, 100-101.
VAN BARRE, 47.
VAN MILDERT, 210, 211.
VAN VLOTEN, 287.
VERGIL, Polydore, cited, 33 *n*.
VIRET, 74-75.
VOLNEY, 221.
VOLTAIRE, 168, 180, 181, 193, 269, 300-302.

W.
WALLIS, Dr., 76.
WALPOLE, 132, 136.
WALTHER, 6.
War and culture, 175.
WARBURTON, 95, 98.

WARD, Mrs. Humphrey, 319, 320.
WATERLAND, 135, 143, 179.
WATSON, Bishop, 196-201, 215, 220.
WATTS, Dr. Isaac, 125.
WESLEY, movement of, 131, 181.
WHATELY, 220-225, 254.
WHIGGISM, 198, 215, 225.
WHISTON, 177.
WHITE, Blanco, 223-4, 259, 284.
WILBERFORCE, 208-9.
—— Bishop, 251, 264.
WILKINS, Bishop, 76.
WILLIAM RUFUS; 15.
WILLIAMS, T., 208.
—— Prof. Rowland. 253, 257.
WILSON, H. B., 254, 257.
WITTEMBERG, 6.
WOLSEY, 21, 37, 43.
WOLSELY, Sir C., 86, 89.
WOOLSTON, 173, 176, 189, 207.
Women and religion, 313-316, 331.
WRIOTHESLEY, 60.
WYCLIFFE, 15, 17, 18, 19, 20, 27, 73.

Y.

YOUNG, 181, 202.

Z.

ZWINGLI, 48.